Quicke

Q

BOBBI

MARTY M.

McGraw-Hill/

New York   Chicago   San Francisco
Lisbon   London   Madrid   Mexico City
Milan   New Delhi   San Juan
Seoul   Singapore   Sydney   Toronto

McGraw-Hill/Osborne
2100 Powell Street, 10th Floor
Emeryville, California 94608
U.S.A.

To arrange bulk purchase discounts for sales promotions, premiums, or fund-raisers, please contact **McGraw-Hill**/Osborne at the above address.

QUICKEN® 2006 QUICKSTEPS

1234567890 WCK WCK 0198765

ISBN 0-07-226266-4

VICE PRESIDENT & GROUP PUBLISHER / Philip Ruppel

VICE PRESIDENT & PUBLISHER / Jeffrey Krames

ACQUISITIONS EDITOR / Megg Morin

PROJECT EDITOR / Jody McKenzie

ACQUISITIONS COORDINATOR / Agatha Kim

SERIES CREATORS & EDITORS / Marty and Carole Matthews

TECHNICAL EDITOR / Marty Matthews

COPY EDITOR / Lisa McCoy

PROOFREADER / Stefany Otis

INDEXER / Valerie Perry

COMPOSITION / G & S Book Services

ILLUSTRATION / G & S Book Services

SERIES DESIGN / Bailey Cunningham

COVER DESIGN / Pattie Lee

To Rob and Rhonda and, always, Sandy:
The ones who make my life a joy; and to Carmen and Joe who put the spark in the eyes of my children.
Bobbi Sandberg

For George Makela (1935-2005):
A truly great human being who deeply loved his family, worked hard for his community and the causes in which he believed, was a brilliant engineer, and knew he was on top of the world while driving his red Porsche with Evie at his side. He left us way too soon.
Marty Matthews

About the Authors

A technical writer, teacher, and retired accountant, **Bobbi Sandberg** has been involved with computers and their vagaries for more than 40 years. She lives on an island with Nick the Wonder Pup.

Marty Matthews has used computers for more than 40 years, from mainframes to the most recent PCs. He has done this as a programmer, as the president of a software firm, and many positions in between. As a result, he has first-hand knowledge of most facets of computing. More than 20 years ago, Marty and his wife Carole began writing computer books and they have now written over 65 of them, including *Windows XP QuickSteps, Microsoft Office Outlook 2003 QuickSteps, Windows Server 2003: A Beginner's Guide, Windows XP: A Beginner's Guide,* and *FrontPage 2003: The Complete Reference,* all published by **McGraw-Hill**/Osborne. Marty, his wife, and son live on an island in Puget Sound.

Acknowledgments

Our thanks go to the following people who put a lot into this book and made it the great finished product that it is:

Megg Morin, acquisition editor at McGraw-Hill, who had the original idea of a Quicken QuickSteps book and made it happen.

Jody McKenzie, McGraw-Hill project editor, who orchestrated all the various elements of book creation and watched over it to make sure they all came together.

Lisa McCoy, copy editor, who caught widely varied inconsistencies and suggested improvements to the text that transformed it into much more readable prose.

Rosa Cuestos, Quicken Beta team coordinator, and to the other folks at Intuit who supported and encouraged us.

Stefany Otis, very talented proofreader, who was able to find the most obscure errors and make us look much better than we would have otherwise.

Valerie Perry, world-class indexer, who so ably lent her skills to our book.

Bobbi Sandberg and Marty Matthews

Thank you Marty Matthews for making this possible and being the one who encouraged, prodded, edited, and fixed.
Bobbi Sandberg

Thank you Bobbi Sandberg for taking this on and being so willing to take to heart and implement the minutia that I believe are important to a good book. You are great to work with!
Marty Matthews

Contents at a Glance

Contents

Chapter 3 Setting Up the Other Centers 47

Chapter 4 Using Quicken Every Day 63

3 1218 00400 3746

7 Chapter 7 Keeping Your Records Up to Date 129

8 Chapter 8 Managing Your Investments 149

Introduction

QuickSteps books are recipe books for computer users. They answer the question, "How do I . . . ?" by providing a quick set of steps to accomplish the most common tasks with a particular operating system or application. The sets of steps are the central focus of the book. *QuickSteps* sidebars show how to quickly perform many small functions or tasks that support the primary functions. Notes, Tips, and Cautions augment the steps, presented in a separate column to not interrupt the flow of the steps. The introductions are minimal rather than narrative, and numerous illustrations and figures, many with callouts, support the steps.

QuickSteps books are organized by function and the tasks needed to perform that function. Each function is a chapter. Each task, or "How To," contains the steps needed for accomplishing the function along with the relevant Notes, Tips, Cautions, and screenshots. You can easily find the tasks you need through:

- The Table of Contents, which lists the functional areas (chapters) and tasks in the order they are presented
- A How To list of tasks on the opening page of each chapter
- The index, which provides an alphabetical list of the terms that are used to describe the functions and tasks
- Color-coded tabs for each chapter or functional area with an index to the tabs in the Contents at a Glance (just before the Table of Contents)

Conventions Used in This Book

Quicken 2006 QuickSteps uses several conventions designed to make the book easier for you to follow. Among these are

- A 🔍 or a ✍ in the table of contents and in the How To list in each chapter references a QuickSteps or a QuickFacts sidebar in a chapter.

- **Bold type** is used for words or objects on the screen that you are to do something with—for example, "Click the **Start** menu, and then click **My Computer**."

- *Italic type* is used for a word or phrase that is being defined or otherwise deserves special emphasis.

- <u>Underlined type</u> is used for text that you are to type from the keyboard.

- SMALL CAPITAL LETTERS are used for keys on the keyboard such as ENTER and SHIFT.

- When you are expected to enter a command, you are told to press the key(s). If you are to enter text or numbers, you are told to type them.

How To...

Chapter 1
Stepping into Quicken

Welcome to Quicken 2006! Quicken is more than a digital checkbook or a way of organizing your finances. It is a ready tool—an easy way to track all of your income, expenses, loan payments, assets, and liabilities information. One of the more popular computer programs available, Quicken can give you peace of mind and a way to control your money instead of letting your money control you. With Quicken, you can print checks; pay bills online; reconcile your bank, credit card, and investment account statements; track your expenses; and plan your financial future.

This chapter introduces you to the various versions of Quicken, shows you how to install it on your computer, explains some terms used by Quicken, reviews a few Windows concepts, walks you through the Quicken Setup Guide, and shows you how to close the program when you're

QUICKSTEPS

UPGRADING QUICKEN

If you purchase any version of Quicken 2006 and later want to upgrade, you can do so easily with your Internet connection.

1. Click **Help** in the menu bar.

2. Depending on the Quicken version you have, you will see one of the following options for upgrading. Click the one that is correct for you:

Help
Quicken Help
Current Window   F1
Add Business Tools
Unlock Again
Product and Customer Support
Submit Feedback on Quicken
What's new in Quicken
Learn About Setting Up Quicken
Learn About Downloading Transactions
User Manuals
Ask a Quicken User
About Quicken
Privacy Statement

   - **Which Quicken Is Best For You?**

   - **Add Business Tools**

3. The displayed window shows the features of the available upgrades. Select the upgrade you want, and then click **Order Online**. You will be prompted for your credit card information.

4. After your order has been accepted, Quicken will send you a confirmation e-mail containing an unlock code.

5. Click **Help** and click **Unlock**.

6. You are prompted to either go online to unlock your file automatically or to enter the code from your confirmation e-mail.

finished using it. Even if you are an experienced user of Quicken, it might be good to review this chapter to see some of the new features of Quicken 2006.

Meet Quicken

Quicken 2006 helps you set up your checking, savings, investment, and credit card accounts; enter transactions into those accounts; balance or reconcile the accounts to the institutions' records; print checks on your printer; create reports; design and print graphs; manage your debt; and see tips to help save your hard-earned dollars. If you are connected to the Internet, you can download information from your bank, investment house, and credit card company. Quicken also makes it quick and easy to transfer your data to TurboTax at year-end to make tax preparation less stressful.

Determine the Version for You

Quicken 2006 comes in four versions: Basic, Deluxe, Premier, and Premier Home & Business. The version you select will depend on the tasks you want Quicken 2006 to perform:

- **Quicken 2006 Basic** is often the best choice for new users. It lets you track your bank accounts, credit cards, investment accounts, and loans. With an Internet connection, you can work online with any of your accounts. It also gives you links to insurance and mortgage information as well as some handy budgeting tools.

- **Quicken 2006 Deluxe** gives you more power to make future financial decisions. It includes all of the features in Quicken 2006 Basic and offers planning tools for taxes, college, and other major financial events. It features free investment information, debt-reduction tips, and a Home Inventory and Emergency Records Organizer.

- **Quicken 2006 Premier** adds investment reports, comparisons, analyses, and a report generator for income tax Schedules A, B, and D.

- **Quicken 2006 Premier Home & Business**, in addition to providing everything in Premier, helps you run your small business. It supplies business estimates, invoices, vehicle mileage tracking, and a host of other features. It prints business financial

NOTE

Quicken 2006 does not allow more than one version of Quicken on your computer. You may install any version of Quicken 2005 or 2006, but not more than one year or one version.

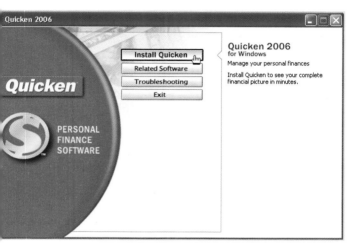

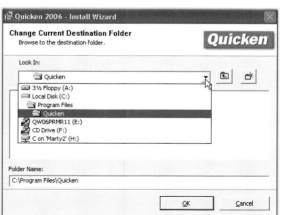

statements in the proper form, creates customer and vendor lists, and helps you track specific projects and jobs.

You can upgrade any of the first three versions directly from your computer with an Internet connection. See the QuickSteps "Upgrading Quicken."

Install Quicken 2006

Quicken 2006 can be installed on your computer for the first time, or it can update an earlier version. Either way, you need only follow the directions in a series of windows and dialog boxes to complete the task.

Install Quicken for the First Time

To install Quicken for the first time:

1. Put the Quicken 2006 CD in the CD drive. The installation dialog box appears. (If it doesn't appear, double-click **My Computer** on your desktop, and then double-click the letter for your CD drive.)

2. Click **Install Quicken**, and then click **Next** to begin the installation. The license agreement appears.

3. Use the vertical scroll bar (see "Use Windows Tools" later in this chapter) to read through the license agreement, and click **I Accept The Terms In The License Agreement** if you agree to its terms. If you do not accept the agreement, the installation stops and Quicken 2006 will not be installed.

4. Click **Next**. If you want to install the program in its default location, click **Next**. If you want to install the program in a folder other than the default folder, click **Change**. With the latter alternative:

   a. The Change Current Destination Folder dialog box appears. Click the down arrow by the **Look In** text box to see a list of the drives and folders on your computer.

   b. Click one of the existing drives and folders, or create a new folder by clicking a parent drive and folder, clicking the **New Folder** icon , and entering the folder name. Then click **OK**. Quicken shows your choice as the Destination Folder. Click **Change** again to change it, or click **Next** to continue.

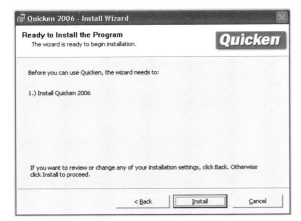

5. In all cases, the Ready To Install The Program dialog box appears. Click **Install** to continue.

Depending on the speed of your computer, it should take between three and five minutes. Once the installation has finished, remove the CD from the drive and store it in a safe place. Should you ever need to reinstall the program, you will need the disk.

Complete the Installation

Near the end of the installation, you will see a dialog box asking if you want to go online for the latest Quicken updates. If you plan to download any financial transactions, it is best to update Quicken now.

If you have a previous version of Quicken installed on your computer, it will uninstall that version before installing Quicken 2006.

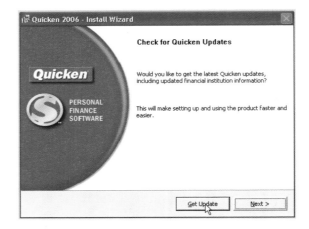

1. Click **Get Update**. This requires an Internet connection. You will see dialog boxes connecting you to the Internet and possibly downloading an update. When the update is complete, click **Use Quicken Now**.

2. If you are updating Quicken from a prior version, you will be asked to convert your Quicken data to the Quicken 2006 format and place it in the Quicken folder within My Documents. Click **OK**. When the conversion is complete, you are led through a series of dialog boxes that will introduce you to Quicken 2006 and tell you what's new. Click **Next** as needed to work through the introductory dialog boxes.

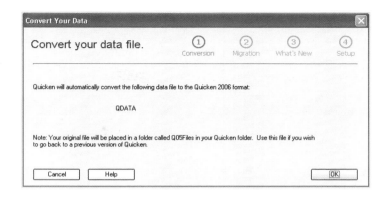

QUICKSTEPS

VIEWING THE INSTALLATION CD

The Installation CD has additional software that you can either buy or install for free and also includes troubleshooting help. Some of the software is only available for a trial period. If you decide to keep using the additional software, you must purchase it after the free trial period is over.

1. Click **Related Software** to view available programs. When finished, click **Back To Main Menu**.

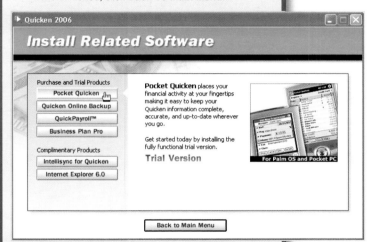

2. Click **Troubleshooting** to open the Quicken 2006 Troubleshooting Information window. If you are connected to the Internet, click **Quicken Install Help** to see information on Intuit's web site. It can answer a number of your installation questions. If you have additional questions and have an Internet connection, click the link to the Quicken support page. Click **Back To Main Menu** when finished.

3. Click **Exit** when finished using the CD.

3. If you are installing Quicken for the first time, you will see the Welcome To Quicken 2006 dialog box. If you are new to Quicken, leave the default option selected (**I Am New To Quicken**.), and click **Next**. You are asked if you want to use the default file name and folder location of QData and My Documents (it is recommended that you do so). Click **Next**.

4. If you are already a Quicken user, select the **I Am Already A Quicken User** option in the Welcome To Quicken 2006 dialog box, and click **Next**. You are asked if you want to use an existing file on the computer with Quicken, restore a file from a CD or disk (could be on another computer on your network), or start a new data file. With the first two choices, a dialog box appears in which you can click the **Look In** down arrow to select the folder, select the file, and click **OK**. With the third choice, a dialog box appears from which you can select the folder in which the new file will be stored, enter a file name, and click **OK**.

5. In any of the cases where you create a new Quicken file, Quicken Guided Setup will start. See "Use Quicken Guided Setup" later in this chapter.

Get Started with Quicken

As part of the installation, Quicken places a number of icons on your desktop. With them, you can order a free credit report, apply for a credit card through Quicken, and use the bill-paying feature free for one month. You also have a shortcut to start the program.

QUICKSTEPS

CREATING A QUICK LAUNCH SHORTCUT

The Quick Launch tool bar, located just to the right of the Start button on the Windows taskbar, is a handy place to store program shortcuts that you use often so you can open them with only one click. It allows you to run one or more programs that hide your desktop icons and still quickly access your important programs without moving or minimizing the programs on your desktop. To create a shortcut on your Quick Launch tool bar:

1. Right-click a blank area of the Windows taskbar to display the Taskbar menu.

2. Click **Toolbars** and, if it is not already selected (as indicated by a check mark), click **Quick Launch** to activate the Quick Launch tool bar.

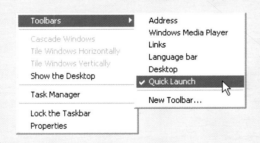

3. Drag the **Quicken** icon from the desktop to the Quick Launch tool bar. A small I-beam appears along with a shadow of the Quicken icon.

4. Drag the I-beam to where you want the Quicken icon, and then release the mouse button. Your icon appears on the Quick Launch tool bar.

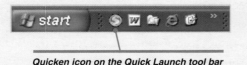

Quicken icon on the Quick Launch tool bar

Start Quicken

Quicken 2006 gives you several different ways to start it:

- Double-click the **Quicken** icon on the Windows desktop.

  Quicken 2006 Premier

- Click **Start** in the Windows taskbar, click **All Programs**, click **Quicken 2006**, and then click **Quicken 2006** again, as shown in Figure 1-1.

- After you have used Quicken several times, you should be able to click **Start**, and then click **Quicken 2006**, also shown in Figure 1-1.

- Click the **Quicken 2006** icon on the Quick Launch tool bar on the Windows taskbar, as explained in the QuickSteps "Creating a Quick Launch Shortcut."

Whatever method you use—whether you click an icon or use the Start menu—Quicken 2006 opens. Periodically you will see the Update Quicken dialog box. See the QuickSteps "Updating Quicken" to handle updating.

Register Quicken

At some point during your initial use of Quicken, the Product Registration dialog box will appear and prompt you to register Quicken and create a Quicken.com member name. This requires an Internet connection.

1. Click **More Info** to display a Help window explaining how you get started with Quicken 2006 and what features are available online, such as Portfolio Export, Historical Quotes and Asset Classes, and Updated Investment Alerts. Click **Close** in the title bar of the Help screen to return to the Product Registration dialog box.

2. Click **Register Now** to open the Quicken Registration dialog box. Enter the information in the required fields, and then scroll down and click **Register** to submit the information.

Figure 1-1: *You should always be able to start Quicken through the All Programs option on the Start menu.*

Quicken Guided Setup is designed to help you set up your accounts, but you may set up new accounts without using the Guided Setup. However, if you use it, you do not have to figure out what to enter—you need only type the information requested.

3. Enter your existing Quicken.com member ID and password, and click **Sign In**; or click **Continue**; enter a new member ID, password, and other information; and click **Submit**.

4. When registration has been completed successfully and you are informed of that, click **Finished**.

You are returned to the Quicken home page and are ready to start entering information into your Quicken file.

Use Quicken Guided Setup

When you have completed the installation and have indicated that you want to use a new file, the Quicken Guided Setup dialog box will appear, as shown in Figure 1-2. Quicken Guided Setup walks you through a series of questions that will tailor the program to fit your needs. At the beginning of this process, you have the opportunity by clicking Watch Quicken Tour to watch a short video explaining some of the features of your version of Quicken.

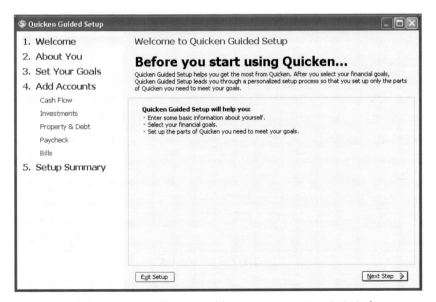

Figure 1-2: *Quicken Guided Setup provides an easy way to get started.*

TIP

If Quicken Guided Setup doesn't open automatically after installing Quicken (probably because Quicken has been run before on that computer), or if you closed Quicken and restarted it, you can open Quicken Guided Setup by clicking the **Tools** menu, and then clicking **Quicken Guided Setup**.

1. Click **Next Step** to begin the guided setup. The About You window asks for your personal information. Quicken uses this information, which is not required, in its planning area. Click **Next Step** to continue.

2. Click the financial area in which you want Quicken to help you, as shown in Figure 1-3. As you make your selections, Quicken highlights that area as a goal. To go to the next window, click **Next Step**. To go back to the previous dialog box, click **Previous Step**.

Each financial area you selected as a goal has its own set of steps to set up its accounts. Quicken Guided Setup will take you through each one. If you want to add an account in an area that you did not pick as a goal, click the name of that area in the column on the left to display the Add Account window.

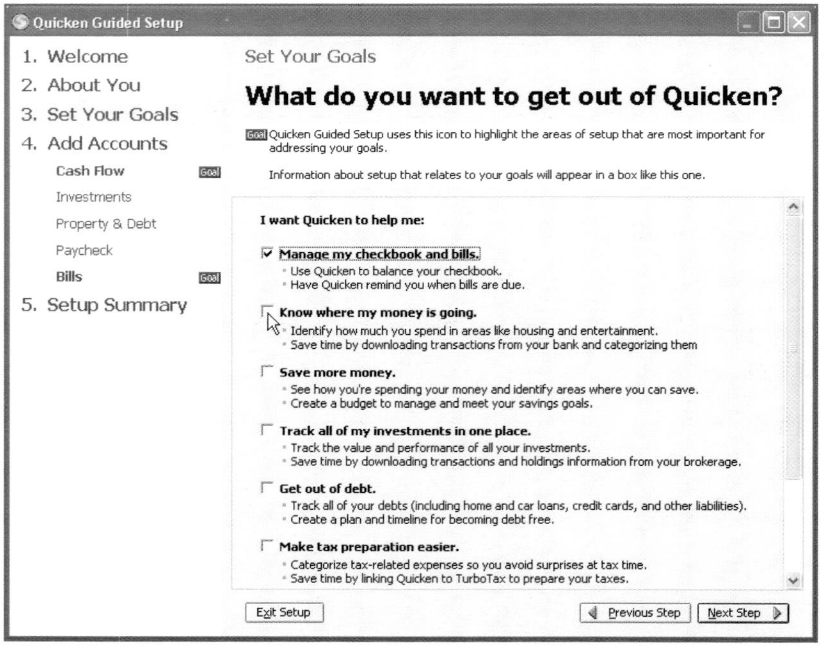

Figure 1-3: *As you identify your goals, Quicken prepares the tools to help you achieve them.*

ADD CASH FLOW ACCOUNTS

The first accounts to be set up in almost all cases are cash flow accounts, as shown in Figure 1-4. These include checking, savings, credit card, and cash accounts. Start with a checking account.

1. Opposite Checking, click **Add Account**. The Quicken Account Setup dialog box appears and asks if this account is held in a financial institution.

2. If you are using a financial institution, type the first letter of that institution. A drop-down list appears showing many of the banks and credit unions in the United States. Scroll down to choose your institution. Click the name of your bank or credit union, and then click **Next** to continue.

3. Click either **Online** or **Manual** to specify the method of setting up a checking account. The Online option is recommended because it is the easiest to use and sets you up to download your transactions.

   Clicking **Online** takes you directly to your financial institution. If you have established a password with them, you only need to log in and download your account information. If you click **Manual**, you will have to enter the information yourself (see the QuickSteps "Setting Up a Checking Account Manually").

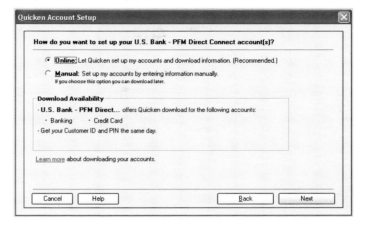

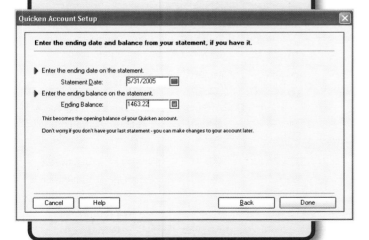

QUICKSTEPS

SETTING UP A CHECKING ACCOUNT MANUALLY

If your bank does not offer downloading services, you can set up your account manually.

1. Click **Manual** in the Quicken Account Setup window, and click **Next**.

2. Type the name you want to use for this account, and click **Next**.

3. Enter the date on the last statement you received. Quicken uses today's date by default.

4. Enter the ending balance shown on that statement. If you don't have the statement available, you can complete this information later.

5. Click **Done**.

*Figure 1-4: **Quicken lets you set up a number of checking, savings, and credit card accounts.***

4. Click **Next** and follow the instructions, which are unique for each financial institution.

5. When you have completed setting up an account, it will appear at the bottom of the window. Repeat steps 1 through 4 for each additional account you want to set up.

6. When you have set up all the cash flow accounts you need, click **Next Step** to add accounts in the next goal area.

Spending & Savings Accounts				
Account	Financial Institution		Ending Balance	
Spending				
Checking	Damariscotta Bank & Trust Co		1,463.22	Edit Delete
Checking Liz	Caldwell Bank & Trust		354.71	Edit Delete
Savings				
Savings	Harrington Bank		7,135.56	Edit Delete

Credit Card Accounts					
Account	Financial Institution	Credit Limit	Available	Balance	
Credit Card John	Regions Bank	10,000.00	9,634.75	-365.25	Edit Delete
Credit Card Liz	Visalia Community Bank	12,000.00	11,787.85	-212.15	Edit Delete

ADD OTHER ACCOUNTS

While cash flow accounts are the most commonly used, Quicken offers four other types of accounts as well: investments, property and debt, paycheck, and bills.

1. Click **Next Step** from the Cash Flow window, or click **Investments** at the left side of the Quicken Guided Setup window, to open the Investment Account dialog box. Quicken tracks four different types of investment accounts: Brokerage, IRA or Keogh, 401(k) or 403(b), and Single Mutual Fund. A description of each account type is displayed to the right of the account.

2. Click one of the **Add Account** buttons to enter information about a particular investment. During Quicken Guided Setup you do not enter investment balances. See Chapter 8 for more information on investment accounts.

3. Click **Next Step** to open the Property & Debt dialog box where you enter information about your house, car, or other major assets. (An asset is something you own that has significant value, like a painting or a stamp collection.)

4. Click **Add Account** next to the type of property or debt for which you want to add an account. Quicken asks if there is a loan against this asset. If so, it prompts you to set up the liability account and leads you through the steps. See Chapter 6 for more detailed information about property and debt accounts.

NOTE

During the guided setup, you are prompted to set up accounts only for the goals you selected at the beginning of the setup. If you forget an account, you can set it up another time or go back to activate the goal setter.

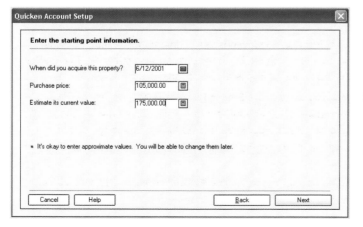

Quicken Account Setup

Enter the starting point information.

When did you acquire this property? 6/12/2001

Purchase price: 105,000.00

Estimate its current value: 175,000.00

• It's okay to enter approximate values. You will be able to change them later.

Cancel   Help   Back   Next

5. Click **Next Step** to enter information about your paycheck. By entering paycheck information, you give Quicken information it uses to help you with tax planning. Quicken can also enter your check automatically and keep track of your payroll deductions. This feature saves you time when entering data and makes your information more complete:

   a. Click **Add Paycheck**. The Welcome To Paycheck Set Up dialog box appears.

   b. Click **Next**. The Tell Quicken About This Paycheck window opens.

   c. Choose whether this is your paycheck or that of your spouse. Type your company name in the Company Name field, and indicate if you want to enter all of your earnings and deductions, including taxes, or have Quicken track just your take-home pay. Click **Next**.

   d. If you chose to enter all of your earnings and deductions, the Setup Paycheck dialog box appears, as shown in Figure 1-5. Click each item to enter your salary, taxes, and other deductions. Click **Done** to close the window.

   e. If you chose to have Quicken track only your take-home, or net, paycheck, a dialog box asks the net amount of your check as well as the dates on which you receive it. When you are paid, Quicken will enter your paycheck information in the account you designate. Click **Done** after you have entered the information to return to the Add Paychecks window.

6. Click **Next Step**. In the Add Bills dialog box you will see the bills and scheduled transactions that result from the mortgages, loans, and paychecks you have already entered. You can also tell Quicken about other recurring bills you owe and select a method by which to pay them. Quicken offers two payment choices: Quicken Bill Pay and Add Bills Manually:

   a. If you click **Quicken Bill Pay**, a window opens with information about a Quicken service that lets you see and pay your bills online. You may try this service free for one month. After the first month, there is a service fee.

   b. Click **Add Bills Manually** to open the Set Up Bills dialog box, shown in Figure 1-6. Use this window to enter your recurring bills. Move between the fields by pressing the TAB key on your keyboard. Enter who you pay, which account to use to pay the bill, the category, the amount of the payment, and how often you pay it.

   c. After you have entered all your bills, click **OK**. The bills you entered are listed in the Add Bills window.

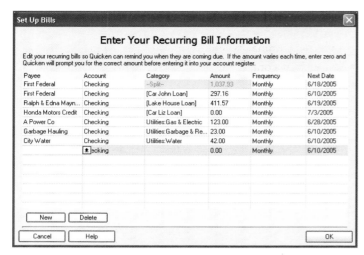

Set Up Bills

Enter Your Recurring Bill Information

Edit your recurring bills so Quicken can remind you when they are coming due. If the amount varies each time, enter zero and Quicken will prompt you for the correct amount before entering it into your account register.

Payee	Account	Category	Amount	Frequency	Next Date
First Federal	Checking	--Split--	1,037.93	Monthly	6/18/2005
First Federal	Checking	[Car John Loan]	297.16	Monthly	6/10/2005
Ralph & Edna Mayn...	Checking	[Lake House Loan]	411.57	Monthly	6/19/2005
Honda Motors Credit	Checking	[Car Liz Loan]	0.00	Monthly	7/3/2005
A Power Co	Checking	Utilities:Gas & Electric	123.00	Monthly	6/28/2005
Garbage Hauling	Checking	Utilities:Garbage & Re...	23.00	Monthly	6/10/2005
City Water	Checking	Utilities:Water	42.00	Monthly	6/10/2005
	ecking		0.00	Monthly	6/10/2005

New   Delete

Cancel   Help   OK

Figure 1-6: Use the Recurring Bill list to set up regular periodic bills.

7. Click **Next Step**. The last window in Quicken Guided Setup is a review of the accounts you created. As you can see in Figure 1-7, each account that you entered in each area is listed in the window. You can make any changes by clicking the links on the right side of the window, or click **Add Account** in the area where you want to put a new account.

8. When you have finished entering all the information you want to start with, click **Done**. After receiving a message that you are now ready to use Quicken 2006, click **OK**. The Quicken home page is displayed.

Figure 1-7: Review your data to make sure you've entered all the accounts you want to use.

Understand the Home Page

The Quicken home page provides a summary of all the accounts you have entered into Quicken. Figure 1-8 shows one of the default displays of the home page. You will see how to customize it in Chapter 2.

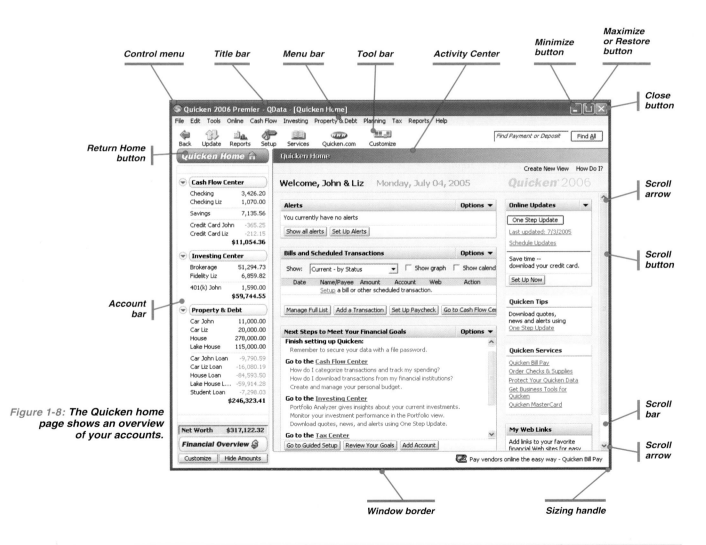

Control menu · **Title bar** · **Menu bar** · **Tool bar** · **Activity Center** · **Minimize button** · **Maximize or Restore button** · **Close button** · **Return Home button** · **Account bar** · **Scroll arrow** · **Scroll button** · **Scroll bar** · **Scroll arrow** · **Window border** · **Sizing handle**

Figure 1-8: **The Quicken home page shows an overview of your accounts.**

The Quicken home page has two major sections, or *panes*: the Account bar on the left shows a summary of your accounts, and the Activity Center on the right shows the detail of whatever you are looking at. Around these panes are a number of objects that are common to other Windows programs, including:

- The **Control Menu icon** opens the Control or System menu and allows you to move, size, and close the window.

- The **title bar** contains the name of the program or folder in the window and is used to drag the window around the screen.

- The **menu bar** contains the menus that are available in the window. Click a menu to open it, and then click one of its options.

- The **tool bar** contains tools related to the contents of the window. Click a tool to use it. The tool bar can be customized; see Chapter 2.

- The **Activity Center** displays the principal object of the window, such as the home page, a register, a transaction list, an analysis, alerts, or a report.

- The **Minimize button** decreases the size of the window so that you see it only as a task on the taskbar.

- The **Maximize button** [icon] increases the size of the window so that it fills the screen. When the window is maximized, the Maximize button becomes a Restore button to return the window to the size it was before being maximized.

- The **Close button** closes the window and any program it contains.

- The **vertical scroll bar** allows you to move the contents of the pane vertically within the window so that you can see information that wasn't previously visible. Scroll bar elements include:

  - **Scroll arrows** move the window contents in small increments in the direction of the arrow.

  - The **scroll bar** itself, when clicked, moves the contents in large increments.

  - A **scroll button** can be dragged in either direction to move the contents accordingly.

- The **sizing handle** allows a window to be sized diagonally, increasing or decreasing its height and width when you drag this handle.

- The **window border** separates the window from the desktop and can be used to size the window horizontally or vertically by dragging either the vertical or horizontal border.

- The **Return Home** button will redisplay the Quicken Home Activity Center when you are displaying a different activity center, such as a checking account register.

TIP

The common Windows objects around the periphery of the Quicken window generally remain fixed. The Activity Center, however, frequently changes to reflect whatever you are working on, such as one of your accounts.

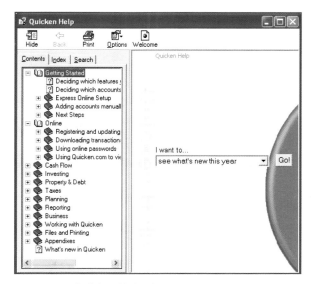

Figure 1-9: *Quicken Help gives you answers to your questions.*

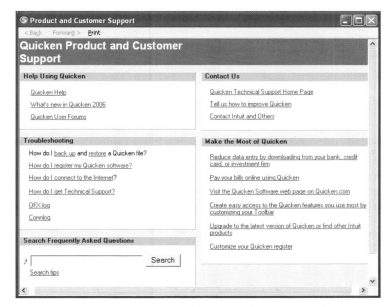

Figure 1-10: *Quicken provides a wide range of support to help you get the most out of it.*

Find Help

The Quicken Help window, shown in Figure 1-9, provides a ready reference to answer your questions about Quicken and to show you how to accomplish tasks. At any point in the program, pressing the **F1** key brings up the Help window with information about the current Quicken window, or you can click the **Help** menu, and click **Quicken Help** to open the Help window for a broad range of information about Quicken.

USE HELP

The Help window gives you four ways to find information:

- The **Contents** tab in the left pane of the Help window allows you to display a topic by clicking the plus sign on its left, open subtopics in the same way, and eventually click and view an article with the information you want.

- The **Index** tab provides an alphabetical list of all articles in Help. In the text box at the top of the list, you can type the topic and Quicken will automatically display matching entries, or you can scroll down the list using the scroll bar, and then click a topic.

- The **Search** tab allows you to type a word or words in the text box at the top of the left pane and see a list of articles, which you can click to display and read in the right pane.

- In the right pane of the initial Help window, shown in Figure 1-9, you can select one of six "I want to" topics and display the article requested.

USE OTHER HELP RESOURCES

The Help menu provides a number of other resources to assist you. Click one of the following options:

- **Product And Customer Support**, shown in Figure 1-10, displays the Quicken Help Options window and troubleshooting tips, as well as a link to Frequently Asked Questions and Quicken Technical Support on the Quicken.com web site (this requires an Internet connection).

QUICKSTEPS

UPDATING QUICKEN

Intuit provides online updates that you can access when you install Quicken and periodically thereafter. Occasionally when you start Quicken, the Quicken Update dialog box appears. If you have an Internet connection, it is a good idea to use this update feature to ensure that your program is completely up-to-date.

1. Click **Update Quicken** to go online. The program connects to the Intuit Update page, checks for new updates, and then downloads and installs them. You can click **Next** to continue if you want to update later or if you do not have an Internet connection.

2. The first time you go online with Quicken, it may ask you for your Internet connection information. After the program verifies an Internet connection, it may then ask for your name and address. You have the option of answering some questions about how you intend to use Quicken.

3. Click **Next** several times to work your way through the update process. To use any of the online tools available through Quicken, you must register and establish a password.

- **Submit Feedback On Quicken** allows you to provide feedback on Quicken. This also requires an Internet connection. It is through feedback from users such as you that Quicken improves its products. Your input is important, and Quicken encourages you to contact them.

- **What Is New In Quicken**, as well as **Learn About Setting Up Quicken** and **Learn About Downloading Transactions**, provides foundational information that will help you get started using the product.

- **User Manuals** provides documentation that you can print or view using Adobe Acrobat Reader. If you don't have Adobe Acrobat Reader, you can click the link in the Quicken User Manual window to download the program for free.

- **About Quicken** shows you which version of Quicken you are using if you need to call Customer Support (they will need this information before they can help you).

- **Privacy Statement** tells you how Quicken protects your personal information.

- **Register Quicken** appears on the Help menu if you did not register Quicken during the installation process. Click this link to register at any time. See "Register Quicken" earlier in this chapter.

Exit Quicken

When you have finished working with Quicken, you should exit the program. You will usually be prompted to back up your work before you exit Quicken. This is always a good idea. Hard drive crashes, power outages, and computer malfunctions happen to all of us at one time or another.

You can exit Quicken in several ways:

- Click the **Close** button on the right side of the title bar.
- Click **File** on the menu bar, and then click **Exit**.
- Click the **Quicken** icon on the left side of the title bar, and then click **Close**.
- You can also hold down the ALT key on your keyboard, and press the F4 key.

Use Quicken and Windows Basics

If you are new to Quicken, take a few minutes to read this section. It discusses terms used with Quicken as well as some that are used with all Windows-based programs. The dialog boxes and windows make more sense when you understand their contents.

Recognize Quicken Terms

Quicken is meant to be intuitive. You do most tasks with one or two clicks, and windows are designed to be easy-to-use and understand. The terms defined here are used throughout Quicken and this book:

- **Accounts** in Quicken represent your separate checking, savings, credit card, and brokerage accounts, as well as your mortgage and car loans, as shown in Figure 1-11. All your account information as a whole is kept within one Quicken data file. In Table 1-1 you can see the different account types used by Quicken, the location in which Quicken stores them, and some examples of each account type. There are standard accounts within each account type.

- **Data files**, or just files, are how Quicken stores the information about your financial records. Just as a word-processing document is stored as a document file in a folder on your hard disk, Quicken stores your data file in a folder on your hard disk. A data file contains information about all of your accounts, assets, liabilities, financial goals, and tax plans. Each family or entity's information is stored in a separate file. For example, if you are taking care of your Aunt Harriet's financial matters, her information is stored in a file separate from your personal data file.

- **Folders** are similar to the manila folders you store in a filing cabinet. Data files for your documents, spreadsheets, and Quicken files are stored in folders. Compare your hard drive to the filing cabinet in which you store paper files in folders to see the relationship with digital files and folders.

- **Centers** are groupings of similar types of accounts, as shown in Figure 1-11 and Table 1-1. There are three main Centers: Cash Flow, Investment, and Property & Debt. If you run your small business using Quicken Premier Home & Business, you have an additional Center just for the business accounts. Quicken combines the information from all of the Centers to calculate and display your net worth in the Financial Overview Center.

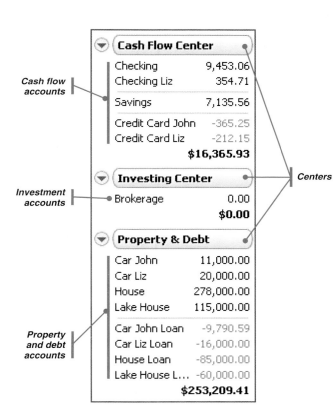

Cash flow accounts

Investment accounts

Property and debt accounts

Centers

Figure 1-11: **Quicken organizes account information into centers.**

ACCOUNT TYPE/ LOCATION	EXAMPLES
Cash Flow Accounts/ Cash Flow Center	These accounts track your checking, savings, and credit card accounts. You can even set up cash accounts for each member of your family to track allowances for the kids or petty cash kept in a cookie jar.
Investment Accounts/ Investment Center	These track your investments. You can track your individual brokerage accounts, your IRAs, your mutual funds, or any other investment. If you have Quicken 2006 Deluxe, Premier, or Premier Home & Business, you can keep track of your 401(k) or 403(b) plans offered by your employer.
Property & Debt Accounts/ Property & Debt Center	These accounts track your home and other mortgages, your car and any loans on it, or any other property you own. You can track loans owed to you or by you. You can even record your stamp collection or your son's baseball card collection.
Business Accounts/ Business Center	If you use Quicken 2006 for your small business, you can keep track of all your business accounts, such as receivables and inventory, as well as your capital equipment and other assets that would normally appear on a balance sheet. If you have Quicken 2006 Premier Home & Business, you can keep track of how much sales tax you owe as well as other bills you must pay, and you can record invoices to keep track of what your customers owe you.

Table 1-1: *Types of Accounts in Each Center*

Registers are similar to the paper check register used with a checking account and show the checks you write and the deposits you make. Each non-investment account in Quicken has its own register. You open a register by clicking the account in the Account bar. The menu items on the top of the register let you locate and delete transactions, write checks, and reconcile the account to a statement. The Overview tab shows the account attributes and status as well as a graphic display of activity for a period of time you designate.

- **Transactions** are the checks you write, the payments you make, and all other individual financial events. Quicken puts each event in either an account register or on an investment account transaction list.

- **Transaction lists** are used with investment accounts, such as a brokerage account or a 401(k) account, instead of a register. Quicken designed these lists to look like a brokerage statement, showing every transaction that has taken place.

- **Categories** are used to group similar transactions. Every time you enter a transaction into a Quicken register, you have the option of assigning it to a category. For example, all payments to the phone company could be put into the Telephone category. Quicken comes with a number of categories, but you can add new ones or delete those you don't want to use. Categories are handy for preparing taxes, budgeting, and analyzing where you are spending and receiving money.

- **Windows** are used to display related information on the screen. In addition to the basic Quicken window shown in Figure 1-8, several other windows are used by Quicken to display various types of information:

    - The **Internet window** uses the built-in Quicken web browser to display the Quicken.com web site.

    - **List windows** display information about related items, such as classes or categories.

    - **Report windows** let you create customized reports from your accounts.

- **Menus** and the **menu bar** are the tools Quicken and other Windows-based programs use to give you access to the commands and features within the program. Click a menu name in the menu bar to open the menu, and then click one of the *options* in the menu to select it. Some menu options have a right-pointing arrow to the right of the option. When you move the mouse pointer over that arrow, a submenu, or *flyout* menu, will open. When you right-click some objects within a window or dialog box, a *context* menu will open. Context menus show options specific to the item clicked.

- **Keyboard shortcuts** allow you to perform tasks from the keyboard rather than with the mouse and menus or tool bars. Table 1-2 lists the more frequently used keyboard shortcuts. If, for example, the shortcut is CTRL+P, you hold down the CTRL key while pressing the P key on the keyboard. Then, release both keys.

NOTE

Some of the more familiar Windows keyboard shortcuts may use a different keyboard combination in some areas of Quicken.

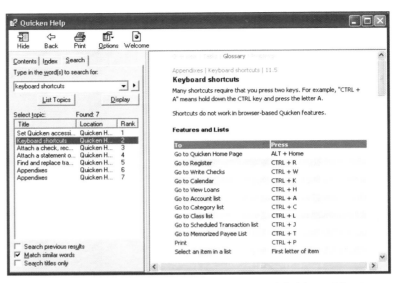

ACTION	KEYBOARD SHORTCUT
Cut	CTRL+X
Copy	CTRL+C
Paste	CTRL+V
Print	CTRL+P
Go to an account	CTRL+A
Create a backup file	CTRL+B
Help	F1
Go to Quicken home page	ALT+HOME
First day of the current month	M
Go to the next field or column	TAB
Go to a register	CTRL+R

Table 1-2: Keyboard Shortcuts

Figure 1-12: Keyboard shortcuts help you get around Quicken without removing your hands from the keyboard.

QUICKSTEPS

FINDING MORE KEYBOARD SHORTCUTS

To see additional keyboard shortcuts:

1. Click the **Help** menu and then click **Quicken Help**.

2. Click the **Search** tab, type keyboard shortcuts, and then press ENTER.

3. Double-click **Keyboard Shortcuts** in the Select Topic list to see the upper part of the list of shortcuts, as shown in Figure 1-12.

4. Click the scroll bar on the right side of the window to see the rest of the shortcuts list.

5. When you are done, click **Close** in the title bar to close the Quicken Help window.

• **Tool bars** are rows of buttons, often located directly below the menu bar. Click a button to perform its task, open a window, or display a dialog box. You can customize your Quicken tool bars. (See Chapter 2 for more information.)

Use Windows Tools

Quicken 2006 has a familiar feel if you are used to working with other Windows-based programs. For example, the Minimize, Maximize, and Close buttons appear in the title bar in the upper-right corner of every window, as shown here from left to right.

As with all Windows programs, if you have more than one window (or program) open at one time, the *active window* is the one with the brightest title bar:

- **Windows** are areas of the screen in which you can see a program that is running and they provide primary control of that program. When Quicken starts, it opens in its own window, as shown in Figure 1-8. Windows generally have menus and can be sized.

- **Dialog boxes** are used by Quicken and other Windows programs to communicate with you as the user and for you to communicate back to the program. They can be message boxes that require no action other than clicking OK, or they can be smaller areas of the screen with check boxes, option buttons, drop-down lists, text boxes, and possibly other controls that let you add information and control what is happening in a program, as shown in Figure 1-13. The primary parts of a dialog box are:

  - The **title bar** contains the name of the dialog box and is used to drag the box around the desktop.

  - A **drop-down list box** opens a list from which you can choose one item that will be displayed when the list is closed.

  - A **list box** (not shown) lets you select one or more items from a list; it may include a scroll bar.

  - **Check boxes** let you turn features on or off.

  - A **text box** lets you enter and edit text.

  - **Command buttons** perform functions, such as closing the dialog box and accepting the changes (the OK button) or closing the dialog box and ignoring the changes (the Cancel button).

  - **Tabs** let you select from among several pages in a dialog box.

  - **Option buttons**, also just called *options*, let you select one among mutually exclusive choices.

  - A **spinner** lets you select from a sequential series of numbers.

  - A **slider** lets you select from several values.

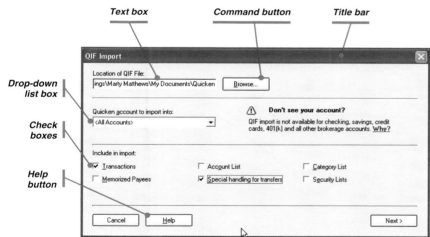

Text box   Command button   Title bar

Drop-down list box

Check boxes

Help button

Figure 1-13: **A dialog box provides the primary means of controlling what is happening in a program.**

Chapter 2
Making Quicken Yours

In Chapter 1 you saw how to install Quicken and how to use Quicken Guided Setup to establish your initial accounts. When you were finished, however, the look and feel of Quicken is the default style built into the product. For many people, this is fine, and their whole experience with Quicken is with the default style. However, Quicken provides a number of ways that you can customize it, both in how it looks and how it operates, allowing you to tailor the program to meet your specific needs. Quicken most likely will become an important program that you use often. As a result, it should reflect what you want. In this chapter you will see how to customize the home page so that it reflects you, how to add and change accounts, how to set up online banking, and how to add and delete categories so they provide the level of organization you want for your finances.

Customize the Home Page

After you have completed Quicken's installation and setup, the default Quicken
home page is displayed, as shown in Figure 2-1. You can customize the home
page by customizing the tool bar, changing the Account bar, managing
accounts, creating additional views, and setting your preferences for the way
various elements on the page are used.

Figure 2-1: *The Quicken home page provides an overview of all the financial
information you have entered into Quicken.*

Customize the Tool Bar

The tool bar can be customized to display any of the more than 60 command icons available in Quicken, as well as any reports you save. To customize the tool bar:

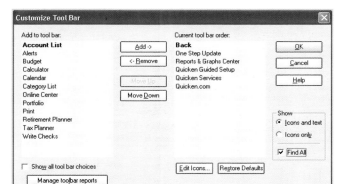

1. Click **Customize** on the right side of the tool bar. The Customize Tool Bar dialog box appears.

2. Click **Show All Tool Bar Choices** to display all possible commands.

3. To add a command icon to the tool bar, click the command in the Add To Tool Bar list on the left, and then click **Add**.

4. To remove an icon from the tool bar, click the command in the Current Tool Bar Order list on the right, and then click **Remove**.

5. To change the order in which icons are displayed on the tool bar, click the command in the Current Tool Bar Order list on the right, and click either of the **Move Up** or **Move Down** buttons. One click moves the icons up or down one place.

6. To assign a keyboard shortcut to a command icon, click the command and then click the **Edit Icons** button. The Edit Tool Bar Button dialog box appears:

   a. Type a letter from the keyboard in the text box opposite Alt+Shift+.

   b. Click **OK** to set the new shortcut and close the dialog box.

7. Choose whether to show both icons and text or only icons by clicking the relevant option. Click the **Find All** check box to have the global search field present on the tool bar.

8. When finished, click **OK** to set the changes and close the dialog box.

NOTE

In the Edit Tool Bar Button dialog box, you can also change the label under a tool bar icon.

TIP

In the Customize Tool Bar dialog box, click Restore Defaults to reset the tool bar settings to their original default state. You can also restore the original settings by pressing ALT+S on your keyboard.

Change the Account Bar

The Account bar on the left side of the home page shows the various activity centers you are using. At the top of this bar is the Quicken Home button. This button is normally in view and clicking it will bring you back to the home page from any place in Quicken. The rest of the Account bar can be changed in the following ways:

- Click the arrow in a circle to the left of each activity center name. If the arrow points to the right, only the total of the accounts in that center is displayed. Click the arrow ⊙ so it points downwards to display all of the accounts in that center as well as its current balance.

- Use the Financial Overview, Customize, and Hide Amounts buttons near the bottom of the Account bar as follows:

  - Click **Financial Overview** to display your financial overview in the Activity Center. This Center has three tabs—Net Worth, Planning, and Tax—that help you manage your finances and taxes as described in later chapters of this book.

  - Click **Hide Amounts** to hide all the amounts in the Account bar and change the button to Show Amt. Click Show Amt. to display the amounts again.

  - Click **Customize** to display the Account List dialog box, as described in the section "Manage Accounts."

Manage Accounts

You manage your accounts and determine how they are displayed using the Account List dialog box, which appears when you click **Customize** at the bottom of the Account bar. The Account List dialog box, shown in Figure 2-2, allows you to review and manage your accounts in more detail using the View Accounts and Manage Accounts tabs:

- Click **View Accounts** to see a list of all accounts in all activity centers with their current and ending balances. Normally, these amounts are the same. However, if you have a scheduled transaction that will occur after today but within the current accounting period (normally a month), the ending balance may be higher or lower than the current balance

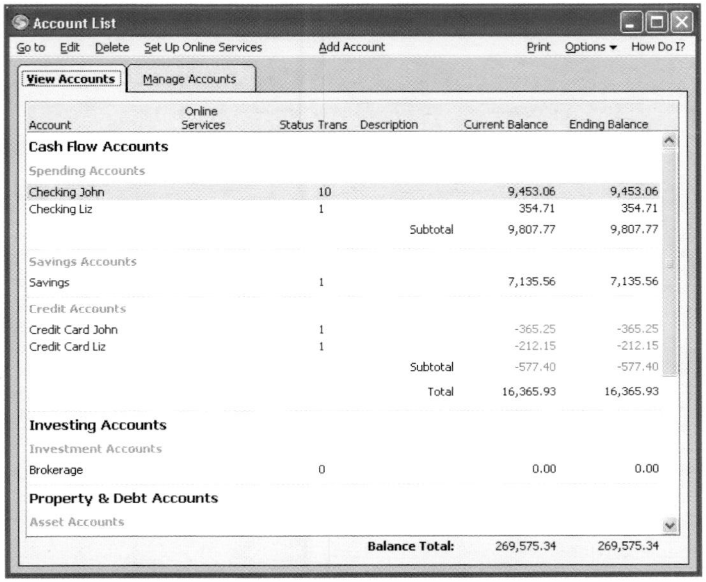

Figure 2-2: *The View Accounts tab in the Account List dialog box shows you your current account balances.*

by the amount of the future transaction. This tab also shows whether the account uses online services, the number of transactions that have been posted against it, and the account description. At the bottom of this window is the total of all of your accounts.

- Click **Manage Accounts** to determine how accounts are displayed and figure into the totals, as shown in Figure 2-3:

  - **Hide In Quicken** removes the account and its balance from the Account bar and View Accounts lists and from the Activity Center totals. The account only appears in the Manage Accounts tab.

  - **Don't Include In Totals** shows the account in its normal location but does not include its balance in the total for that Center.

  - **Remove From Bar** hides the name of the account from the Account bar and View Accounts lists but includes its balance under the name "Other Accounts"; it is also included in the Center total.

Figure 2-3: *The Manage Accounts tab in the Account List dialog box lets you determine whether an account is displayed and included in the totals.*

WORKING WITH THE ACTIVITY CENTER

The Activity Center, which takes up the majority of the Quicken home page, contains two major areas: the activity area, which is in the center of the home page, and the links bar on the right, as shown in Figure 2-4.

- The **activity area** displays Alerts, Bills And Scheduled Transactions, and Next Steps To Meet Your Financial Goals sections. Each section has an Options menu that you can use to set up and change what displays in that section.

- The **Links bar**, on right side of the home page, displays a number of links to various Intuit and other Internet sites. The One Step Update button provides the means to quickly update your financial accounts and obtain tips, quotes, and alerts from investment houses, banks, and Quicken. If you need to set up this service, there is a Set Up Now button at the bottom of the Online Updates section that connects you to one of the financial institutions you use so that you can set up an account with them. In addition, there are links to Quicken.com and other Quicken services, as well as the My Web Links service, which allows you to add links to your own financial web locations.

CAUTION

Be careful when changing an account from one activity center to another. Some accounts should not be moved, such as a checking account linked to a liability. (A *liability* is something that you owe.)

Activity area   *Links bar*

Figure 2-4: *The Activity Center contains the activity area on the left and the links bar on the right.*

- Rearrange the order in which your accounts are displayed by clicking an account, and then clicking **Move Up** or **Move Down** to change the account's position.
- **Change Group** allows you to move a selected account from one Center (or group) to another.
- Click **Close** to close the Account List dialog box.

Design a New Home Page View

Other than the modifications described in the previous sections of this chapter, the home page itself cannot be changed. You can, however, create a new, alternate view of the home page that will appear as a tab on the Quicken Home title bar of the Activity Center. To create a new view of the home page:

TIP

Click the **Options** menu in any area to display links to reports, planning tools, and customization tools.

NOTE

Clicking the How Do I? button opens the Help dialog box. You can also access the same dialog box by clicking **Help**, clicking **Contents**, and clicking **Index**.

Quicken Home **Home** **View 1**

1. Click **Create New View** in the upper-left corner of the Activity Center. The Customize View dialog box appears. From here you can add items to your view from the Available Items list on the left, and remove items from the Chosen Items list on the right.

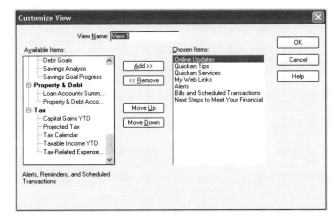

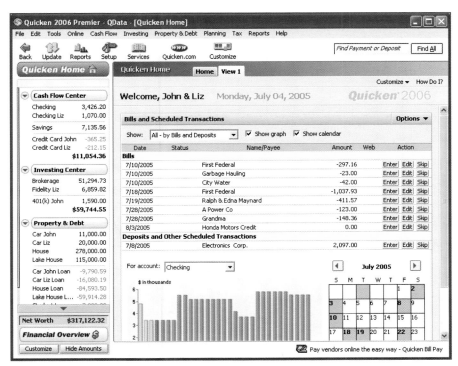

Figure 2-5: *You can create many different views for the Activity Center of the home page.*

2. Click an item on the Available Items list, and click **Add**. The item appears in the Chosen Items list.

3. Click an item on the Chosen Items list, and click **Remove**. The item disappears from the Chosen Items list but does not disappear from the Available Items list.

4. Click an item on the Chosen Items list, and then click **Move Up** or **Move Down** to change the position of the item on the list.

5. Repeating steps 2–4, create one or more views that meet your needs. When finished, click **OK**. Your new view(s) will appear in the Activity Center, as shown in Figure 2-5.

Set Preferences

Preferences are the ways in which you make Quicken behave the way you want. For example, when you start Quicken, instead of displaying the home page, you can display the Cash Flow Center. This is a startup preference. Other types of preferences in Quicken include backup preferences, register preferences, and report preferences. This section will discuss startup and setup preferences. The remaining preferences will be discussed elsewhere in this book. To change the startup and setup preferences:

1. Click the **Edit** menu, click **Preferences**, and then click **Quicken Program**. The Quicken Preferences dialog box appears with the startup preferences displayed, as shown in Figure 2-6.

2. Click the **On Startup Open To** down arrow, and choose the center or account that you want to appear when you start Quicken.

3. Click **Setup** in the left column. The setup preferences are displayed.

4. Choose whether to display the Account bar on the left or right side of the window or not at all.

5. Choose whether to map keyboard shortcuts to Quicken or Windows standards. See Table 2-1 for what these shortcuts do in each case. The Windows standard is the default (see Chapter 1 for more information).

Figure 2-6: You can control many of the nuances of Quicken through the Quicken Preferences dialog box.

6. Choose whether to turn off the Quicken sounds—for example, the "ka-chung" sound that plays every time you enter a transaction—by clicking that option to deselect it.

7. Click **OK** to close the dialog box when you are finished.

NOTE

The reason most people keep the Windows standard for the CTRL+C, CTRL+V, CTRL+X, and CTRL+Z shortcut keys is that the Windows commands are heavily used in Windows programs, while the Quicken commands are infrequently used.

SHORTCUT KEYS	WINDOWS	QUICKEN
CTRL+C	Copy	Open the Category List
CTRL+V	Paste	Void a transaction
CTRL+X	Cut	Show the matching entry, for example, in a liability register
CTRL+Z	Undo	Display more detail about a report amount

Table 2-1: Alternative Windows and Quicken Mapping of Shortcut Keys

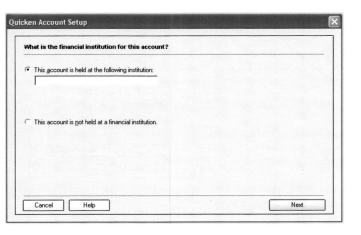

TIP

If you have a small business, it is a good idea to maintain a separate account for business transactions, rather than paying business expenses from your personal checking account.

Add and Change Accounts

Accounts are central to Quicken's operation, whether they are checking, investment, or property and debt accounts. In Chapter 1 you saw how to get started setting up accounts with Quicken Guided Setup. As you use Quicken, it is likely that you will want to add additional accounts and modify the accounts you already have. This section will look at adding and modifying cash flow accounts. In later chapters you'll see how to add and modify accounts in other centers.

Add Cash Flow Accounts

If you did not use Quicken Guided Setup to create the checking, savings, and credit card accounts you want, you can here:

1. Right-click the **Cash Flow Center** button in the Account bar, and click **Add New Account** in the context menu that opens.

   –Or–

   Click the **Cash Flow Center** button in the Account bar to open it in the Activity Center, and then click the **Add Account** button at the bottom of the applicable section: Spending & Saving Accounts or Credit Card Accounts.

   –Or–

   Click the **Cash Flow** menu, click **Cash Flow Accounts**, and then click **Add Account**.

   All three methods open the Quicken Account Setup dialog box.

2. Type the name of your financial institution. Often you can begin typing the first few letters of the name of your institution to display a list, and then click yours. To set up an account without online banking services, click **This account is not held at a financial institution**. You can set up online banking later.

3. Click **Next**. Click either **Online** or **Manual** to choose how you want to set up the account. If the Online choice is not available, your financial institution does not support online banking, so click **Manual**.

   If you click Online:

   a. You are told you will need to have an ID, account number, or user name and a PIN (personal identification number) or password given to you by your bank. Indicate to Quicken that you have these, and click **OK**.

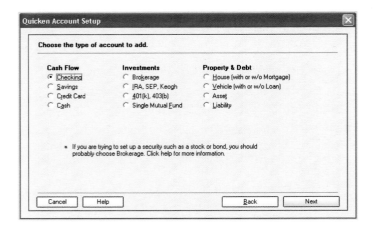

Quicken Account Setup

Choose the type of account to add.

Cash Flow
- Checking
- Savings
- Credit Card
- Cash

Investments
- Brokerage
- IRA, SEP, Keogh
- 401(k), 403(b)
- Single Mutual Fund

Property & Debt
- House (with or w/o Mortgage)
- Vehicle (with or w/o Loan)
- Asset
- Liability

- If you are trying to set up a security such as a stock or bond, you should probably choose Brokerage. Click help for more information.

[Cancel] [Help] [Back] [Next]

b. Quicken will then connect to the bank over the Internet, your bank's web site will appear, and you will be prompted to enter your ID and PIN.

c. You then need to locate on the bank's web site a command to download the current transactions (in most cases, this is a Download button). Click it and follow your bank's instructions to download your account information.

d. When the download is complete, sign out and exit the bank's web site.

e. Upon returning to Quicken, you are asked if this download is for an existing account or for a new account. Select the latter, type a name, and click **Continue**. You are notified when the download is complete. Click **Done**.

If you click Manual:

a. You will be asked the type of account you want to set up. For example, to add a checking account, click **Checking** and click **Next**.

b. Type a name for the account, and click **Next**.

c. Enter the last statement date and the ending balance, and then click **Done**.

Modify Cash Flow Accounts

Once you have set up an account, you will likely need to make some changes to, or even delete, the account. To change or delete an account:

1. In the Account bar on the left, click the account you want to change. The account is shown in the Activity Center with the register displayed.

2. Click the **Overview** tab to view the account attributes and current status, as shown in Figure 2-7.

3. To delete an account, click **Delete Account** in the Activity Center's menu bar. Type yes to confirm the deletion, click **OK** to carry out the deletion, and then click **OK** again in response to the message that the account was deleted. If you change your mind before clicking **OK**, click **Cancel** and then click **OK** in response to the message that the account was not deleted.

4. To modify the account, click **Edit Account Details** at the bottom of the Account Attributes area. The Account Details dialog box appears.

You can also open the Account Details dialog box by right-clicking an account in the Account bar, and clicking **Edit Account** in the context menu that opens.

TIP

For the account name, you can use any combination of letters, numbers, and spaces except the following characters: right and left brackets ([ ]), the forward slash (/), colon (:), caret (^), and vertical bar (|). If you do not type a name, Quicken uses "Checking" as the default name.

NOTE

If you do not have a bank statement handy, you can enter the statement date and ending balance later. If you have a current bank statement, enter the date in the format MM/DD/YYYY. For example, you would enter October 18, 2005, as 10/18/2005.

UICKSTEPS

ADDING A CASH ACCOUNT

Cash accounts are useful for tracking where your money goes. You can set up cash accounts for each member of the family. To set up a cash account:

1. Click the **Cash Flow** menu, click **Cash Flow Accounts**, and click **Add Account**.

2. Click **This Account Is Not Held At A Financial Institution**, and then click **Next**.

3. For the type of account, click **Cash**. Click **Next**, type a name, such as Nick's Allowance, and click **Next**.

4. If you want to start keeping track of your cash spending as of today, leave the default of today's date. If you want to use another date, enter it in the MM/DD/YYYY format.

5. Press TAB, enter the amount of cash you are starting with, and click **Done**. If you want to go back to earlier dialog boxes, click **Back**. If you decide you do not want to enter this account, click **Cancel**.

Tracking your spending with cash accounts allows each member of the family to see exactly where his or her money goes. It can be a valuable tool for anyone, but especially for young people as they learn to handle money.

TIP

When you use a cash account, make sure you include ATM withdrawals and deposits to your cash account. You could even set up a cash account just for ATM withdrawals.

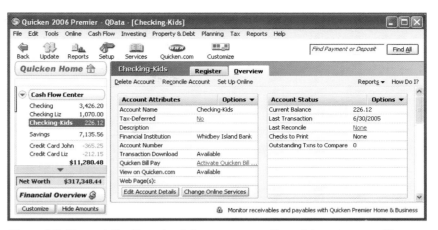

Figure 2-7: *Through the Overview tab on an account's register, you can edit or delete an account.*

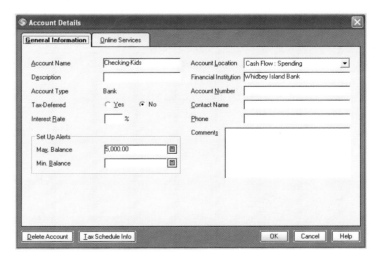

5. In the General Information tab, you can change the account name, description, location, financial institution, and other information, as shown above.

6. In the Online Services tab, you can activate or deactivate online transaction downloading and Quicken bill paying, as described in "Use Quicken Online," next.

7. When finished, click **OK**.

Use Quicken Online

Most banks and credit unions, as well as brokerages, mortgage lenders, and insurance companies, give you the option of connecting to them online and potentially interfacing with Quicken. With banks and credit unions, at least two services are usually offered: online account access and online bill paying. With the online account access service, you use an Internet connection to connect to your financial institution's computer to see what checks have cleared, what deposits have been posted, and what service charges or other *automatically recurring* transactions have been posted to your account. (Automatically recurring transactions are transactions that you have agreed to be automatically deducted from or added to your account on a regular basis, such as property tax, car loan payments, or Social Security checks.) Online banking also allows you to transfer between accounts—from checking to savings, for example, or from your savings account to your credit card account to pay your credit card bill.

The online bill-paying service lets you pay bills electronically rather than by writing a check. You tell the bank the name of the payee, the address, and the amount to pay, and the bank facilitates the payment, either electronically or by writing the check. You can usually set up regularly scheduled payments, such as insurance or mortgage payments, so that those payments are never late.

Quicken also offers bill-paying services through Quicken Bill Pay. Available for any U.S. checking account, the service stores payee information for you, so whenever you make a new payment, account numbers and payee information appear automatically. You just fill in the correct amount to pay. As with many banks, there is a charge for this service.

Understand Online Services

Today, most financial institutions offer some type of online financial service. This saves them money and offers consumers a valuable tool. All such online services require an Internet connection. Some institutions charge a fee for these services, although many do not. Over time your costs may be less than working with paper statements, paying bills by check, mailing payments, and buying stamps. Check with your institution to determine its costs for the services they provide. Table 2-2 explains these services.

SERVICE	DESCRIPTION
Online Account Access	This service allows you to look at your account through the financial institution's web site. You can see which checks or deposits have been posted and any fees charged to your account. Some institutions allow you to transfer money between accounts. Some also allow you to transfer funds from your banking account to your credit card account to pay your bill. This type of access is now available through many types of companies. Firms as diverse as insurance, utility, telephone, and even gasoline companies are beginning to offer forms of online account access.
Online Bill Payment	With this service, your bank or credit union pays your bills from your existing account. Working with information you give them, the institution will either wire-transfer money from your account to your payee's account or actually prepare a check they send to your payee. While not all institutions support this service, you can get the same service by subscribing to Quicken Bill Pay.
Transaction Download	With this service, you can *download* (copy from the bank's computer to Quicken) all of your account activity. There are two ways to download transactions. Which type you use will depend on your financial institution: ● **Web Connect** This service requires that you log on to the institution's web site, enter your identifying information, and indicate which items you want downloaded to Quicken. ● **Direct Connect** If your institution offers this service, click **One Step Update** in the Quicken Home Activity Center. After entering the identifying information supplied by your institution, Quicken will obtain the information and place it in the proper accounts.

Table 2-2: Online Services Offered by Many Financial Institutions

Working online can save you time and money, but as more financial institutions are going online, their security procedures are becoming more stringent. Many institutions discuss these procedures on their web sites, and others provide brochures about maintaining security online. You can help by ensuring you keep your password and PIN in a secure place, by keeping your antivirus program up-to-date, and by using a good firewall. When using any online service, remember that with any benefit comes some risk.

Understand Internet Security

As the Internet has gained popularity, so have the risks in using it. Viruses, worms, spyware, and adware have become part of our vocabulary. As you start to work online, take a moment to understand what each problem is and how to guard your computer and data, as described in Table 2-3.

Before you start your online financial transactions, understand the online security issues and take steps to protect your computer. Your financial institution is working to protect your information on its end, but you need to do your part as well.

Set Up Online Banking

Before you can use online banking services, you must first have a working Internet connection. You get such a connection through an *Internet service provider*, or ISP.

QUICKFACTS

DECIDING TO USE ONLINE BANKING SERVICES

In making the decision whether to use online banking services, consider the following points:

- While electronic banking is becoming more common, not all financial institutions make it available through Quicken or even offer it at all. Ensure your bank or credit union has the service available.

- To ensure security, carefully protect the identification number and PIN provided by your financial institution. Most financial institutions transmit with *encrypted* data. That means anyone intercepting the transmission would see only gibberish. Quicken uses the same method to send information to your financial institution.

- Your records should be up-to-date and your last paper statement reconciled before you start the services.

- You should understand how to use Quicken to record a check, create a deposit, reconcile your accounts, and transfer between accounts before you use the electronic services.

- Most financial institutions charge a fee for these services. Compute the cost of doing it yourself (postage, gas to go to the post office, envelopes, and so on). Compare those costs to the fees charged by Quicken or your financial institution.

PROBLEM	DEFINITION	SOLUTION
Virus	A program that attaches itself to other files on your computer. There are many forms of viruses, each performing different, usually malevolent, functions on your computer.	Install an antivirus program with a subscription for automatic updates, and make sure it is continually running.
Worm	A type of virus that replicates itself repeatedly through a computer network or security breach in your computer. Because it keeps copying itself, a worm can fill up a hard drive and cause your network to malfunction.	
Trojan horse	A computer program that claims to do one thing, such as play a game, but has hidden parts that can erase files or even your entire hard drive.	
Adware	The banners, pop-ups, and ads that come with programs you download from the Internet. Often these programs are free, and to support them, the program owner sells space for ads to display on your computer every time you use the program.	Install an anti-adware program.
Spyware	A computer program that downloads with another program from the Internet. Spyware can monitor what you do, keep track of your keystrokes, discern credit card and other personally identifying numbers, and pass that information back to its author.	Install an antispyware program.

*Table 2-3: **Security Issues Associated with the Internet and How to Control Them***

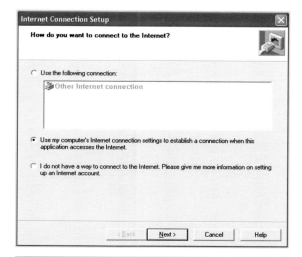

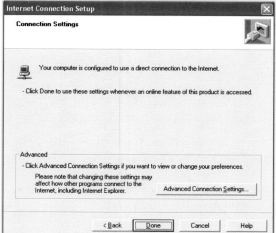

Check your phone book or call your local telephone company or cable TV company to find an ISP in your area. The ISP will give you the information you need to get an Internet connection and set it up in Windows. To set up your Internet connection in Quicken:

1. Click the **Edit** menu, click **Preferences**, and then click **Internet Connection Setup**. The Internet Connection Setup dialog box appears.

2. Choose one of the following three options:

   - Click **Use The Following Connection** to use a listed connection that is different from what your computer normally uses. For example, if your ISP or financial institution requires that you run a program before connecting, or if you are unsure of or unable to use your Windows Internet connection, select this method.

   - Click **Use My Computer's Internet Connection Settings To Establish A Connection When This Application Accesses The Internet**, which is the default, when Quicken can detect an Internet connection in Windows.

   - Click **I Do Not Have A Way To Connect To The Internet. Please Give Me More Information On Setting Up An Internet Account** for information that may help you connect to the Internet.

3. Click **Next**. The Connection Settings dialog box appears and confirms the way you are to connect to the Internet. Click **Done** if you're satisfied with this connection. Otherwise, click **Back** to return to the previous dialog box and make another selection.

Once you have established your Internet connection, you are prepared to contact your bank to sign up for their online services. Many financial institutions allow you to sign up on their web site, while others require that you call your local branch. Either way, most institutions need you to fill out an application, send a voided check or complete other paperwork, and agree to their fees. Then, you may need to wait a few days to get your identification number, password, or PIN sent to you by mail.

Implement Online Banking

Once you have received the information from the bank, you have several ways to implement the online service.

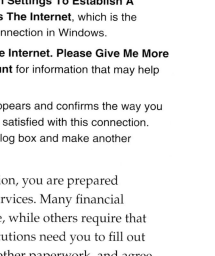

TIP

While you are waiting for the bank to send you your information to use online banking, ensure that all your transactions are recorded and your latest paper statement has been reconciled.

TIP

If you don't see Set Up Online in the register menu bar, it means that the account has already been set up.

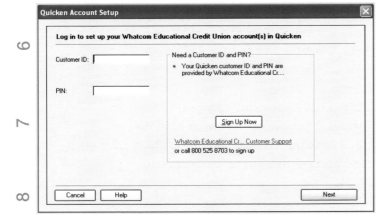

1. For an existing account, open its register by clicking the account name in the Cash Flow Center. When the register appears, click **Set Up Online** in the register menu bar. The Quicken Account Setup dialog box appears.

2. If you have previously entered the name of your financial institution and the institution provides Direct Connect services, the dialog box asks for your Customer ID number or account number and PIN number or password.

   If Quicken is unable to determine the name of your institution, the dialog box displays a list of possible institutions from which to choose. This dialog box may also provide a link to the complete list of financial institutions that work with Quicken to provide online services.

3. If your bank uses Web Connect, you will be directed to log on to your institution's web site and follow their instructions. See the QuickSteps "Setting Up Web Connect."

4. Click **Next**. Some institutions may display a dialog box that asks for more information. Fill in the information as needed, and then click **Next**. A dialog box appears notifying you that you have successfully set up the account.

5. Click **Next** to download your first set of transactions. When you are notified that you have successfully completed the download, click **Done**.

Use Quicken Bill Pay

If your financial institution does not supply online bill-paying services, or if you choose not to use them, Quicken offers a similar service. Quicken Bill Pay is available for all U.S. customers. Using this service allows you to pay bills to any United States vendor from anywhere in the world with an Internet connection.

1. On Quicken's home page, under Quicken Services in the Links bar on the right, click **Quicken Bill Pay** to read a complete description of this service. As seen in Figure 2-8, the Overview tab in the Quicken Bill Pay window provides information on the service, while the other tabs give you more detailed information.

Quicken Services

Quicken Bill Pay
Order Checks & Supplies
Protect Your Quicken Data
Get Business Tools for Quicken
Quicken MasterCard

QUICKSTEPS

SETTING UP WEB CONNECT

You can use Direct Connect, as described in "Implement Online Banking," to perform online banking transactions directly with Quicken if your financial institution offers that service. Otherwise, you must use Web Connect, which requires that you get started through the bank's web site and use their instructions to download your transactions. Quicken will then read and post those transactions.

1. To find out what services your institution offers, in Quicken, click the **Online** menu, and then click **Participating Financial Institutions**.

2. To set up for Web Connect, in your web browser, not Quicken (but Quicken should be running), log on to your financial institution's web site, entering your ID and PIN if needed. Find and click a button or link that says **Download** or **Download To Quicken**. This is often located where you view the detail for an account. If necessary, contact your financial institution to determine its location.

3. If you are proceeding to download information, you'll be asked for the format the file should be in. Choose **Quicken** or **QFX**.

4. If prompted for a range of transaction dates, select or type the dates.

5. When you are asked if you want to save or open the file, click **Open** and choose the **QFX** file type if asked.

Continued . . .

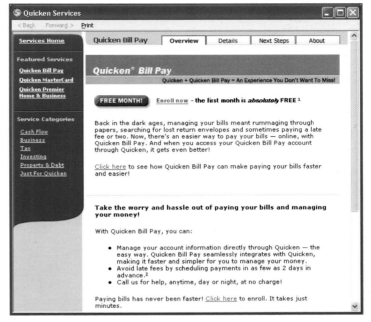

*Figure 2-8: **Quicken Bill Pay offers a safe, quick way to pay your bills on time.***

This service is especially useful if you have a small business or travel extensively. The service allows you to choose the account from which to pay, how much to pay, when to pay, and schedule recurring payments. The cost for this online service may be offset by postage, time in check preparation, and ease in handling this task.

Understand Categories

A *category* is a description or label for an expense or a source of income. For example, payments to your telephone company might use the Telephone category. You can create subcategories for each category. For example, your trash pickup service might be a subcategory of Utilities. There are two types of categories: Income and Expense. As you set up your accounts and prepare to enter transactions, it is a good idea to set up categories at the same time.

Quicken supplies a number of preset categories for you to use. It also remembers the category you assign for each payee. Quicken customizes your list of categories in response to your answers in Quicken Guided Setup. You can add new categories as well as delete any of the preset categories that do not apply to you.

Work with Categories

To view the preset category list and add and remove categories:

1. Click the **Tools** menu and then click **Category List**. Your Category List opens, as shown in Figure 2-9. The list shows all of the income categories in alphabetical order and then the expense categories in alphabetical order.

2. Click **Options** on the right side of the menu bar to choose whether to display the category description, group, and type, and to assign groups to categories:

   a. Click **Assign Category Groups**. The Assign Category Groups dialog box appears.

   b. Click a category from the Category Name List.

   c. Click a category group from the Category Group List. Click the **Assign Category To Group** button. The Category Group column displays in the middle. If you have not assigned a category group, there is no entry in the Category Group column.

   d. Click **OK**. Repeat the process for all the assignments you want to make.

   e. To clear a Category Group assignment, click the category name and click the **Clear Assignment** button. When you are done, close the dialog box.

3. Click the **Display Tax Information** check box. An additional pane opens displaying the income tax line and form assigned to a category, as shown in Figure 2-10.

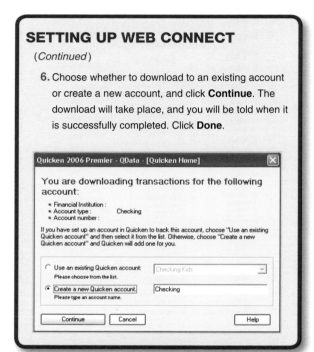

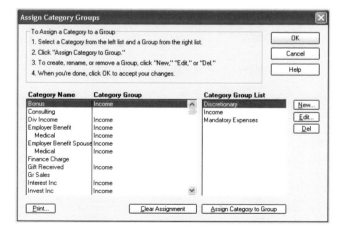

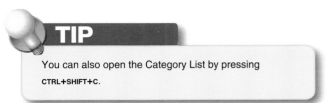

TIP

You can also open the Category List by pressing
CTRL+SHIFT+C.

TIP

Assigning tax-line items to categories makes it easier to
create tax reports and plan for tax time.

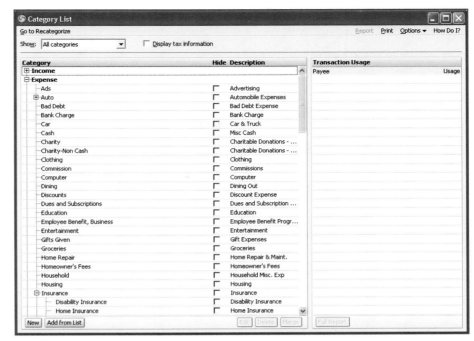

Figure 2-9: *The Category List displays the categories you can use to organize your finances.*

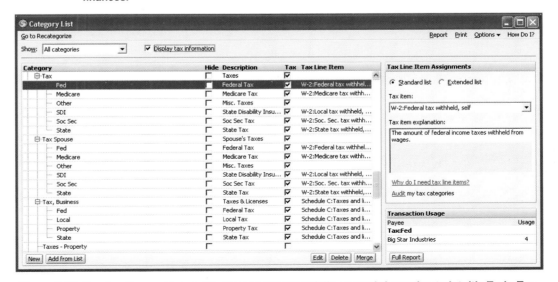

Figure 2-10: *Tax-line item assignments allow you to more fully export information to Intuit's TurboTax, a companion to Quicken.*

TIP

If your screen cuts off part of the information in the Tax Information pane, click the name of the category, and click **Edit** at the bottom of the dialog box to see all of the information.

QUICK**FACTS**

USING TAX-LINE ASSIGNMENTS

While Quicken does not require that you include tax information in categories, entering this information can save a lot of time when preparing your taxes. By using them, Quicken can:

- Display up-to-date tax information in the Tax Center window. By knowing your tax position, you can talk to your tax professional about options well before year-end.

- Prepare tax reports by tax schedule or form. These reports will assist your tax professional and perhaps save you some money in tax-preparation fees.

- Create reports that report taxable and nontaxable dividends, interest, and other items separately.

- Help you use the Tax Planner within Quicken (see Chapter 10).

- Export your data directly into Intuit's TurboTax to help you prepare your income tax return.

The few minutes you spend assigning tax-line items to your categories can save a lot of time and money at the end of the year.

If the Display Tax Information check box is not selected, the list of transactions used in this category appears on the right side of the dialog box. If tax information is being displayed, this list appears below the Tax Information pane.

4. The bottom of the list shows each of your accounts under Transfers And Payments. If there is a small plus sign to the left of Transfers And Payments, click it to display the list. A minus sign indicates that all accounts are currently displayed.

Add an Income Category

To add a new income category:

1. Click the **Tools** menu, click **Category List**, and click **New** in the bottom-left corner of the list. The Set Up Category dialog box appears.

2. Type a name for your new category. Press TAB or click in the **Description** field.

3. Type any description necessary, such as Part-time job or the name of the company from whom you get this income.

4. Press TAB or click in the **Group** field. You have the option to assign this category to a group. Quicken

predefines three groups: Discretionary, Income, and Mandatory Expenses. You may add new groups or choose not to use groups.

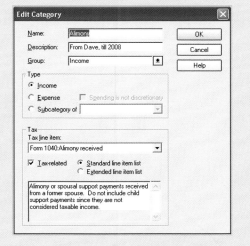

QUICKSTEPS

RENAMING A CATEGORY

You can rename a category to make it more meaningful.

1. In the Category List window, right-click the name of the category, and click **Edit**.

   —Or—

   In the Category List window, click the name of the category, and then click **Edit** at the bottom of the list.

2. In either case, the Edit Category dialog box appears.

3. Click in the **Name** field to select it, and type a new name.

4. If this category is tax-related, review the tax-line item to ensure it is still correct.

5. Click **OK** to close the Edit Category dialog box.

5. Click **Income** to designate this category as an Income item.

6. If this category is tax-related, click **Tax-Related**. Then, choose the tax-line item to which it applies:

   a. Click the **Tax Line Item** down arrow to bring up a list of possible tax lines from which to choose.

   b. Click the relevant line, or you may choose to leave this field blank. A small explanation appears in the box below when a tax-line item is chosen.

7. Click **OK** to finish adding the category.

Enter Multiple Categories at Once

Quicken includes several preset lists of categories:

- Standard
- Married
- Homeowner
- Business
- Children
- Investment
- Rents & Royalties

The one you automatically start out with when you install and begin using Quicken, and the one we have been talking about in previous sections, is the Standard Category List. If you want to include another preset list, you can add all the categories in that list to your Category List at the same time.

1. Click the **Tools** menu and click **Category List**.

2. Click **Add From List** at the bottom of the dialog box. The Add Categories dialog box appears.

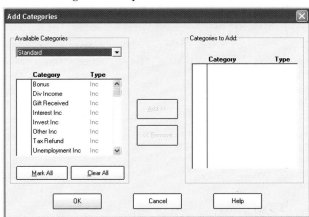

TIP

Do not combine alimony payments you receive with child support payments you receive. Instead, create a separate category for each item. Check with your tax professional for further information.

TIP

When selecting categories in the Add Categories dialog box, you can select multiple contiguous categories (categories that are next to each other) by holding down the SHIFT key while clicking the first and last categories. You can select multiple noncontiguous categories (categories that are not next to each other) by holding down the CTRL key while clicking each of the categories.

TIP

Just because Quicken uses a specific category or subcategory does not mean you have to use it in the same way. For example, if you want all of your insurance expenses to be one category, delete the subcategories.

3. Click the **Available Categories** down arrow to display the lists of preset categories.

4. Click the preset list you want to add to the Standard list. The categories included in the list display in the Category List.

5. Choose the categories you want to use, or click **Mark All** to select all of them.

6. Click **Add** to move the categories into the Categories To Add list on the right side of the dialog box.

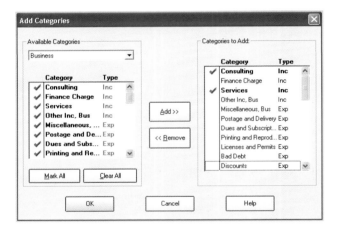

7. If you want to remove one or more of the new categories from the Categories To Add list, click the category and click **Remove**.

8. Click **OK** to add the categories and close the dialog box.

Insert an Expense Category with Subcategories

Expense categories are the best way to find out just where you are spending your money. You can use any of the predefined categories or add your own. You can also create subcategories to show more detail. When you categorize each item, you can create reports and graphs that show spending patterns and habits. You can even create budgets for categories or groups of categories.

1. Click the **Tools** menu and click **Category List**, or press CTRL+SHIFT+C.

2. Click **New**. The Set Up Category dialog box appears. Type the name of your new expense category in the Name field.

3. Press TAB to move to the Description field, and type a description. (The Description field may be left blank.)

4. Press TAB to move to the Group field, click the down arrow, and make your selection from the drop-down list. (The Group field may be left blank.)

5. Click the **Expense** option. If this expense has tax implications, click **Tax-Related**. Click the **Tax Line Item** down arrow, and click the applicable item to select it.

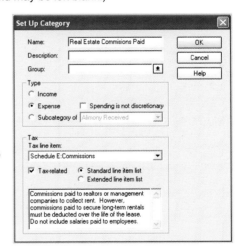

6. Click **OK** to close the dialog box.

7. To add a subcategory to your new category, click the parent category in the Category List, and click **New** at the bottom of the Category List. The Set Up Category dialog box appears.

8. Type the name of your subcategory. Press TAB to move to the Description field, and type a description if you want.

9. Leave the **Group** field blank, or click the **Group** down arrow, and make a selection from the drop-down list.

10. Click the **Subcategory Of** option. Type the name of the parent category, or choose it from the drop-down list.

11. If this expense has tax implications, click **Tax-Related** and choose the tax-line item from the drop-down list. Otherwise, leave the **Tax** field empty.

12. Click **OK** to close the dialog box.

QUICKSTEPS

DELETING CATEGORIES

As you are working with your Category List, you may see some items that you want to delete.

1. Click the **Tools** menu and click **Category List**, or press CTRL+SHIFT+C, to open the Category List.

2. Click the category you want to delete, and click **Delete** in the bottom-right corner of the dialog box.

   –Or–

   Right-click the category you want to delete to open a context menu. Click **Delete**.

3. A warning message appears, notifying you that this account is about to be deleted. Click **OK** if you want to delete the account, or click **Cancel** if this was an error.

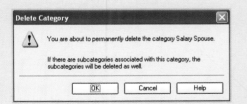

4. If you click **OK**, the category disappears from the Category List.

5. Click **OK** to close the Category List.

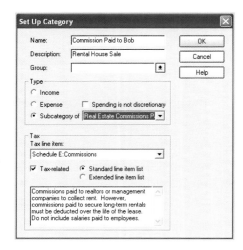

TIP

You can choose to hide a category by clicking the **Hide** check box. Hidden categories do not appear on the Category List but are still included in the Quicken data file.

You will see the new category as a subcategory on the Category List. The Category List displays the categories in alphabetical order and each subcategory in alphabetical order indented underneath the parent category.

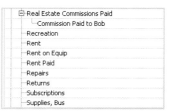

Chapter 3

Setting Up the Other Centers

In the first two chapters, the focus was on setting up the Cash Flow Center using Quicken's tools. In this chapter you'll look at the Investing Center and the Property & Debt Center, learn how to set up their accounts, and examine some of the Quicken tools that are available in those areas. Both Centers are optional, depending on how much detail you want to maintain in Quicken.

Understand Financial Terminology

Before you begin working with the Investing and Property & Debt Centers, review the terms that are used in these areas, as explained in Table 3-1.

3

TERM	DEFINITION
Asset	Something you own that you expect to increase in value.
Brokerage	A company that buys and sells stocks and bonds for a fee on behalf of their clients.
Default	A setting or other value used by a computer program. Quicken names an account "Asset" by *default* if you do not choose another name.
Depreciation	A decrease or loss in value due to age, wear, or market conditions.
Equity	The market value of an asset, less any debt owed on that asset.
Interest	Rent on borrowed money.
Interest Rate	The percentage of a debt charged for borrowing money.
Investment	Something you expect to increase in value or to generate income.
Market Value	The amount for which an asset can be sold today.
Mutual Fund	An investment company that invests in the securities of other companies and sells shares of those investments.
Performance	How a specific investment behaves over time, for example, how much money it earns.
Portfolio	The total of your investments.
Principal	The original amount of a debt on which interest is calculated.
Real Property	Assets that consist of land and/or buildings.
Securities	Documents that show ownership, such as a stock certificate or bond.
Stock	Capital raised by selling portions (*shares*) of the ownership of a corporation. Stockholders receive a share of profits called *dividends* based on the number of shares they own.

*Table 3-1: **Definitions Pertaining to the Investing and Property & Debt Centers in Quicken***

TIP

If you have an Internet connection, you can look up financial terms with which you are not familiar. Go to www.quicken.com/glossary/ for an extensive list.

Use the Investing Center

The Investing Center can contain four types of investment accounts:

- **Standard Brokerage accounts** allow you to track stocks, bonds, mutual funds, and annuities. You can download information directly from your brokerage company or enter items manually to keep track of your capital gains or losses, cash balances, market values, performance, and shares for one or more securities.

- **IRA or Keogh accounts** track your retirement plans.
- **401(k) and 403(b) accounts** track your pre-tax contribution investment accounts for your retirement. It is important to set up a separate account for each plan.
- **Single Mutual Fund accounts** track capital gains or losses, income, market value, share balance, and performance of a single mutual fund. This type of account does not track cash balances, interest, or miscellaneous expenses or income.

Table 3-2 describes which type of account to use for a particular type of investment.

	USE THIS ACCOUNT TYPE
...3(b)	401(k) or 403(b)
	Standard Brokerage account
...count	Standard Brokerage account
...Market Account	Standard Brokerage account (Note: You can also set these up as Standard Savings accounts in the Cash Flow Center.)
...estment Program	Standard Brokerage account
...Options or Employee Stock Purchase	Standard Brokerage account
IRA (any type)	IRA or Keogh account
Real Estate Investment trusts (REIT)	Standard Brokerage account
Real property	Asset account
Single mutual fund (no cash balance)	Single Mutual Fund account
Stocks and bonds (certificates that you hold, including U.S. savings bonds)	Standard Brokerage account
Treasury bills	Standard Brokerage account

*Table 3-2: **Types of Quicken Investment Accounts to Use with Various Investments***

TIP

If you hold bonds or stock certificates in a safe deposit box or other secure location, you can still track your information in a Standard Brokerage account.

Track Investments

Using Quicken to track your investments allows you to consolidate all of your investment information so you can easily see the value of your total portfolio at any time. Understanding the performance history of several different types of investments and being able to calculate capital gains quickly can be extremely helpful throughout the year as well as at year-end for tax purposes.

You open the Investing Center by clicking **Investing** on the menu bar or by clicking **Investing Center** in the Account bar of the Quicken home page. Figure 3-1 shows the Investing Center.

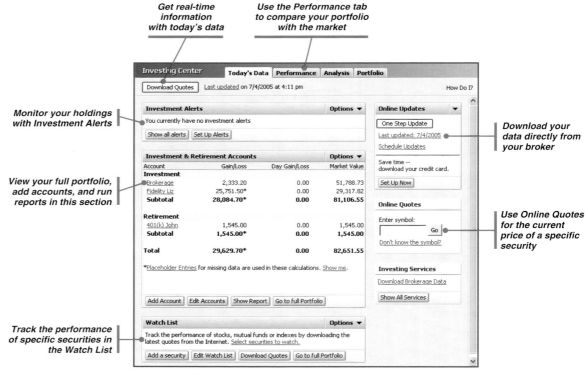

Figure 3-1: The Investing Center allows you to see your investment accounts, track the performance of specific stocks or funds, and quickly update your portfolio using an Internet connection.

Set Up a Standard Brokerage or IRA Account

Setting up an Investing Center account is similar to setting up an account in the Cash Flow Center.

1. Click **Investing Center** in the Account bar to open the Investing Center in the Activity Center, and then click **Add Account** at the bottom of the Investment & Retirement Accounts window.

   —Or—

   Click the **Investing** menu, click **Investing Accounts**, and click **Add Account**.

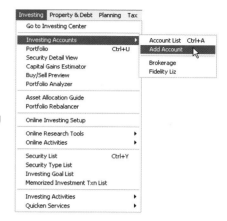

2. Either way, the Quicken Account Setup dialog box appears. If your financial institution offers automated data entry, type the name of the institution, and click **Next**.

3. If your brokerage firm or other institution supports online setup, you'll see a dialog box that asks if you want to set up your new account online or manually.

4. If you do not choose online setup, or if your institution does not support online setup, the next dialog box, shown on the left, asks what type of investment account you want to add. Refer to Table 3-2 for some suggestions as to which Quicken investment account you should use for each of your investments.

5. Click the type of account you want to set up, and then click **Next**.

6. Type a name for this account. You may type any name that identifies the account for you. You might consider using the name of the brokerage firm or other institution. If this account is an IRA, you are asked if this is for you or your spouse. Click **Next** to continue.

7. Using either your last statement or your account on the firm's web site, enter the last statement date or the "as of" date, the ending cash balance in the account, and any money-market fund balances in the account, and then click **Next**.

8. Enter the securities that are in the account. If you want Quicken to download current information about each security, type its symbol. If you do not have an

NOTE

Most financial institutions require that you sign up for their download service prior to using the Quicken download. Most institutions require an account number or ID and a password or PIN that they assign.

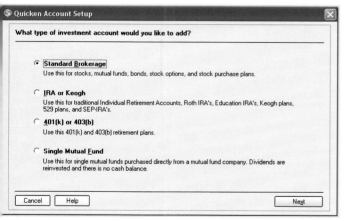

TIP

Some firms call the cash amounts not invested on a given date a *sweep account*.

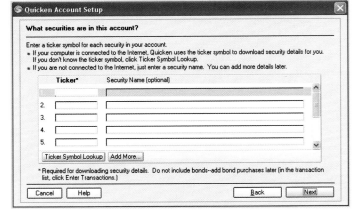

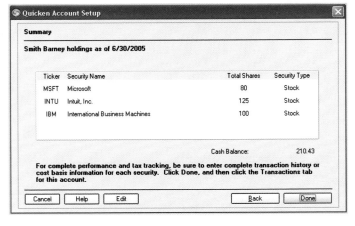

Internet connection, you can just type the name of the security. You can add more information later. Click **Next** to continue.

9. In the Quicken Account Setup Current Holdings dialog box, enter the number of shares you hold for each security. Click **Next** to see a summary of the securities in the account. Click **Done** to complete the account setup.

Your new account information appears in the Investing Center, as shown in Figure 3-2. Quicken cannot calculate your gain or loss on each investment without knowing what you paid for your securities. This amount is your cost basis. Quicken displays an asterisk in the Gain/Loss columns called a *placeholder entry* until you complete the information. You may enter this information now or later. To enter the cost for your security:

1. Click **Enter** under the Cost Basis column. The Enter Missing Transactions dialog box appears.

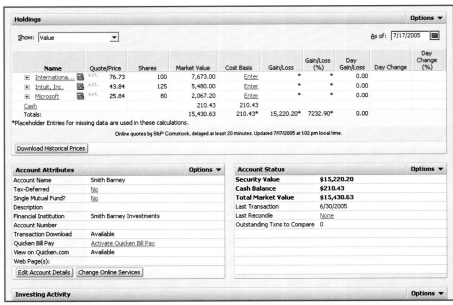

Figure 3-2: *Quicken automatically updates the current price of your securities if you're online, and it can calculate your gain or loss if you enter the cost.*

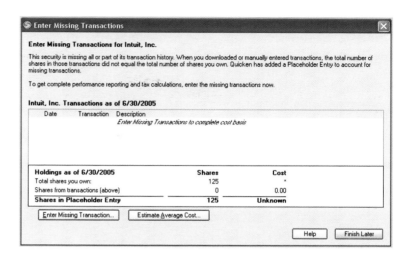

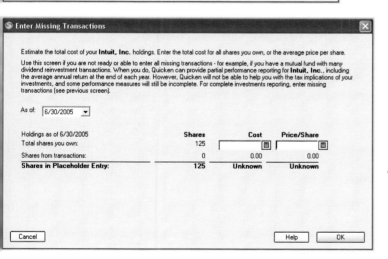

2. Click **Enter Missing Transaction**. The Buy-Shares Bought dialog box appears. Enter the transaction date, number of shares, the price per share that you paid on that date, and the commission you paid. Quicken will calculate a total cost. Click **Enter/Done** when finished.

If you purchased the shares over a period of time, click **Estimate Average Cost**. Enter values in either the total Cost or the Share Price fields, and click **OK**. This option is not as accurate as entering each batch of shares you purchased, but it is quicker and may be enough if you don't need all the detail. You can come back and enter the individual transactions at a later date.

3. Repeat steps 1 and 2 for each security you own.

Add a 401(k) or 403(b) Account

Entering a 401(k) or 403(b) account is similar to setting up an investment account, as described in "Set Up a Standard Brokerage or IRA Account" earlier in this chapter. Use steps 1 through 6 in that

QUICKSTEPS

USING THE TICKER SYMBOL LOOKUP

Normally, the paper statement from your brokerage firm or the firm's web site shows the ticker symbol for each security you own. If you cannot find the ticker symbol for your security and you have an Internet connection, you can use Quicken's Ticker Symbol Lookup button in the Security Listing dialog box.

1. Click the **Ticker Symbol Lookup** button. The Symbol Lookup dialog box appears.

2. Click the type of security you want to look up: **Stock**, **Mutual Fund**, **Index**, or **Any**.

3. Type a name or a partial name of the security, and click **Search**. A list of all the possible securities appears.

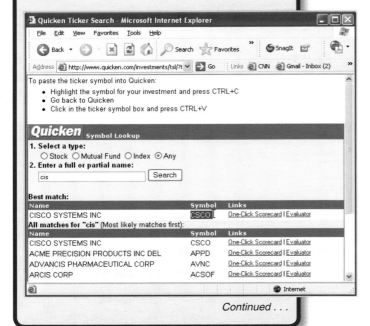

Continued . . .

section, choosing **401(k)** or **403(b)** as the type of account. Then, in the Tell Us About This Account dialog box:

1. Enter the date of your last paper statement (optional), enter your employer's name, select whether this account is from your current employer or a previous employer, and designate whether this account is your account or that of your spouse.

2. If your statement shows how many shares you own, click **Yes**. If not, click **No**. Click **Next** to continue.

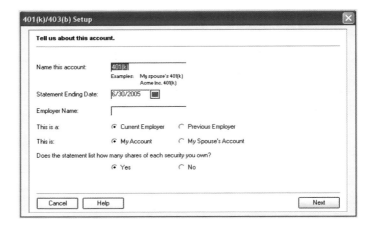

3. When asked if there are any outstanding loans against this account, click **No** if there are no loans. If there are loans against this account, click **Yes** and enter the number of loans. Click **Next** to continue.

4. If you clicked Yes in step 3, you are asked for a description of this loan and its current balance. Click **Set Up An Account To Track The Remaining Balance Of This Loan**, type the original loan amount, and click **Next**.

5. You are asked abut the securities in this account. Type the ticker symbol if you know it, or type the name of the security. You can enter all the details later if you want. Click **Next** to continue.

USING THE TICKER SYMBOL LOOKUP

(Continued)

4. Find your security and click its symbol to highlight it. Click the **Edit** menu and click **Copy**, or press CTRL+C.

5. Return to the Quicken Account Setup dialog box, click in the ticker symbol text box, and press CTRL+V—or right-click the ticker symbol box, and click **Paste**—to paste the symbol into the ticker symbol text box.

6. Type the name of the security if you want.

7. Repeat these steps for each symbol you need, and then close the Quicken Ticker Search dialog box.

While some 401(k) plans allow you to take loans against the funds in the plan, it may not be a good idea. The interest payments on these loans are not tax-deductible, and you lose the growth you would have gotten on the amount of the loan. See your tax professional for more information.

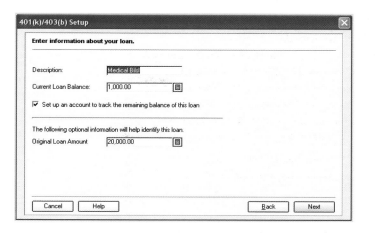

6. Enter the total shares you own and, if Quicken hasn't entered it for you, the market value shown on your last statement. Click **Next**.

7. Review the summary of what you have entered. If you have chosen to enter the information from your paper statement, the summary should match the total shown on that statement. Click **Done** to finish setting up this account.

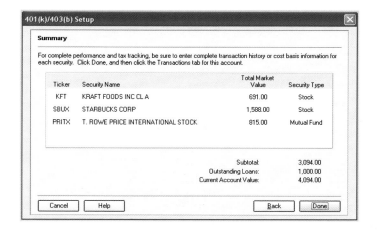

CREATING A SINGLE MUTUAL FUND ACCOUNT

If you own or buy a single mutual fund from a mutual fund company, you can use a Single Mutual Fund account to track it. Typically, these funds pay no dividends and there is no cash balance. To add this type of account, follow the first six steps in setting up an Investment account as described in "Set Up a Standard Brokerage or IRA Account" earlier in this chapter. Then:

1. Choose **Single Mutual Fund** as the type of account, type a name for this account, choose whether this account is tax-deferred, and click **Next**.

2. Enter the date of your last paper statement, and click **Next**.

3. If you want to download the security details, type the ticker symbol for the security in this account. If you are not connected to the Internet or want to add information later, simply type the name in the Security Name field, and click **Next**.

4. If you do not enter the name, you will see a warning message that since this is a Single Mutual Fund account, you must provide the name.

5. Type the number of shares you own, and click **Next**. The Summary dialog box appears. Review your account and, when you are ready, click **Done** to complete the setup.

Use the Property & Debt Center

The Property & Debt Center provides a way to integrate all your other financial information into Quicken so you can see your total financial position at any given moment. Property & Debt Center accounts include:

- **House** accounts are used for your main residence, vacation home, rental properties, or other real estate. You can create a Liability account for each property at the same time you create the Asset account.

- **Vehicle** accounts are used for all types of vehicles, including cars, trucks, motorcycles, boats, motor homes, and campers. You can create Liability accounts for the loans on each vehicle at the same time you create the Asset accounts.

- **Asset** accounts are used for assets other than real property, vehicles, or investments. Examples include sterling silver, antiques, baseball card collections, first-edition and rare books, and business equipment.

- **Liability** accounts are used for personal debts other than credit cards, which use the Cash Flow Center. Examples include personal loans and promissory notes you owe banks, loan companies, and individuals, as well as student loans.

Work with the Property & Debt Center

You use the Property & Debt Center to:

- Record your major assets and debts to better understand your overall financial standing.
- Allow Quicken to calculate the amount due on your mortgage and other obligations.
- Allow you to track the amount of interest you are paying on any specific debt and in total.

Not all Quicken users need to enter the information in the Property & Debt Center, but if you have a mortgage, make car payments, or have other assets and liabilities, you might want to consider adding the information to Quicken so you can see your true financial picture.

Set Up a House Account with a Mortgage

For most people, their biggest asset is their home. To enter this asset and any associated liability:

1. Click the **Property & Debt** menu, click **Property & Debt Accounts**, and click **Add Account**.

–Or–

Click **Property & Debt** in the Accounts bar, and then click **Add Account** at the bottom of the Property & Debt Accounts listing in the Activity Center.

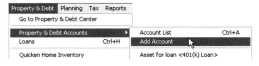

In both cases, the Quicken Account Setup dialog box appears with several choices.

2. Click **House (With Or Without Mortgage)**, and click Next.

3. Type a name for the account. Quicken uses "House" as the default. If you have more than one house account, Quicken uses "House 2," "House 3," and so forth unless you type another name. Click **Next**.

4. Enter or select the date you acquired the property. You can use the small calendar icon to the right of the date of acquisition field to select the date. Press **TAB** to move to the next field.

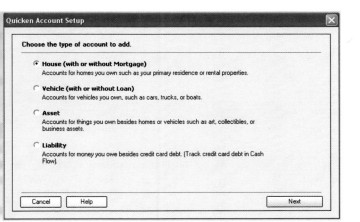

5. Enter the purchase price, and again press **TAB**. Estimate the value of your home today. Quicken requires that you enter an amount, so use your best guess. You can change the value later. Click **Next**.

6. Choose if and how you want the Liability account set up for the house:

   - Click **Yes, Create A Liability Account For Me** if you have not already created a Liability account for the mortgage.

   - Click **There Is A Mortgage And I'm Already Tracking It In Quicken** if you have entered the Liability account. Choose which account is associated with this asset in the Account drop-down box.

   - Click **The House Is Paid For, So I Don't Need A Liability Account** if you have no mortgage or do not want to track your mortgage through Quicken.

7. Click **Done** to create the Asset account. A new dialog box appears asking for the loan information. It shows the opening date of the loan as being the acquisition date of the property.

8. Enter the original balance and length of the loan, how it is compounded, and how often you make payments, pressing **TAB** to move from field to field. Use the small calculator icon to the right of the Original Balance field if you want. Click **Next** to continue.

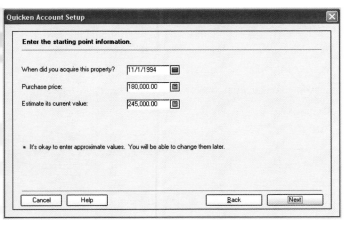

Try using the 10-key pad on your keyboard to enter numbers (make sure the NUMLOCK light on the keyboard is lit; press the NUMLOCK key if it isn't). The 10-key pad will give you an experience similar to that when using a calculator.

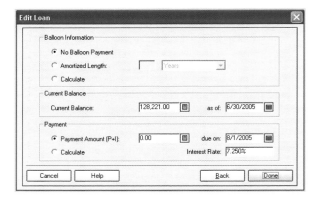

The compounding period reflects how your lending institution computes the interest charged on the loan. The more often the institution calculates the interest, the more interest you pay. Most institutions compound interest daily.

Some variable or adjustable-rate loans change the interest rate with the next payment that is due. Others change the interest rate for all future payments.

9. If you are unsure of the payment amount, enter the interest rate and click **Calculate**. Quicken will compute the amount of principal and interest for each payment. Click **Done**. A message appears advising you that Quicken has calculated the next loan payment.

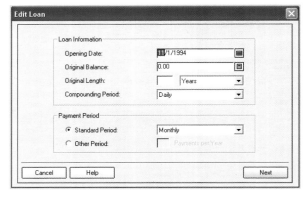

You are instructed to click **OK** to return to the View Loans dialog box. You see the estimate of the next payment amount and the date on which it is due. You can change this later if you want.

10. Click **Done**. The Edit Loan Payment dialog box appears. If desired, change the interest rate and/or adjust the principal and interest payment.

11. Click **Edit** to include other amounts you pay with your mortgage payment, such as real estate taxes and homeowners' insurance. In the Split Transaction dialog box, enter the category for each portion and the amount for each category, and then click **OK**.

12. Click in the **Payee** field to enter the name of your mortgage lender. Adjust the next payment date, and, if desired, change the interest category. By default, Quicken uses Mortgage Int:Bank as the category.

13. After you have completed editing the loan, click **OK** to return to the Property & Debt Center. Depending on how you set up your payment, you may see a message stating that Quicken automatically set up the payment transaction. If you see such a message, click **OK**.

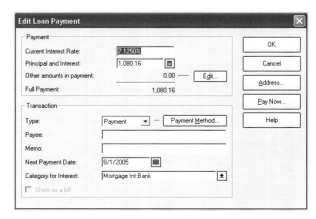

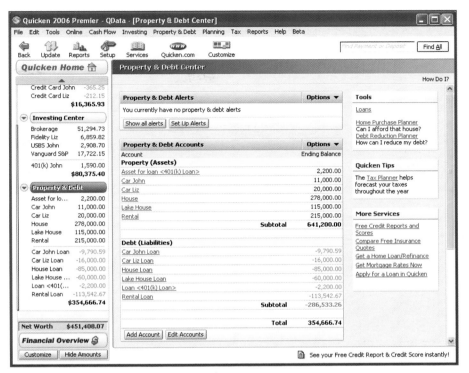

Figure 3-3: *The Property & Debt Center completes your financial picture.*

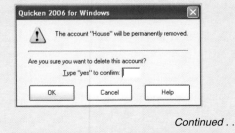
Your new Asset account and its related Liability account appear in both the Activity Center and the Quicken Account bar, as shown in Figure 3-3. Information about each loan appears in the Loan Accounts Summary section.

Add Other Property and Debt Accounts

You can create other accounts within the Property & Debt Center. As you work with the dialog boxes, you will see similarities between the various accounts. To add a vehicle, for example:

1. Click **Add Account** from the Account List or Property & Debt Center Activity Center, click **Vehicle**, and click **Next**.

DELETING AND HIDING ACCOUNTS

(*Continued*)

HIDE AN ACCOUNT

1. Click the **Tools** menu and click **Account List**, or press CTRL+A, to display the Account List.

   –Or–

   Right-click the account in the Account bar, and click **Delete/Hide Accounts In Quicken**.

2. Click the **Manage Accounts** tab, and click the **Hide In Quicken** check box.

2. Enter the name of the vehicle, and identify its make, model, and year, pressing TAB to move from field to field. Click **Next** to continue.

3. Enter the date you acquired the vehicle, its purchase price, and its estimated current value, and then click **Next**.

4. Choose whether to create a Liability account for this vehicle, identify an existing loan account, or indicate that there is no loan on it. In all instances, click **Done** to create the account.

5. If you indicated that you wanted to create a loan, the Edit Loan dialog box appears. Enter the opening date, original balance and term, and the compounding period. When finished, click **Next**.

6. Indicate whether the loan has a balloon payment, the current balance, and payment information, and click **Done**. (A balloon payment is usually larger than regular payments and is often the last payment.)

7. If you asked Quicken to calculate the payment, click **OK** and then click **Done** again to accept Quicken's calculation.

8. Review the loan payment information; enter the payee and any additional information you want, such as the payee's address; and click **OK**.

Add Other Liability Accounts

Liability accounts can be used for loans other than for your house or vehicle. These types of loans can be promissory notes, student loans, loans against insurance policies, loans for medical expenses, or any other liability.

1. Click **Add Account** in the Property & Debt Center Activity Center or Account List.

2. Type a name for the liability, and click **Next**.

3. Enter the starting date of the loan or the date on which you want to start keeping track of this loan, and enter the value of the loan—that is, what you owed on that date.

4. If the liability has tax implications, click **Tax**. Consult your tax professional for information on tax implications, and, if needed, enter the recommended information. Click **Done**.

NOTE

If one of your vehicles is a motor home, consult your tax professional to see if you should consider this your primary home or a second home.

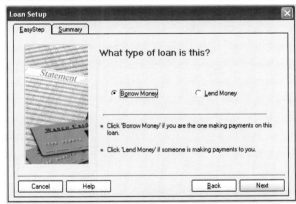

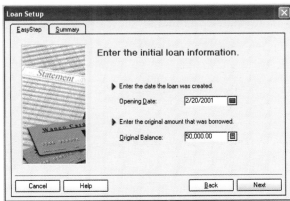

5. A dialog box appears asking if you want to set up an amortized loan to be associated with this account. This provides a payment schedule. If so, click **Yes**, and the EasyStep Loan Wizard will start (see "Use the EasyStep Loan Wizard"). If not, click **Done**.

Use the EasyStep Loan Wizard

Quicken provides the EasyStep Loan Wizard to help you set up an amortized loan. This feature can be opened automatically, as described in the previous section, or you can open it directly.

1. Click the **Property & Debt** menu, and then click **Loans**, or press CTRL+H. Either way, the View Loans dialog box appears.

2. Click **New** in the menu bar. The EasyStep Loan Setup window opens. Click **Next** to continue.

3. Choose between borrowing money and loaning money. Borrowing is the default. Click **Next**.

4. Enter the name of a new account, or link this loan to an existing account, and click **Next**.

5. If you have made payments on this loan, click **Yes** and then click **Next**. You are asked for the initial loan information. If this is a new account, you are required to provide the opening date and original balance of the loan. If this is an existing account, Quicken provides the information for you. Click **Next** to continue.

6. If there is a balloon payment, click **Yes**; otherwise, click **No** and then click **Next**. Enter the original length of the loan, and click **Next**. Select how you pay the loan (the default is monthly), and click **Next** again.

7. Enter how often interest is compounded, and click **Next**. If you know the current balance click **Yes**, click **Next**, enter the date and amount of the current balance, and click **Next** again. Otherwise, click **No** to have Quicken calculate the amount for you. Click **Next**.

8. Enter the date on which the next payment is due, and click **Next**. If you know the amount of the next payment, click **Yes**, enter the payment, and click **Next** again. If not, click **No** to have Quicken calculate it for you. Click **Next** to continue.

9. Type the interest rate for this loan. If your interest rate fluctuates, use the rate that will be applicable for the next payment due. Click **Next**.

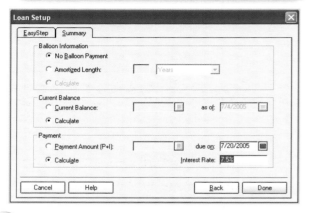

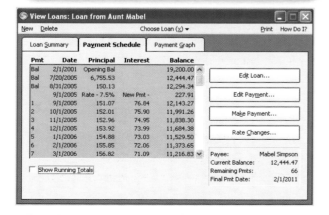

10. Review the summary in the next three dialog boxes, and make any necessary adjustments. Click **Done** to have Quicken calculate the next payment.

11. You are told that Quicken has calculated the next loan payment. Click **OK** and, if all is in order, click **Done** again.

12. Review the loan payment information, and enter the name of the payee. The default is the standard Interest Exp category, but you can change it to another category or create a new category. At the bottom-left corner of the dialog box is the Show As A Bill check box, which Quicken selects by default. Click the check mark to deselect the check box if you want. If all appears to be correct, click **OK**.

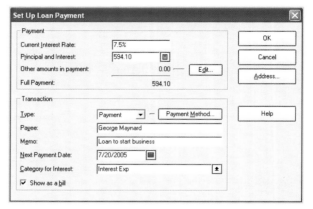

13. If there is an associated asset with this loan and you want to enter the asset, click **Yes** to create the Asset account; enter the asset name, acquisition date, and current value; and then click **Done**. Otherwise, click **No** to finish creating the Liability account and return to the Property & Debt Center Activity Center.

Print an Amortization Schedule

As you continue to work with loans in Quicken, you may want to print a payment schedule. To print this payment schedule (often called an *amortization schedule*):

1. Click the **Property & Debt** menu, click **Loans**, click the **Choose Loan** down arrow, and click the loan for which you want to print the schedule.

2. Click **Payment Schedule** and click **Print**.

3. Close the View Loans dialog box.

Chapter 4
Using Quicken Every Day

In earlier chapters you learned how to install Quicken and set up your Quicken accounts. In this chapter you will learn how to use Quicken every day to record your checks and deposits and other transactions. You'll learn to use the check register and credit card registers, with both manual and online transactions. Before we begin, we'll introduce you to some definitions that are used throughout this chapter.

Understand Basic Transactions

A *transaction* in Quicken is something that affects the balance in an account. You enter a transaction into the *register* of an account. A register looks like a checkbook register where you enter the activity, or transactions, into your accounts. Table 4-1 explains some of the terms used when talking about transactions. When using these terms it is important to distinguish between:

- **Checking or savings accounts** in which you deposit your money and write checks or make withdrawals against your own funds. In essence, the bank owes you your money.

TERM	DEFINITION
Charge or debit	A transaction that increases the balance in a credit card account or decreases the balance in a checking account, like a check you write. A charge can also be something you purchased with a credit card or a fee from a financial institution.
Credit	A transaction that decreases the balance in a credit card, like a payment, or increases the balance in a checking account, like a deposit.
Deposit	A transaction that increases the balance in a checking or savings account.
Field	An area where you can make an entry, such as the date *field* or the amount *field*.
Payee	The company or person to whom you make a payment.
Payment	A transaction that lowers the balance in a credit card account.
Reconcile	To make what you have entered into a Quicken account agree with the statement you receive from your financial institution.
Transaction	An action that changes the balance in an account.
Transfer	To move funds from one account to another.

Table 4-1: Terms Used with Quicken Transactions

- **Credit card accounts** in which the bank extends you a credit line, you make charges against that line, and then make payments to it. In essence, you owe the bank their money.

You create a transaction when you write a check, make a deposit, enter a credit card charge, or make a payment on your credit card. To keep your account register up-to-date, you need to enter the transaction into the account register, either manually or by downloading the information from the financial institution. You also need to reconcile your accounts on a regular basis against your financial institution's records. Quicken offers an Automatic Reconciliation feature. Chapter 7 discusses that and other methods of reconciling your accounts in more detail.

Establish Preferences for Your Registers

Before you use a register for the first time, you may want to set your preferences. Preferences are the ways in which you tell Quicken how to display and process your information.

Set Register Preferences

To set your preferences for an account:

1. Click the **Edit** menu, click **Preferences**, and then click **Quicken Program**.

2. Click **Register**. The Quicken Preferences dialog box appears, as shown in Figure 4-1. Select the order in which you want the register fields displayed:

   - **Show Date In First Column**, which is selected by default, can be deselected to show the check number as the first field and the date as the second field.

   - **Show Memo Before Category**, which is not selected by default, can be selected to display the Memo field first, instead of showing the Category field on the left.

Num	Payee	
	Memo	Category

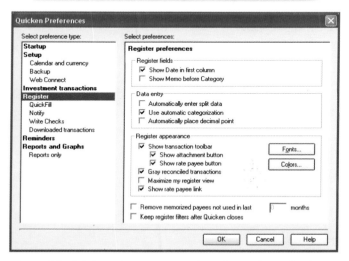

Figure 4-1: Quicken gives you a number of ways to customize the register to meet your needs.

Click to return to the normal view

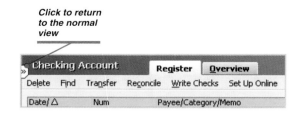

3. In the Data Entry area, click the relevant check boxes:

   • **Automatically Enter Split Data** changes the way you enter a split transaction (see "Create a Split Transaction" later in this chapter). This check box is not selected by default.

   • **Use Automatic Categorization** lets Quicken choose the category for a transaction based on an internal database or on the category you used before for this payee. This check box is selected by default.

   • **Automatically Place Decimal Point** sets the decimal point to two places. By default, Quicken enters zero cents when you enter a number. For example, if you type the number 23 in the Amount field, Quicken displays it as $23.00. If you choose to set the decimal point automatically, the number 23 becomes .23 or 23 cents. This check box is not selected by default.

4. In the Register Appearance area, select how you want the register to look:

   • **Show Transaction Toolbar** allows you to display the transaction tool bar on the right-hand side of your transaction entry field. It has Enter, Edit, and Split buttons by default. Quicken 2006 has added the Attachment and Rate Payee buttons. The Attachment button allows you to add notes, images, or flags to a transaction. The Rate Payee button allows you to rate each of your payees.

   • **Gray Reconciled Transactions**, which is selected by default, displays all reconciled transactions in gray rather than in black. This feature allows you to quickly scan your register and find transactions that have not yet cleared the bank.

   • **Maximize My Register View** fills your screen with the register. Use the small arrows in the upper-left corner to return to the normal view.

   • **Show Rate Payee Link** displays a small link in the bottom-left corner of your register. See "Rate Your Payees" later in this chapter for more information.

5. Click the **Fonts** button to see a menu of available fonts for the register. You can choose from several different font sizes, depending on the font you choose, and from a wide range of type faces. Click the font name and size to see in the preview box how the register would look using this font. When finished, click **OK**.

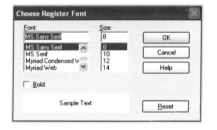

NOTE

Some fonts display better than others. Look at how your choice appears in the register. If you can't read it easily, choose another type face or size.

If you choose too large a font, Quicken displays a warning message. Click **OK** to close the message box.

6. Click the **Colors** button to display the available colors for each register. Click the down arrow to the right of each account name to see the available choices. You can choose from seven different colors, including the default color. Click **OK** to close the dialog box.

7. Click the **Remove Memorized Payees Not Used In Last ___ Months** check box to limit the list of memorized transactions displayed. By default, Quicken retains the first 2,000 transactions that you enter and then does not memorize any more. When you click this check box and type a number in the field, for example, <u>5</u>, Quicken saves only the transactions you've entered over the last five months. See Chapter 5 for more information on memorized transactions.

8. Click the **Keep Register Filters After Quicken Closes** check box, which is not selected by default, to use the filter utility to quickly find specific types of transactions, such as all unreconciled transactions or all payments made within a certain period.

9. Click **OK** to close the dialog box when you have selected your register preferences.

Determine QuickFill Preferences

Quicken saves you time during data entry with what Intuit calls *QuickFill* features. For example, Quicken provides drop-down lists from which to choose categories and payees. You can choose to complete a field after typing only a few letters using Quicken's memorization of payees and transactions. You can determine how these features work in the QuickFill Preferences dialog box, shown in Figure 4-2.

1. Click the **Edit** menu, click **Preferences**, click **Quicken Program**, and then click **QuickFill**. The QuickFill Preferences dialog box appears.

2. Choose whether to use the ENTER key in addition to the TAB key to move between fields in your registers. By default, the ENTER key is used only to complete a transaction.

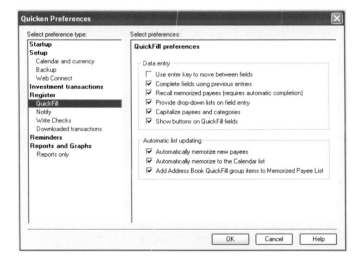

Figure 4-2: QuickFill preferences help you tailor your registers to the way you want to enter and view your data.

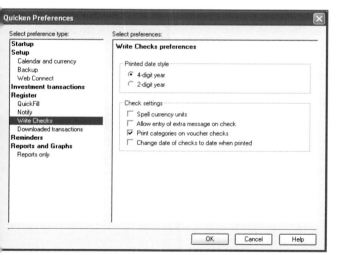

Figure 4-3: Quicken's check-writing options allow you to format checks the way you want.

3. Choose whether to automatically complete each field using the entry previously made for this payee. If you choose this option, which is selected by default, you can also choose whether to have Quicken recall your memorized payees.

4. Choose whether to have Quicken display a drop-down list for the number, payee, and category fields (this is selected by default).

5. Choose whether you want payee and category names capitalized and whether to display the drop-down list button every time you click in a number, payee, or category field (both of these check boxes are selected by default).

6. Choose whether you want Quicken to memorize new payees, memorize transactions to the Calendar List, and add Address Book items to the Memorized Payee List.

7. Click **OK** when finished.

Set Notify Preferences

Notify preferences tell Quicken the circumstances in which you want to receive warning messages. By default, all warnings are activated.

1. Click the **Edit** menu, click **Preferences**, click **Quicken Program**, and then click **Notify**. The Notify Preferences dialog box appears.

2. Choose whether to get an alarm when:

    • Entering transactions that are not in the current year

    • Changing an existing transaction

    • Entering a transaction without a category

    • Not running a reconciliation report after you complete a reconciliation

    • Using a check number more than once

3. Click **OK** when finished.

Set Preferences for Writing Checks

Quicken gives you six options from which to choose when using the program to write checks, as shown in Figure 4-3. To set those options:

1. Click the **Edit** menu, click **Preferences**, click **Quicken Program**, and then click **Write Checks**. The Write Checks Preferences dialog box appears.

If you choose a two-digit year, the on-screen image still shows four digits, but when you print the check, only the right-most two digits are printed.

QUICKSTEPS

SETTING DOWNLOADED TRANSACTION PREFERENCES

Downloaded transactions preferences

☑ Apply renaming rules to downloaded transactions
  ☑ Automatically create rules when manually renaming
  ☐ Don't display a message when renaming
  [Renaming Rules...]

☑ Capitalize first letter only in downloaded payee names

You can set two preferences for transactions you download from financial institutions:

• Choose whether to apply renaming rules to downloaded transactions. Renaming rules change the name of a payee on a downloaded transaction, for example, "Grocery 198775" becomes "Corner Grocery" in your register. Renaming rules are discussed further in Chapter 5.

• Choose whether to capitalize only the first letters in the payee names you are downloading.

2. Choose whether you want a four-digit year, such as 4/5/2007, or a two-digit year, such as 4/5/07, to be printed on your checks.

3. Click the **Spell Currency Units** check box to have Quicken print the currency amount on your check with the currency unit displayed, for example, "Twenty Dollars and 37 cents" rather than "Twenty and 37/100."

4. Click the **Allow Entry Of Extra Message On Check** check box if you want to include information for the payee's records, such as your account number or the invoice number you are paying with this check.

5. Click the **Print Categories On Voucher Checks** check box if you want to include that information. A voucher check has a perforated portion that can include additional information. This setting allows Quicken to include up to 16 lines of category information on this voucher.

6. Click the **Change Date Of Checks To Date When Printed** check box if you enter data over time and print all your checks at once.

7. Click **OK** to close the dialog box.

Work with the Register

The register in Quicken looks a lot like the paper check register you may have used in the past. It displays in the color choices you selected in your preferences setup. You can open a register in two ways:

• Click the **Tools** menu and then click **Account List**. Click the name of the account whose register you want to open.

–Or–

• Click the name of the register's account on the Account bar on the left of your Quicken home page.

Either way, the register opens. Figure 4-4 displays a register window for a checking account.

Enter a Check

To enter a check into the register:

1. If it is not already selected, click in the empty line at the bottom of the Date column. This activates the transaction line.

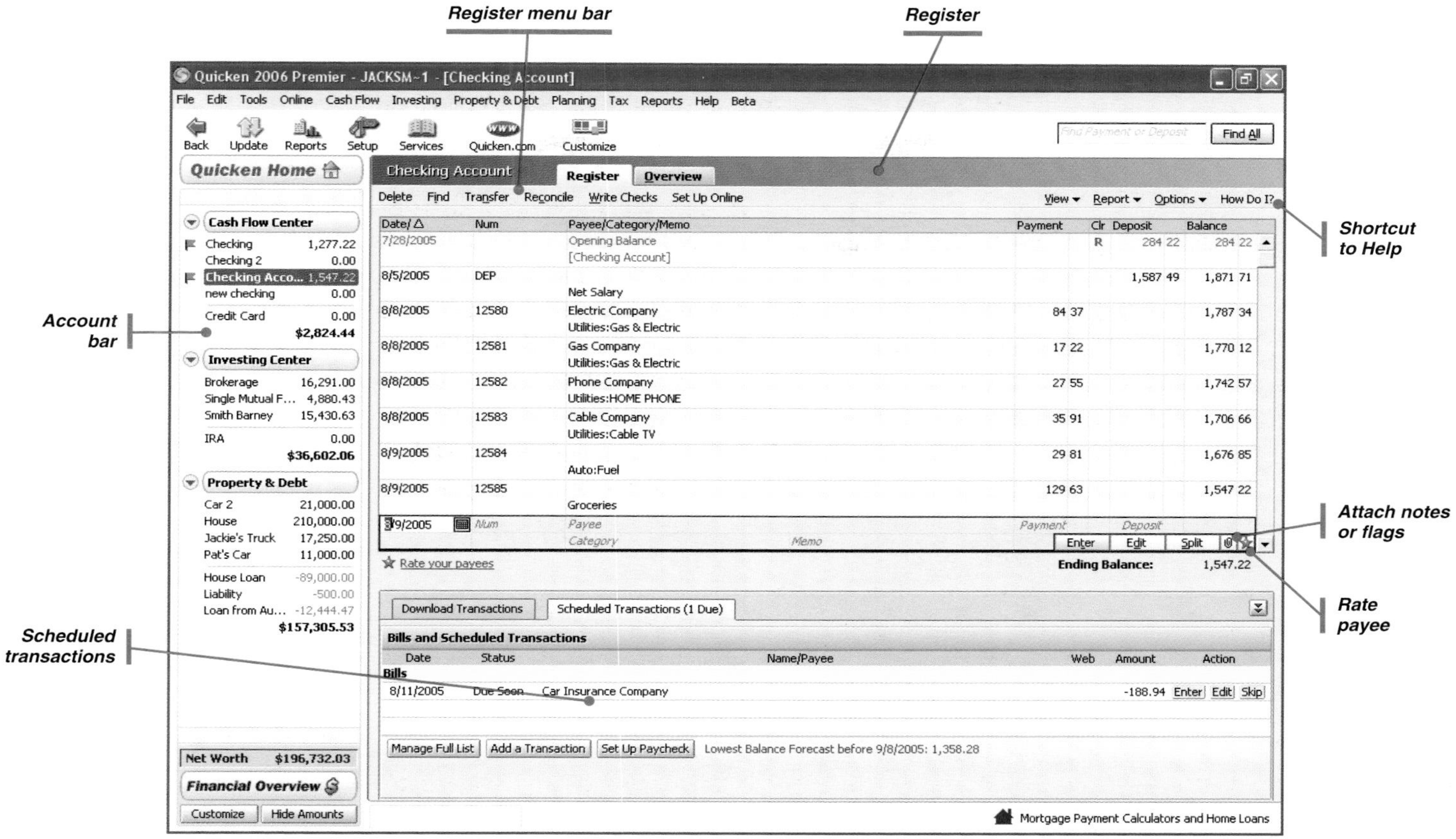

Register menu bar

Register

Shortcut to Help

Account bar

Scheduled transactions

Attach notes or flags

Rate payee

Figure 4-4: The account register window for a checking account looks a lot like a paper-based register.

NOTE

When you click in the Date field, the month is selected, which you can change by typing a new number. To move to the day, press the RIGHT ARROW key, and press it again to move to the year. Change the day and year again by typing.

2. Accept today's date, type a date using either the numeric keys at the top of the keyboard or the 10-key pad on the right of the keyboard (with NUMLOCK activated), or click the small calendar 🔲 to the right of the field. In the calendar, click the date you want using the arrows in the upper-left and upper-right corners to select a different month.

TIP

You can press the plus sign (+) key on your 10-key pad to increase the date one day at a time while you are in the Date field. Use the minus sign (–) key on the 10-key pad to decrease the date one day at a time.

TIP

Press the plus sign (+) or minus sign (–) keys on your keyboard to increase or decrease the check number in increments of one.

CAUTION

Unless you have specifically set your preferences to use the ENTER key to move between fields (see the earlier "Determine QuickFill Preferences" section), pressing ENTER has no effect on the Num field.

NOTE

When you enter a payee for the first time, you might notice that Quicken assigns it to a category. A special feature of Quicken, Automatic Categorization assigns a category based on a list of thousands of payees.

3. Press **TAB** to move to the Num field, or click in the **Num** field. By default, a drop-down list of potential entries will display. Type the check number if you haven't entered one before, or use the drop-down list by pressing the following keys on your keyboard:

   - Press **N** to move to the next check number if you have been using the check register.
   - Press **A** if you want "ATM" to appear in the Num field.
   - Press **D** if you want "DEP" (for "Deposit") to appear in the Num field.
   - Press **P** if you plan to print this check later and want "Print" to appear in the Num field.
   - Press **T** if you want "TXFR" (for "Transfer") to appear in the Num field.
   - Press **E** if you want "EFT" (for "Electronic Funds Transfer") to appear in the Num field.

4. Press **TAB** to move to the Payee field. Type the first letter of the payee's name to display a list of all the payees that start with that letter. Choose the name you want, or type a new payee name.

5. Press **TAB** to move to the Payment field. Type the amount of the check. You can use either the 10-key pad with **NUMLOCK** activated or the numbers at the top of the keyboard. If you have paid this payee before and have set your preferences to automatically enter it, the amount of the most recent transaction for this payee appears.

6. Press **TAB** to move to the Category field. Type the first letter of the category you want to use. By default, the category you used the last time you paid this payee appears in the Category field. If you want to change the category, click the name in the drop-down list. If the transaction is for more than one category, you can create a split transaction. See "Create a Split Transaction" later in this chapter.

7. Press **TAB** to move to the Memo field. Type any special information, such as an invoice number or what you purchased.

8. Press **ENTER** or click the **Enter** button to complete and save the transaction.

Print Checks with Quicken

Quicken will print checks for you if have special paper checks for your printer. You can order these checks through your bank, through Quicken, or through third-party companies (do an Internet search on "Quicken checks"). Printing your checks makes them easier to read and potentially saves you time in that you can enter information directly into a check form or print checks already entered into the register. Before you start, you need to load the special paper checks into your printer.

PRINT CHECKS IN THE REGISTER

If you have transactions to print in your register with "Print" in the Num field, you can directly print them instead of entering them into the check form to be printed. When you use the form, however, the information is automatically entered into the register.

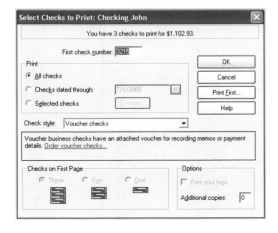

1. Click the **File** menu and then click **Print Checks**. If you do not have transactions in your register with "Print" in the Num field, you will see a message that you do not have any checks to print. If you do have transactions with "Print" in the Num field, the Select Checks To Print dialog box will appear.

2. Enter the number of the first paper check in the printer.

3. Choose which checks to print:

   - **All Checks** prints any checks that have not yet been printed. This includes any postdated checks you may have entered.

   - **Checks Dated Through** allows you to print unprinted checks through a date you enter or select.

   - **Selected Checks** allows you to choose which checks to print. Click **Choose** and clear the check marks for any checks you don't want to print at this time:

   - Click **Mark All** to print all of the checks.

NOTE

Standard style checks are normally thought of as business checks and are 8½ x 3½ inches. Wallet style checks are normally thought of as personal checks and are 6 x 2¾ inches.

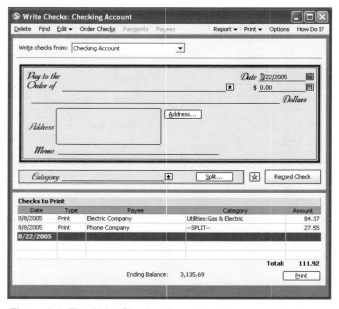

Figure 4-5: The Write Checks dialog box gives you a way to visualize the checks you are writing.

• Click **Clear All** to clear all of the listed checks, and then click in the Print column just the checks you want to print.

• Click **Done** to close the dialog box and print the checks.

4. Click the **Check Style** down arrow and choose a style. Depending on the style you are using, click the number of checks on the first page with your style.

5. Click **Print First** to print the first check and see how it looks. Click **OK** if your check printed correctly. Otherwise, enter the check number of the check, and Quicken will reprint it. Make any necessary corrections to how checks are printed.

6. Click **OK** to print all the checks you selected. When the printing is completed, click **OK** if all checks printed correctly. Otherwise, enter the check number of the check on which there was a problem so that Quicken can reprint the check.

PRINT CHECKS FROM THE CHECK FORM

If you would like to see a representation of the check you will be sending, Quicken provides a form into which you can enter the information you want on the final printed check, as shown in Figure 4-5. To use the check form:

1. Click **Write Checks** from your register pane. The Write Checks dialog box appears with a blank check displayed that you can fill in.

2. Click in the **Pay To The Order Of** line, or the down arrow at the end of the line to display a drop-down list box of previous payees.

3. Type as much of the payee's name as needed to select the payee you want, or click the payee you want in the drop-down list.

4. Press TAB to move to the amount field. If you have sent checks to this payee previously, the most recent amount you paid them will be filled in. Press TAB again to accept the previous amount and move to the Address field. Otherwise, enter the new amount and then press TAB.

5. Type the address if one is not already attached to the payee. If you want to edit the address, click **Address** to open the Address Book. Make any changes or additions to the address, and click **OK**.

6. Press TAB twice to move to the Memo field. Type a memo entry if you want, and press TAB again to move to the Category field.

7. Begin to type the category. If there is an existing category starting with the letters you've typed, it will be filled in. Alternatively, you can click the down arrow at the end of the Category line, and click the category you want to use.

Groups: <QuickFill>

8. If you want to have portions of the money you are paying go to different categories, click **Split** and follow the instructions in the section "Create a Split Transaction" later in this chapter.

9. If you don't want to use the default of today's date, click in the **Date** field, and enter a new date using any of Quicken's date-entering features described in "Enter a Check" earlier in this chapter.

10. When the check looks the way you want it, click **Record Check**. The new check appears on a list of checks to be printed at the bottom of the window, and the check form is once more blank.

11. When you have entered all the checks you want to print, click **Print**. The Select Checks To Print dialog box appears. To continue, see "Print Checks in the Register," and complete the steps in that section (starting with step 2).

Create a New Transaction Category

When you enter a check or a deposit, you can easily create a new category if there isn't one in the Category List that you want to use.

1. Click in the **Category** field, or press TAB to move there, and open the list of existing categories.

2. Click **Add Cat**. The Set Up Category dialog box appears.

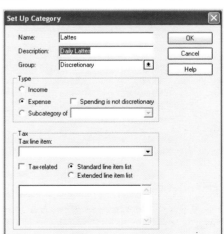

3. Type the name and description of the new category, and select the group you want it in. Press TAB to move from field to field.

4. Click **Income** or **Expense** to tell Quicken what type of category this is.

5. Enter the tax-line item if this category has tax implications.

6. Click **OK** to close the dialog box.

QUICKSTEPS

ENTERING A DEPOSIT

Entering a deposit is like entering a check, except you type the amount in the Deposit field rather than the Payment field. To enter a deposit:

1. If it is not already selected, click in the empty line at the bottom of the Date column.

2. If you want to change the date, use one of the techniques described in "Enter a Check."

3. Press TAB to move to the Num field, and press D to have "DEP" placed in the field.

4. Press TAB and enter the name of the payer, or select it from the drop-down list that is displayed.

5. Press TAB to move to the Deposit field, and enter an amount.

6. Press TAB to move to the Category field. Type a category or choose one from the drop-down list.

7. Click **Enter** to complete the transaction.

The only register item you cannot change is the Balance column.

QUICKSTEPS

CHANGING, VOIDING, OR DELETING A TRANSACTION

From time to time, you may need to edit, or change, a transaction in your check register.

CHANGE A TRANSACTION

1. With the register containing the transaction displayed, click in any field of the transaction you want to change.

2. Type or select the new or revised information.

3. Click **Enter** or press **ENTER** to save the changes.

VOID A TRANSACTION

You can void any transaction in an account register. Quicken keeps the check number, removes the dollar amount, and inserts ****VOID**** in front of the payee name. If you make a mistake, you can restore the transaction to the way it was originally.

| 7/2/2005 | 1514 | **VOID**John Staley | | Payment | c | Deposit | 3,134 25 |
| | | Auto:Insurance | Memo | | Enter | Edit | Split | |

1. With the register containing the transaction displayed, click the transaction you want to void.

2. Click the **Edit** menu, click **Transaction**, and click **Void transaction(s)**. The transaction is voided.

3. If you have not yet pressed **ENTER** or clicked **Enter** and the transaction is still selected, you can restore it by clicking the **Edit** menu, clicking **Transaction**, and clicking **Restore Transaction**.

4. Press **ENTER** or click **Enter** to complete voiding and possibly restoring it.

Continued . . .

Perform Activities with Check Registers

Not all transactions in your register are as straightforward as a check or a deposit with one category. Some transactions require you to split categories or transfer funds from one account to another. Quicken makes all of these transactions easy to enter. Other activities you may want to perform are locating, sorting, or filtering transactions; attaching check copies or other images to your transactions; rating your payees; and printing your check register.

Create a Split Transaction

A *split* transaction is one that has more than one assigned category. For example, a check you write to the insurance company might be for both homeowners' and automobile insurance or a payment might be for both the principal amount of a loan and interest. You can assign up to 30 categories for any single transaction. To enter a split transaction:

1. Click the empty line at the bottom of your register.

2. Enter the date, check number, payee, and the total amount of the check as described in "Enter a Check" earlier in this chapter.

3. Click **Split** in the bottom-right of the transaction.

   –Or–

   Press **TAB** or click in the Category field to open the drop-down list. Click **Split** at the bottom of the category list.

   In either case the Split Transaction dialog box appears, as shown in Figure 4-6.

4. Click the **Category** field on the first line and choose or type a category. Press **TAB**, type any additional information or notes in the Memo field, and again press **TAB**.

5. The total amount of the transaction appears under Amount on the first line. Over that amount, enter the amount for the first category. Click **Next**.

6. Quicken computes the remainder and shows it in the Amount field of the second line. Enter or select the next category, press **TAB**, if desired enter in the Memo field, press **TAB**, and either accept the computed amount, or type a new one, and click **Next**.

CHANGING, VOIDING, OR DELETING A TRANSACTION

(Continued)

DELETE A TRANSACTION

When you delete a transaction, Quicken recalculates all balances and permanently removes that transaction from the register.

1. With the register containing the transaction displayed, click the transaction you want to delete.

Continued . . .

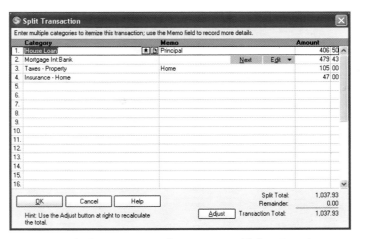

Figure 4-6: Splitting a transaction among multiple categories allows you to refine your accounting and get better control of where your money goes.

7. Repeat step 6 until you have all the categories you want, then click **Next** once more. If you need to adjust any of the entries, click the amount that needs to be adjusted.

8. If the entries are correct and you have a difference, either positive or negative, with the original check amount, click **Adjust** to make the total for the transaction the sum of the split categories.

9. Click **OK** to close the Split Transaction dialog box. Instead of a single category appearing in the Category field, Quicken displays --Split-- to remind you that there are multiple categories for this transaction.

3/18/2005	3215	First Federal	1,037 93	*Deposit*	9,936 88
		--Split-- ✓✗🗋 *Memo*		Enter	Edit	Split	📎☆

10. Hover your mouse pointer over "--Split--" in the Category field to see the amounts in each split category.

First Fed	🗋 House Loan	-406.50
--Split-	🗋 Mortgage In...	-479.43
Ralph &	🗋 Taxes - Pro...	-105.00
--Split--	🗋 Insurance - ...	-47.00

11. Click the transaction and three buttons appear next to "--Split--."

a. Click ✓ to open the Split Transaction dialog box where you can edit the split.

CHANGING, VOIDING, OR DELETING A TRANSACTION

(*Continued*)

2. Press **CTRL+D** and click **Yes** to delete the transaction.

–Or–

Click the **Edit** menu, click **Transaction**, and click **Delete**.

–Or–

Click **Delete** in the register menu bar.

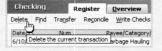

3. The transaction is completely deleted, and your balance is recomputed.

CAUTION

Quicken can restore a deleted transaction only in the Quicken session in which it was deleted (that is, before you exited Quicken). To restore a deleted transaction, click the **Edit** menu, click **Transaction**, and click **Undo Delete**.

b. Click 🗙 to clear all of the split categories and amounts, so you can replace them with a single new category.

c. Click 🗋 to open the activity dialog box where you can see the sum of the amounts in the categories used in this transaction.

Transfer Funds from One Account to Another

You can easily record the transfer of funds from one account to another in Quicken. The quickest way is to open the register of the account the money is from. Then:

1. Click **Transfer** in the register's menu bar.

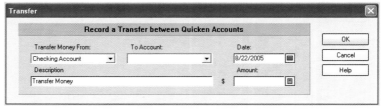

2. Click the **To Account** down arrow and select the account into which you are transferring the funds.

3. Press **TAB** and enter the date of the transfer if it is different than today's date.

4. Press **TAB** and, if you want either a different description, other than "Transfer Money," type that description or addition, such as "Transfer Money to savings."

5. Press **TAB** and type in the amount.

6. Click **OK** to make the transfer and close the dialog box.

Locate Transactions

There are several ways to find a transaction within Quicken.

1. Click **Find** on the register's menu bar.

–Or–

Click the **Edit** menu, click **Transactions**, and then click **Find**.

–Or–

Press **CTRL+F**.

–Or–

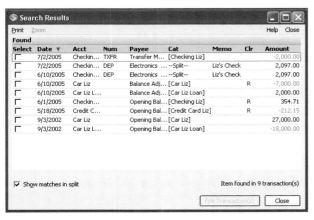

Figure 4-7: Quicken's transaction search feature allows you to find, for example all the transactions to a given payee, or all the transactions over a certain amount.

Click the **Edit** menu, click **Find & Replace**, and then click **Find**.

In all cases the Quicken Find dialog box will open.

2. Click the **Search** down arrow to open a list of fields on which to search. Click the field you want to search on.

3. Click the **Match If** down arrow to open a list of expressions to use in the search. Click the expression you want to use.

4. Click in the **Find** text box and type what you want to find.

5. Click **Find** to select the most recent transaction that matches your criteria.

–Or–

Click **Find All** to open the Search Results dialog box showing all the transactions that match your criteria. Figure 4-7 shows all the transactions containing the word "Liz" in any field.

Filter Transactions for More Information

Quicken can help you filter the transactions you see in a register, so only the ones you are interested in are shown. This can help you quickly locate specific information.

1. Click the **View** menu in the register menu bar and then click **Filter Register View**. The filter options appears at the top of the register.

2. Click the **View** down arrow to see a list of available filters.

3. Click the **Date Range** down arrow and click a specific period, like **Current Month** or **Last Quarter**, or click **Custom** to enter or select a specific date range.

4. Click the **Close Filter** button to close the filter toolbar.

Attach Digital Images to a Transaction

If you use Quicken 2006 Deluxe, Premier or Premier Home & Business, you can attach up to three digital images to each transaction in your register, a check image, a receipt image, and one other image. These attachments are then stored in the same file as your Quicken data. A digital attachment can be a picture of your new snowboard, a receipt for a donation, or any other item you may want to scan or download and keep with your transaction for tax or warranty purposes. You must first bring these items into Quicken, and then attach them to a transaction.

BRING ATTACHMENTS INTO QUICKEN

1. Click the **Edit** menu, click **Transaction**, and then click **Attachments**.

2. Click the **Check Image**, **Receipt Image**, or **Other Attachment** tab depending on the type of attachment you want to use.

3. Click **Add Attachment** at the bottom of the window to open the Select Attachment dialog box.

4. Locate the file you want to attach and click **Open**. The image is displayed in the Transaction Attachment Viewer.

5. Click **Close Viewer** to attach the image and close the window.

ADD A FLAG, ALERT, NOTE, OR IMAGE TO A TRANSACTION

1. Click 🔘 in the bottom-right of the transaction to open a drop-down menu.

2. Choose to add or attach the object you want from the menu.

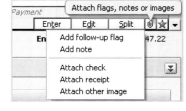

The way the sort options and direction of sorting is described by Intuit for the Payment and Deposit fields is confusing. When you hover the mouse pointer over Payment, you get the message "Sort By Amount (Smallest First)." Yet when you do the sort you get a downward pointing arrow and the largest numbers are at the top of the register. When you hover the mouse pointer over Deposit you get "Sort By Amount (Largest First)" and get the same results as you get when sorting Payment. In the View menu there is the option "Sort By Amount (Largest First)" that sorts the Deposits field with the largest numbers at the top. Also in the View menu there is the option "Sort By Amount (Smallest First)" that sorts the Payment field with the largest numbers at the top.

Figure 4-8: Quicken's Zipingo rating system is similar to eBay's feedback. Both help you know the reliability of who you are dealing with.

a. Click **Add Follow-Up Flag** if you need to mark the transaction. The Transaction Notes And Flags dialog box opens. Choose the color of the flag from the drop-down list. Click the **Alert** option and enter a date to have this transaction appear on your Alert List in the selected day on the Quicken home page. Click **OK** to close the dialog box. A small flag appears beneath the date of the transaction.

b. Click **Add Note** and type a note in the Transaction Notes And Flags dialog box that opens. Click **OK** to save the note. A small note icon appears beneath the date of the transaction. Click the note icon to read or change the note.

7/1/2005	3216
⚑	

6/10/2005	3482
🗒	

c. Click **Attach Check**, **Attach Receipt**, or **Attach Other Image** to open the Transaction Attachments dialog box. Add an attachment as previously discussed in "Bring Attachments into Quicken" and click **Close Viewer**. A small attachment icon appears beneath the date of the transaction. Click the attachment icon to see or change the attachment.

6/11/2005	3483
📎	

Rate Your Payees

Did you ever want to tell the world about a really great deal or wonderful service at a local store? Quicken now has a service, called Zipingo, that allows you to do just that, anonymously and quickly. The Zipingo service allows all Quicken users in the U.S. to rate their experiences at any business by clicking the blue star ⭐ in the lower-right of a transaction or in the Write Checks dialog box, and answering some questions. To use this service:

1. Click in or enter a transaction you wish to rate and click the **Rate This Payee** blue star icon.

   –Or–

   With the transaction selected, click the **Edit** menu, click **Transaction**, and click **Rate This Payee**.

   In either case, the first time you try rating a payee you will get a message about Zipingo and how it works. Click **Try It!** The Rate It! dialog box will open, as shown in Figure 4-8.

2. Type a name in the **Payee Name** field if it does not appear. Press TAB and type either the ZIP code or the city and state of the company you are rating.

3. Click the number of stars you are awarding, one for poor and five for the best.

4. Press TAB and type any comments about the transaction others should know.

5. Click the verification that you or anyone in your family do not work for nor compete with this business.

6. Click **Preview My Rating** to ensure you have completed each required field, review the rating, and make any necessary changes.

7. Click **Don't Display Payment Range** if you don't want that information to be displayed on your rating.

8. Click **OK To Publish** to transmit this rating to the Zipingo site, or **Change My Comments** to return to the Rate It! dialog box.

Set Up Your Printer and Print a Register

As you continue to work with Quicken you may want to print a register. Before you do, you may need to set up your printer to print reports or graphs.

SET UP YOUR PRINTER

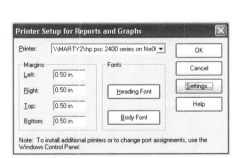

1. Click the **File** menu, click **Printer Setup**, Choose **For Reports/Graphs**. The Printer Setup for Reports and Graphs will open.

2. Click the **Printer** down arrow to show a list of your printers and click the one you want to set up.

3. Click in each of the margin text boxes you want to change and type the new margin.

4. Click **Heading Font** to change the font name, style, and size; click the name of the font, the style, and the size from their respective lists; and then click **OK**.

5. Click **Body Font** and repeat the tasks in step 4. These choices will appear on all of the reports or graphs you print on this printer.

6. Click **OK** to close the Printer Setup dialog box.

PRINT A REGISTER

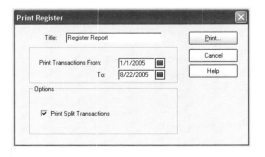

1. With the register you want to print open, click the **File** menu, and click **Print Register**.

   –Or–

   Press CTRL+P.

2. Type a title for the report. The name of the account appears on the report by default.

3. Select a time period for which you want to display the transactions.

4. Clear the **Print Split Transactions** option if you do not want the multiple categories in your split transaction to be included on the report.

5. Click **Print** to print the report. In the Print dialog box that opens, make any needed changes and click **OK**.

Use Other Cash Flow Center Registers

When you first open the register for a credit card account, its appearance is much like a check register. However, there are a few differences that you should recognize as shown in Table 4-2.

CHECK REGISTERS	CREDIT CARD REGISTERS
Date: The date of the transaction	**Date**: The date of the transaction
Num: The check number or an alphabetic description of the transaction. There is a drop-down list to assist you in choosing.	**Ref**: The type of transaction such as Charge, Payment, or Finance Charge. There is no drop-down list.
Payee/Category/Memo: The person or organization paid and the categorization of it. Drop-down lists are available for Payees and Categories.	**Payee/Category/Memo**: The person or organization paid and the categorization of it. Drop-down lists are available for Payees and Categories.
Payment: The amount of the check, charge, or deposit. There is a calculator available if you need it.	**Charge**: The amount of the charge, payment, or fee. There is a calculator available if you need it.
Clr: Whether a transaction has appeared on a statement from your financial institution and has been cleared.	**Clr**: Whether a transaction has appeared on a statement from your financial institution and has been cleared.
Deposit: The amount that has been deposited into this account. A calculator is available if you need it.	**Payment**: The amount you have paid on this credit card. A calculator is available if you need it.
Balance: The amount of money you have in this account after entering all of your deposits and checks.	**Balance**: The amount of money you owe on this credit card after entering all of your charges and payments.

Table 4-2: Differences Between Checking and Credit Card Registers

ENTER A CREDIT CARD CHARGE, FINANCE CHARGE, OR CREDIT

If you are familiar with entering checks into your checking account register, the process is similar in your credit card register.

1. Click the credit card account in the Account bar to open that card's register. The empty transaction line at the bottom of the register should be selected as shown in Figure 4-9.

2. If it isn't already selected and you want to change the date, click in the **Date** column and use the date techniques described in step 2 of "Enter a Check" earlier in this chapter.

3. Press TAB to move to the **Ref** column and type a description of the transaction.

4. Press TAB or click **Payee** and enter the name of the business.

5. Press TAB or click **Charge** and enter the amount of the charge.

6. Press TAB or click **Category** and select from the drop-down list or type the category.

TIP

A credit card payment is easily made in one of your checking account registers. Simply identify the credit card you want paid in the category field of the check using one of the "Transfer to/from" categories. When you go back into the credit card register, the amount of the payment and the checking account from which it was paid appear on the next transaction line.

Transfer to/from...	**[Checking 2]**
Transfer to/from...	**[Checking Account]**
Transfer to/from...	**[new checking]**
Transfer to/from...	**[Savings]**
Transfer to/from...	**[Credit Card]**
Transfer to/from...	**[Cash Account]**
Transfer to/from...	**[Car 2]**

Split	Transfer	Add Cat
Show List		Show Hidden

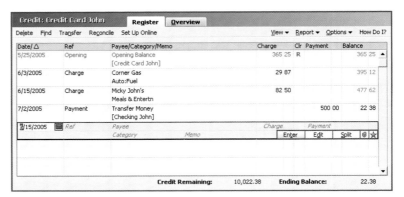

Figure 4-9: Credit card registers have many similarities to check registers.

7. Press TAB or click **Memo** and enter any identifying information, such as "Dinner with Meg and Jack" or "School clothes for Sally."

8. Click **Enter** or press ENTER to complete the transaction.

WORK WITH A CASH ACCOUNT REGISTER

Creating an account to track your cash spending can be useful. It is a great learning tool for young people to track where they spend their money. You can enter data each time money is spent, or add information in bulk at the end of each week or month. Many people who use this type of account enter only whole dollar amounts. Use the same procedures described earlier in this chapter for entering checks and credit card transactions.

1. Create a cash account as described in Chapter 3. Open that account's register, and, if it isn't already selected, click in the empty transaction line.

2. If needed, change the date, press TAB, type a description in the **Ref** column and select or type a payee to identify the transaction.

3. Enter the amount spent in the **Spend** column or the amount received in the **Receive** column.

4. Click **Enter** or press ENTER to complete the transaction.

Chapter 5
Taking Control with Quicken

After using Quicken to enter your day-to-day transactions, you may want to step up to the next level and start using more of the features Quicken provides to help you save time as you manage your finances. Quicken can even alert you to recurring bills you forgot to pay! In this chapter you will learn how to automate Quicken, memorize payees, schedule transactions, use the Calendar, automate transactions or schedule your bills online, create reports, and produce useful graphs from accounts in your Cash Flow Center.

Memorize Your Entries

When you set your preferences (see Chapter 4), you told Quicken how to use QuickFill to make data entry faster and whether to automatically update new payees. You might recall that one choice was to automatically memorize new payees and then recall them when you next entered them. Whether or not you chose to have Quicken do this, you can also memorize transactions and payees manually.

Create a Memorized Payee

Memorizing saves you valuable data-entry time. Use the Memorized Payee List, shown in Figure 5-1, to create a memorization.

1. Click the **Cash Flow** menu, and click **Memorized Payee List** to display the list.
   –Or–
   Press CTRL+T.

2. Click **New** in the menu bar. The Create Memorized Payee dialog box appears.

3. Click the **Type Of Transaction** down arrow to choose the transaction type.

NOTE

The Address button found in the Create Memorized Transaction dialog box is available only when you select Print Check as the transaction type.

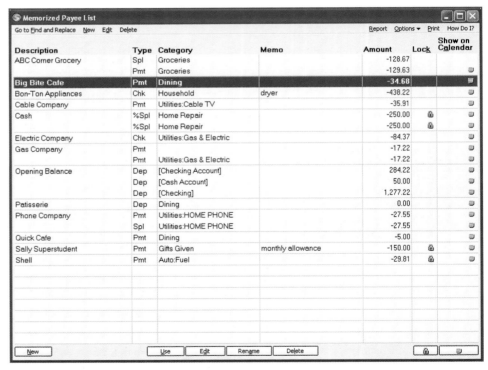

Figure 5-1: *The Memorized Payee List lets you create, edit, use, rename, and delete your memorized payees.*

4. Press TAB and type the name of the payee in the Payee field.

5. Press TAB and type an amount if you pay the same amount each time.

6. Click the **Category** down arrow, and choose a category from the list, or type one in the Category text box.

7. Enter any note in the Memo field, and click **OK** to memorize the payee.

Change Memorized Payees

You can work with the Memorized Payee List in several ways. As you look at the list shown in Figure 5-1, you see the menu bar at the top of the list, as well as the buttons on the bottom of the list. Some of the things you can do with the Memorized Payee List include:

- If your Memorized Payee List isn't already displayed, press CTRL+T. Then click **New** in either the menu bar or using the buttons at the bottom to create a new memorized transaction.

- Click **Go To Find And Replace** in the menu bar to find an existing transaction and replace any of its information.

- Choose any payee on the list, and click **Edit** on either the menu bar or at the bottom to make changes to existing information.

- Select any payee and click **Delete** in either the menu bar or in the buttons at the bottom, to delete that payee. A dialog box appears asking if it is all right to delete one item. Click **OK**.

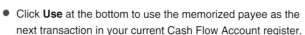

- Click **Use** at the bottom to use the memorized payee as the next transaction in your current Cash Flow Account register.

Use Renaming Rules for Downloaded Transactions

When banks assign a payee name to a transaction, they might not use the name you want in your check register. Quicken allows you to establish renaming rules so that these transactions can be matched. You can add renaming rules from the Memorized Payee List or from the Quicken Preferences dialog box.

ADD RENAMING RULES FROM THE MEMORIZED PAYEE LIST

1. Click the **Cash Flow** menu, and click **Memorized Payee List**.
   –Or–
   Click CTRL+T.
   In either case the Memorized Payee List appears.

2. Click the name of one or more payees that you want to rename. To choose multiple names and rename them with the same name, hold down CTRL while clicking them. This method allows you to fix several entries to the same payee with different spellings. For example, you may have entered J. Jameson and John Jameson. You can create one payee, John L. Jameson, with this method.

3. Click **Rename** at the bottom of the window. Type the name in the New Name field. If you want to create a renaming rule for a downloaded transaction using this name, click that option and click **OK**. The Edit Renaming Rule dialog box appears.

4. Make any changes to the rule, and, if needed, click **Add New Item** to add additional names that should be renamed with this renaming rule. Click **OK** to close the Edit Renaming Rule dialog box.

ADD RENAMING RULES FROM QUICKEN PREFERENCES

Quicken Preferences allow you to add a renaming rule when you don't have a current memorized name to work with.

1. Click the **Edit** menu, click **Preferences**, and click **Quicken Program**.

2. Click **Downloaded Transactions** and then click **Renaming Rules**. The Renaming Rules For Downloaded Transactions dialog box appears.

3. Click **New**. The Create Renaming Rule dialog box appears. Enter the new payee name and the name or names that should be renamed to that name, and click **OK**.

4. Click **Done** to close the Renaming Rules For Downloaded Transactions dialog box, and then click **OK** to close Quicken Preferences.

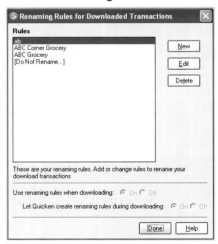

Create and Memorize a Split Transaction Using Percentages

When you create a split transaction, there may be times when you want to use a percentage and have Quicken calculate an amount rather than entering the specific dollar amount for each category. To create such a memorized transaction:

1. Open the Cash Flow Account register that will contain the transaction, and enter the date, number or reference, payee, and total amount as you normally would.

2. Click **Split** in the Transaction tool bar.
   –Or–
   Click in the **Category** field, and click **Split**.
   In either case, the Split Transaction dialog box appears, as shown in Figure 5-2.

3. Click the **Category** down arrow, and select a category. Press TAB, enter a memo or description if you choose, and press TAB again.

4. In the Amount field, which contains the total amount, replace the existing amount by typing a percentage as a number followed by the percent (%) sign. Quicken automatically calculates the dollar amount for the category by multiplying the total amount of the transaction times the percentage and then displays the balance on the next line. For example, if the check is for $200.00 and you type 75% on the first line, the amount displayed on the first line will be $150.00 and $50.00 will be displayed on the second line.

5. Press TAB to move to the next line, and repeat steps 2 through 4.

6. Click **OK** to apply the split and close the window.

7. Click **Edit**, click **Transaction**, and then click **Memorize Payee** to memorize the transaction
   –Or–
   Press CTRL+M.

Figure 5-2: *The Split Transaction dialog box allows you to assign multiple categories to one transaction by either dollar amount or percentages.*

Create a Schedule

Most of us have bills we pay every month. Your list may seem endless, with utility bills, rent or mortgage payments, property tax payments, and so on. Quicken's Scheduled Transaction feature helps you automate the process. You can select and schedule all recurring transactions so you don't overlook a

QUICKSTEPS

LOCKING A MEMORIZED PAYEE

If you choose to automatically memorize new payees in Quicken Preferences, each time you use a memorized payee, the transaction amount associated with that payee is updated. You can lock a memorized payee transaction so that the transaction amount won't change if you enter a transaction with a different amount for that payee. For example, let's say you send your daughter in college, Sally Superstudent, an allowance of $150.00 per month for spending money and have locked that transaction. If you send her a birthday check for $250, the locked transaction will not change. If you do not lock it, the new memorized payee amount will be $250.00. To lock a transaction that is already in the Memorized Payee List:

1. Click the **Cash Flow** menu, and click **Memorized Payee List**.

2. Select the transaction you want to lock.

3. Click the **Lock** column to display the small lock icon.
   –Or–
   Click the **Lock** icon at the bottom of the Memorized Payee List.

| Sally Superstudent | Pmt | Gifts Given | Monthly Allowance | -150.00 | 🔒 |

4. Click **Close** to close the list.

You can unlock a transaction in the same way. When a transaction is unlocked and your preferences are set to automatically memorize new payees, the next time you enter a transaction for this payee, the new amount is memorized.

regular payment. Quicken can even enter them automatically. You can set up reminders or record transactions several days earlier than they are actually due to remind yourself to put money in the bank to cover them. You can keep track of your paycheck using Quicken Guided Setup to enter your gross wages and deductions to help with tax planning. (See Chapters 9 and 10 for information on taxes and budgeting.)

Understand Scheduled Transactions

Quicken has two types of scheduled transactions: recurring transactions, such as insurance or mortgage payments, and one-time transactions, such as the balance due on the new deck you're having built. Other scheduled transactions can include:

- Income
  - Paychecks (see "Schedule Your Paycheck" later in this chapter)
  - Alimony or child-support payments
  - Social Security or retirement checks
- Payments
  - Mortgage or rent payments
  - Car payments
  - Health and other insurance payments
  - Taxes
  - Membership dues

Find Recurring Transactions

Quicken helps you find transactions you pay on a recurring basis to let you determine if they should be paid on a regular schedule. Use this feature to ensure you've paid all your recurring bills each month.

1. Click the **Cash Flow** menu, and click **Go To Cash Flow Center**.

2. Scroll to the **Bills And Scheduled Transaction** section at the bottom of the screen.

3. Click the **Show** down arrow, and click **All - By Bills And Deposits**.

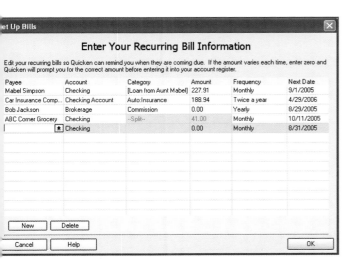

Figure 5-3: *The Set Up Bills dialog box allows you to enter several recurring bills at once.*

4. Click **Options** on the right of the Bills And Scheduled Transactions title bar, and click **Scan Now For Recurring Transactions**. A message appears stating that a list of transactions appears at the bottom of Bills And Scheduled Transactions.

5. Scroll to the bottom of the list. Click the **Yes** button for each bill you want to include as a scheduled transaction, or click the **No** button if you don't want it included in the list.

Schedule These?				
9/8/2005	Gas Company	-17.22	Checking A...	Yes No
9/8/2005	Electric Company	-84.37	Checking A...	Yes No
9/8/2005	Cable Company	-35.91	Checking A...	Yes No

If you click **Yes** for a bill you want scheduled, the Edit All Future Transactions dialog box will appear so you can make any changes you want to the transaction. Click **OK** when finished.

If you click **No** for a bill, you will be asked to confirm that decision by clicking **OK**.

If a newly scheduled transaction causes you to exceed your budget, you will be notified of that and given the opportunity to update your budget. See Chapter 9 for a discussion of budgeting.

Schedule a Transaction with Guided Setup

You can use Quicken Guided Setup to schedule regular bills.

1. Click **Setup** on the tool bar.

–Or–

Click the **Tools** menu and click **Quicken Guided Setup**.

2. Click **Bills** in the left column to display the Add Bills pane. Click **Add Bills Manually** to schedule transactions you handle yourself instead of using Quicken Bill Pay. The Set Up Bills dialog box appears, as shown in Figure 5-3.

3. Click **New** to add a new recurring bill. Type the payee name or choose one from the drop-down list, and press TAB.

UNDERSTANDING SCHEDULED TRANSACTION METHODS

Quicken provides nine different methods for completing a scheduled transaction. These methods are based on the type of account the transaction affects and what version of Quicken you use, so not all choices are available for every transaction.

OUTGOING TRANSACTIONS

Scheduled disbursements can be used in all types of accounts. The methods for completing outgoing transactions are:

- **Payment** is used by Quicken for all transactions that pay money out of an account, including handwritten checks and direct charges, such as the deduction for your annual safe-deposit box fee.
- **Printed Check** is a check that is printed with Quicken.
- **Online Payment** from Quicken is the option you use when you use an online bill-paying service through your financial institution or Quicken Bill Pay.
- **Business Bill** schedules a regular bill, such as rent or telephone, when you use Quicken Premier Home & Business.

INCOMING TRANSACTIONS

The methods for completing incoming transactions are:

- **Deposit** is used by Quicken to indicate any transaction that puts money into an account.
- **Transfer** is the method used when you move funds from one account to another, for example, from your checking account to your savings account each month.

Continued . . .

4. Choose the account from which this transaction will be taken. Press TAB.
5. Type the category name or click the down arrow to choose one from the drop-down list. Press TAB.
6. Enter the amount if it is the same each time. You can enter zero and Quicken will prompt you each time for the amount. This works well for bills you pay regularly that are not the same amount, such as your telephone bill. Press TAB.
7. Enter how often this transaction occurs in the Frequency field. The default is **Monthly**, but you have other choices, as shown in Table 5-1. Press TAB.

FREQUENCY FOR SCHEDULED TRANSACTIONS	EXPLANATION
Only Once	This is for transactions that will only happen once, such as an upcoming balloon or final payment.
Weekly	Use this if the transaction occurs every week. Quicken uses the starting date of the transaction to determine which day of the week it will occur. With all frequencies other than Only Once, you have the option to set the date on which this transaction will end, the number of times it will occur, or no ending date.
Every Two Weeks Every Four Weeks	You have the same options as with the Weekly occurrence. The transaction repeats every two or four weeks from the start date.
Twice A Month	You tell Quicken on which two days each month to schedule this transaction.
Monthly	This is the default setting since most recurring transactions happen monthly. You can designate a specific date or a specific day, such as the third Tuesday of each month.
Quarterly	Use this if you have something that occurs every three months, such as estimated income tax payments.
Twice A Year	This option allows you to choose two days per year on which to schedule the transaction. Auto insurance and property tax payments are often paid twice each year.
Yearly	This option is for annual payments. You can set a specific date, such as August 10 or the second Wednesday of August.

Table 5-1: *Choices for the Frequency of Scheduled Transactions*

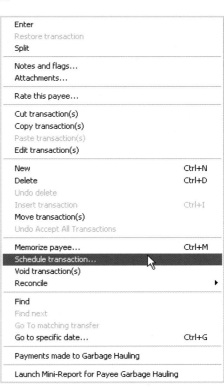

Figure 5-4: *The Create Scheduled Transaction dialog box lets you schedule payments and deposits so you won't forget to enter them.*

---

8. Enter the next date on which this transaction is to occur.

9. Click **OK** to close the dialog box, or repeat these steps for another transaction.

Create a Scheduled Transaction

You can create a scheduled transaction directly from a transaction in a register or by opening the Scheduled Transaction List.

SCHEDULE A TRANSACTION FROM ITSELF

1. With a register open, right-click the transaction you want to memorize to display a context menu. Click **Schedule Transaction**. The Create Scheduled Transaction dialog box appears, as shown in Figure 5-4.

2. Click the **Account To Use** down arrow, and choose an account.

3. Click the **Transaction Method** down arrow, and choose a method.

4. Type an address in the **Web Page Address (Optional)** field if you want.

5. Click in the **Payee** field, and type a name, or choose one from the drop-down list.

6. If you want, click **Address** and enter the payee in the Address Book. Click **OK** when you are finished.

7. Click **Amount** and enter one if this transaction has a standard amount paid each time, or enter zero to have Quicken prompt you for the amount each time. You can also instruct Quicken to estimate the amount based on a chosen number of previous payments you have made.

8. Click **Category** and type a name, or choose one from the drop-down list.

9. Click **Split** to assign multiple categories. Click **Memo** and enter additional information on this transaction if needed. Click **OK** when you are finished.

10. Click **Start On** and enter the first scheduled transaction date.

11. Click the **Remind Me** down arrow, and optionally click **Automatically Enter**.

12. Select the number of days in advance to be reminded of this transaction, up to 180 days.

13. Click the **Frequency** down arrow, and select the frequency with which this transaction will occur. If required, select the date or day in the month (May 9ᵗʰ or second Tuesday, for example) for this transaction.

14. Click **No End Date** or enter an ending date or number of occurrences.

15. Click **Options**. The Create Scheduled Transaction Options dialog box appears:

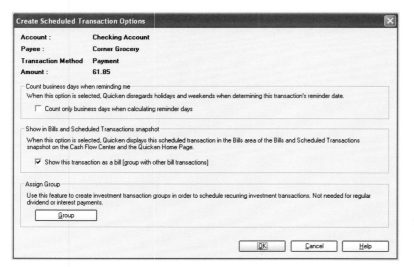

a. Click **Count Only Business Days When Calculating Reminder Days** if you want Quicken to ignore weekends and holidays when determining which day to remind you about a scheduled transaction.

b. Clear **Show This Transaction As A Bill** if you do not want Quicken to display this transaction in the Bills And Scheduled Transactions on both the Cash Flow Center and Quicken home page.

c. Click **Group** to assign a group to an investment transaction.

d. Click **OK** to return to the Create Scheduled Transaction dialog box.

16. Click **OK** to close the Create Scheduled Transaction dialog box.

SCHEDULE A TRANSACTION FROM THE SCHEDULED TRANSACTION LIST

1. Press CTRL+J.

   –Or–

   Click the **Cash Flow** menu, and click **Scheduled Transaction List**. In either case, the Scheduled Transaction List displays.

2. Click **Create New** and click **Scheduled Transaction**. The Create Scheduled Transaction dialog box appears.

3. Follow the procedure described in "Schedule a Transaction from Itself" to create a new scheduled transaction.

Use the Calendar

Sometimes it's helpful to see events on a calendar to reinforce them in your mind. The Calendar in Quicken lets you see at a glance your financial events for each month, as shown in Figure 5-5.

1. Press **CTRL+K**.

    —Or—

    Click the **Tools** menu and then click **Calendar**.

    —Or—

    Click the **Cash Flow** menu, and then click **Calendar**.

    In all instances, the Calendar window opens.

Figure 5-5: Quicken's Calendar helps you organize your financial transactions.

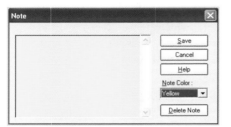

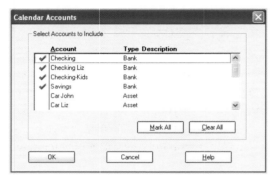

2. Click **Prev Month** or **Next Month** in the menu bar to move between months. The current month is displayed by default.

3. Click **Go To Date** in the menu bar to open a dialog box in which you can enter any specific date you want to view. Click **OK** to close the dialog box.

4. Click a specific date and then click **Add Note** to add a reminder note to that date. Type the note you want on that date, select the color of the note, and click **Save**.

5. Click **Select Accounts** to view the list of accounts whose transactions are displayed on the Calendar. If an account is not selected, click it to display its transactions on the Calendar. If an account is selected, click it to remove the check box and not display its transaction on the Calendar. Click **OK** to close the dialog box.

6. Click **Print** to print the current month's calendar. A list of all transactions for that month is displayed on the bottom of the printed page.

7. Click **Options** to determine what will be displayed on the Calendar and to edit the Memorized Payee List.

8. Double-click any date to view the details of transactions for that day.

9. Click **New** to add a new transaction for that day, fill in the applicable transaction fields, and click **OK** when you are finished.

10. Click **New Scheduled** to add a new scheduled transaction for that day, fill in the applicable scheduled transaction fields, and click **OK** when you are finished.

11. Click an existing transaction and click **Edit** to change it for the future. Make the needed changes and click **OK**.

12. Click an existing transaction, click **Delete**, and click **OK** to confirm the deletion of the transaction.

13. Click **Register** to open the register containing the selected transaction. When you are finished with the register, click **Calendar** at the bottom of the Quicken window to return to the Calendar.

14. Click an existing transaction and click **Schedule** to change its schedule information. When you are finished, click **OK**.

15. Right-click any date to display a context menu. You can:

- Click **Transactions** to open the Transaction dialog box for that date.

- Click **Note** to create a note for that date on the Calendar.

- Click **Previous Month** or **Next Month** to move between calendar months.

| Transactions |
| Note |
| Previous month |
| Next month |
| Calendar accounts |

- Click **Calendar Accounts** to choose the accounts whose contents will be displayed on the Calendar.

16. Click **Close**, or press ALT+F4, to close the Calendar.

Use the Scheduled Transaction List

Quicken displays scheduled transactions on the Calendar, on the Quicken home page, on the Cash Flow Center, and at the bottom of each cash flow check register that has scheduled transactions. The Scheduled Transaction List can display scheduled transactions for all of your accounts, for several accounts, or for only one. In addition, you can add, edit, and delete transactions to, on, or from the list, as well as enter a transaction into the check register or skip it for this time period.

1. Press CTRL+J.

–Or–

Click the **Cash Flow** menu and click **Scheduled Transaction List**.

In either case, the Scheduled Transaction List window opens. One view of it is shown in Figure 5-6.

2. If it is not already selected click the **Monthly Bills & Deposits** tab to display the payment and deposit transactions you have scheduled for the current month. Click the arrow to the right or left of this month's name to move to other months.

3. Click **Show Graph** to display a graph showing the balances each day in all, some, or one of your accounts.

☑ Show graph   ☑ Show calendar

TIP

The account graph shown in the Scheduled Transaction List and other locations within Quicken uses colored bars so you can easily differentiate between the days. Yellow is used for previous dates, green for today, and blue for future dates.

NOTE

Scheduled transactions can be reminders of special days, such as family birthdays or anniversaries. You can also use them to remind yourself of important appointments!

TIP

Create scheduled transactions or notes about tax payment due dates or other important dates, such as insurance premiums you pay semi-annually.

Figure 5-6: *Scheduled transactions help you plan and account for your income and expenses.*

4. Click **Show Calendar** to display the current month's calendar. Days on which you have paid transactions or have scheduled transactions are shown in gray.

5. Click the **All Types** tab to display all scheduled transactions, not just the payments and deposits.

6. Click **Options** to choose how the transactions are sorted: by description, by amount, or by the next payment date.

7. Click **Print** to print a list of the scheduled transactions.

WORK WITH AN EXISTING SCHEDULED TRANSACTION

An existing scheduled transaction—one that has not been handled and entered on a register—can be changed in the Scheduled Transaction List. When you select such a transaction, several additional options on the menu bar become available.

1. Click an existing scheduled transaction, and click **Enter**, either in the menu bar or on the right of the transaction, to enter that transaction into its register. The Edit Current Transaction And Enter Into Register dialog box appears, as shown in Figure 5-7:

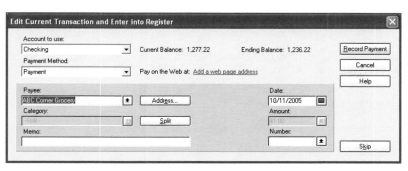

Figure 5-7: *The Edit Current Transaction And Enter Into Register dialog box allows you to move a scheduled payment directly into the register.*

CAUTION

When using scheduled transactions, remember that you still actually have to go to the bank to make the deposit or physically mail the handwritten or printed checks.

Bills and Scheduled Transactions   Options ▼

Show: All - by Bills and Deposits ▼ ☐ Show graph ☐ Show calendar

Date	Status	Name/Payee	Amount	Account	Web	Action
Bills						
7/8/2005	Overdue!	City Utilities	-87.00	Checking		Enter Edit Skip
7/8/2005	Overdue!	Western Insurance	-425.00	Checking		Enter Edit Skip
7/10/2005	Due Soon	First Federal	-297.16	Checking		Enter Edit Skip
7/10/2005	Due Soon	Garbage Hauling	-23.00	Checking		Enter Edit Skip
7/10/2005	Due Soon	City Water	-42.00	Checking		Enter Edit Skip
7/20/2005		George Maynard	-594.10	Checking		Enter Edit Skip
7/28/2005		A Power Co	-123.00	Checking		Enter Edit Skip
8/1/2005		National Union	-1,650.00	Checking		Enter Edit Skip
8/1/2005		National Union	-1,650.00	Checking		Enter Edit Skip
9/3/2005		Al's Motors Credit	-365.18	Checking		Enter Edit Skip
Deposits and Other Scheduled Transactions						
7/22/2005		Electronics Corp.	2,097.00	Checking		Enter Edit Skip

Manage Full List | Add a Transaction | Set Up Paycheck | Go to Cash Flow Center

a. Review the payment method, payee, category, date, and amount, and make any necessary changes.

b. Click **Record Payment** to record the transaction.

2. Click **Skip**, either in the menu bar or on the right of the transaction, to skip the scheduled payment this time only. It will still be available in the future.

3. Click **Edit**, either in the menu bar or on the right of the transaction, to modify the transaction.

4. Click **Delete** in the menu bar to remove the transaction. This only removes the scheduled transaction; it has no effect on transactions that have already been recorded.

5. Click **Close** to close the Scheduled Transaction List.

WORK WITH TRANSACTIONS ON THE CASH FLOW CENTER OR THE QUICKEN HOME PAGE

You can access your scheduled transactions from both the Cash Flow Center and the Quicken home page.

1. Click **Quicken Home**.

–Or–

Click the **Cash Flow** menu, and click **Go To Cash Flow Center**. Using either method, you may need to scroll to the bottom of the Activity Center to open the Bills And Scheduled Transactions section.

2. Click the **Show** down arrow, and click one of the following:

- **All – By Month** displays both recurring bills and scheduled transactions for each month. You can move between months by clicking the right and left arrows.

- **All – By Bills And Deposits** shows all scheduled transactions by the due dates. Use this view to ensure you have not missed any scheduled transactions.

- **Current – By Status** displays a list that is sorted according to transactions that are overdue, due today, and due soon.

- **Upcoming** displays transactions that you asked Quicken to remind you about.

- **Current – By Bills And Deposits** displays bills that are due first, then deposits, and then gives you possible transactions to schedule.

UICKSTEPS

SCHEDULING ONLINE PAYMENTS

When you schedule your transactions using the Online Payment From Quicken option, you can send the first set of instructions and then tell the bill-paying service to repeat that payment a certain number of times on specific dates. This way, the financial institution does not need to receive instructions every time.

1. Press CTRL+J to display your Scheduled Transaction List.

2. Click Create New.

3. Choose the account. This account must have been set up to download transactions and have online payment available.

4. Click Transaction Method and click Online Payment.

5. Click **Repeat This Online Payment Automatically** to set up the repeating online payment.

6. Enter the amount.

7. Enter the number of times this payment is to be made.

8. Click **OK**.

NOTE

If you have an existing paycheck already set up, when you choose to track a new paycheck in Quicken, the Manage Paychecks dialog box will appear. It displays the existing paycheck(s) and allows you to edit or delete them. To enter a new paycheck, click **New**.

---

3. Click the **Show Graph** and **Show Calendar** check boxes to activate the Calendar and graph (clear these check boxes if you do not want these items displayed).

4. Click **Options** to open a menu that offers more choices when working with scheduled transactions.

Schedule Your Paycheck

As you continue to work with all of the features Quicken provides, you will see one of the most important is planning for income tax time. To make this even easier, Quicken has a special paycheck setup feature that tracks your deductions and benefits to save you time at the end of the year.

1. Click the Cash Flow menu, and then click Scheduled Transaction List.

2. Click **Create New** and then click **Paycheck**. The Paycheck Setup Wizard starts. You will need your last pay stub to continue.

3. Click **Next** to begin.

4. Click either **This Is My Paycheck** or **This Is My Spouse's Paycheck**.

5. Enter the name of the company, especially if you will be exporting your Quicken data into TurboTax at the end of the year. Optionally, enter any identifying information in the Memo field.

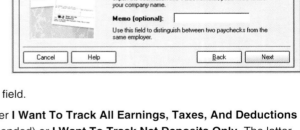

6. Click **Next** and click either **I Want To Track All Earnings, Taxes, And Deductions** (the default and recommended) or **I Want To Track Net Deposits Only**. The latter choice will simply schedule a deposit of your net pay into the account you designate.

7. Click **Next** to continue. The Set Up Paycheck dialog box appears, as shown in Figure 5-8.

8. Verify the company name and the account into which the funds are deposited, and add a memo if desired.

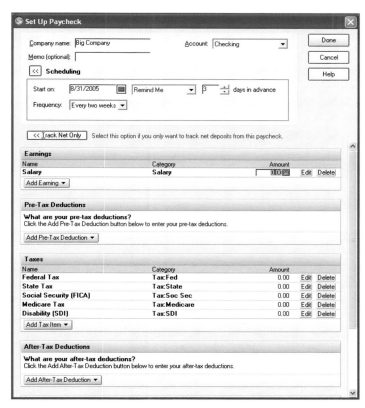

NOTE

There is a specific difference between *Every Two Weeks* and *Twice A Month*. Being paid every two weeks means you get paid every other Thursday, for example, and you receive 26 paychecks each year. Twice a month means you are paid on two specific dates each month, such as the 10th and the 25th. This option means you receive 24 paychecks each year.

*Figure 5-8: **The Set Up Paycheck dialog box saves time and helps with tax planning.***

9. Click **Scheduling**, if it isn't already open, and indicate the start date, whether Quicken should remind you or enter the deposit automatically, and how many days in advance either action should be performed. Set the frequency of this paycheck.

10. Click **Track Net Only** if you only want to schedule the deposit of the take-home portion of your check. The Set Up Paycheck dialog box changes and displays only the company name and scheduling information.

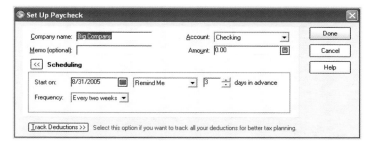

11. Click **Track Deductions** to track your gross pay and deductions.

12. Click **Add Earning** to choose the type of pay you are entering. The default is Salary; additional choices include:
    - Bonus
    - Profit Sharing
    - Vacation
    - Holiday
    - Sick Pay
    - Other Earnings

13. Enter the amount of your gross salary.

14. Click **Add Pre-Tax Deduction** to enter 401(k), medical insurance, or other pre-tax deductions. Click the deduction you want to create, enter a name, choose an account, enter the amount, and, if you choose the 401(k) or PERS options, you may also enter any funds contributed by your employer. Click **OK** when finished.

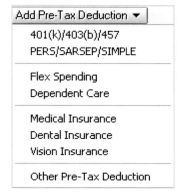

15. Click **Add Tax Item** to display the list of federal and state taxes that may be deducted. You can also use the **Edit** button to the right of each field. Click the tax you want to track, change the name and category as needed, enter the amount, and click **OK**.

16. Click **Add After-Tax Deduction**, select the deduction, enter the name, select or enter the category, enter the amount of the deduction, and click **OK**.

17. If you want a portion of your paycheck put in an account other than the primary account chosen at the top of the dialog box, such as a savings account, click **Add Deposit Account**, select the account, add a memo if desired, and add the amount.

18. Scroll down to see your net pay as well as the gross taxable (W2) amount of wages.

19. Click **Done** to complete the entry and close the Set Up Paycheck dialog box. A dialog box appears asking if you want to enter your year-to-date information.

20. If you want to enter year-to-date information, leave the default, click **OK** and enter this information. It normally is included on your pay stub. When you're done, click **Enter**. Otherwise click **I Do Not Want To Enter This Information**, and click **OK** to close the dialog box. You will see a message that you can enter it later in the Tax Planner (see Chapter 9 for a discussion of Quicken's several planning tools).

Taxes

Name	Category	Amount		
Federal Tax	Tax:Fed	364.00	Edit	Delete
State Tax	Tax:State	0.00	Edit	Delete
Social Security (FICA)	Tax:Soc Sec	111.60	Edit	Delete
Medicare Tax	Tax:Medicare	26.10	Edit	Delete
Disability (SDI)	Tax:SDI	18.22	Edit	Delete

Add Tax Item ▼

After-Tax Deductions

What are your after-tax deductions?
Click the Add After-Tax Deduction button below to enter your after-tax deductions.

Add After-Tax Deduction ▼

Deposit Accounts

Account	Memo	Amount
Checking	Primary Account	1,280.08

Add Deposit Account

Net Pay		1,280.08
W2 Gross		1,800.00

21. If you originally added a new paycheck from the Manage Paychecks dialog box, click **Done** to close it. Click **Close** to close the Scheduled Transaction List dialog box.

Use Reports and Graphs

After you have been working with Quicken for a while, it may be easier to see information in a report or graph format rather than viewing the various Centers, lists, or registers. You can create reports directly from registers or transactions, use one of the many standard reports included with Quicken, customize an existing report in a number of ways, and memorize the reports you use regularly. You can print reports and graphs, and you can copy or transfer the data on a report to other programs, such as Excel, TurboTax, or Microsoft Money. By setting your preferences, you can change how reports use color and display information, and you can set the default date range for your reports. In this chapter we discuss some of the standard reports and graphs available. In later chapters we discuss ways you can customize and change reports, and you'll learn about reports you can create regarding your investments, taxes, and net worth.

Set Report Preferences

You can determine how each report displays your data from two different locations in Quicken: through the Reports menu and through the Preferences menu.

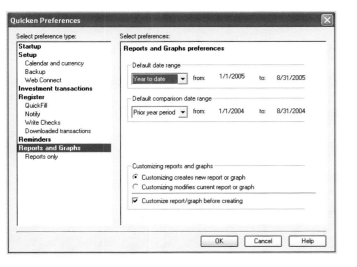

1. Click the **Reports** menu and click **Reports & Graphs Center**. The Reports & Graphs window opens, as shown in Figure 5-9. Click **Preferences** on the right of the menu bar.
   –Or–
   Click the **Edit** menu, click **Preferences**, click **Quicken Program**, and click **Reports And Graphs**
   In both cases the Quicken Preferences dialog box appears displaying reports and graphs preferences:

   - Click the **Default Date Range** down arrow to choose the range you will most often use when running reports. Year To Date is selected by default.

   - Click the **Default Comparison Date Range** down arrow to choose the range that you will compare the current data to when creating a report. **Prior Year Period** is selected by default.

   - In the Customizing Reports And Graphs area, click **Customizing Creates New Report Or Graph** or **Customizing Modifies Current Report Or Graph**.

   You can also click **Customize Report/Graph Before Creating** to customize reports or graphs before creating them. (This is selected by default.)

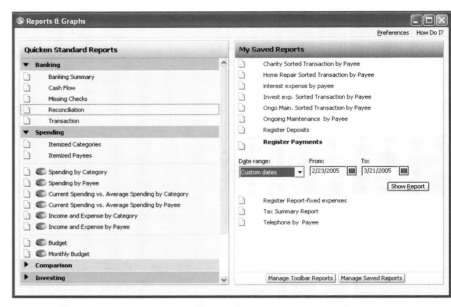

Figure 5-9: *The Reports & Graphs window allows you to choose from the many standard reports and graphs supplied in Quicken.*

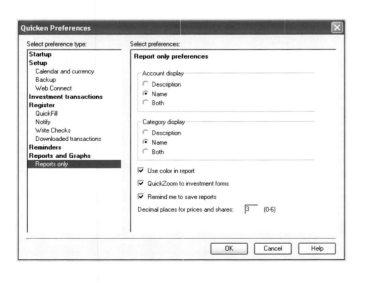

2. Click **Reports Only** to view the options for how reports will display information. For the display of both accounts and categories:

   • Click **Description** to include each account or category's description in your reports.

   • Click **Name** (selected by default) to include the name of an account or category.

   • Click **Both** to include both the name and description in each report.

3. For other display options:

   • Clear the **Use Color In Report** check box if you want to print your report in black and white.

   • Click **QuickZoom To Investment Forms** to have the capability of seeing what information makes up each line of data on an investment report.

   • Clear the **Remind Me To Save Reports** check box if you don't want Quicken to remind you to save any reports you have created.

QuickZoom is a Quicken feature that allows you to see more detail about items in a report or graph. In some reports and graphs, this feature opens the original transaction.

QUICKSTEPS

CREATING A MINI-REPORT

Quicken's standard reports are designed to give you broad information about your accounts and activities. However, sometimes you might only want to find out how much you have paid to one payee to date or how much money you have spent eating out during the last three months. You can create a mini-report from any register regarding a payee or a category.

1. Open a register that has either the category or the payee on which you want your mini-report.

2. Click in either the **Payee** or the **Category** field.

3. Click the **mini-report** icon. You will see a small report on your screen displaying the last few transactions for this category or payee.

Payee mini-report

| Electric Company | ⬇ 🗋 |
| Utilities:Gas & Electric | *Memo* |

Continued . . .

• Type a number in the **Decimal Places For Prices And Shares** field if it is different from the default choice of 3.

4. Click **OK** to close the Quicken Preferences dialog box.

Create a Standard Report

To create a standard report in Quicken:

1. Click the **Reports** menu and click **Reports And Graphs Center** to display the Reports & Graphs List (see Figure 5-9).

2. Click the small **triangle** icon in the area from which you want the report created. The standard reports available in this area are displayed in the window.

3. Click the report you want to create.

4. Choose the date range if it is different from the default range you set under Preferences.

5. Click **Customize** to open the Customize dialog box for this report (see Chapter 6 for more information.)

6. Click **Show Report** to see the report.

7. Click **Print Report** in the menu bar to print the report.

8. Click **Save Report** in the menu bar to save the report.

Create a Standard Graph

Quicken supplies you with several standard graphs for each report area, some of which can be customized. On the Standard Reports list, if there is a standard graph associated with a report, you will see both a report and a graph icon by the report name. To create a graph:

1. Click the **Reports** menu and then click **Graphs**. A list of available graphs appears.

CREATING A MINI-REPORT

(Continued)

4. Click **Show Report** to see a full report, similar to what is shown in Figure 5-10. In the Transaction Report window, a standard report appears about this payee or category. From this window, you can:

close ✕

Electronics Corp.

Last 3 years ▼ (All accounts)

Date	Amount
7/8/2005	2,097.00
6/24/2005	2,097.00
6/10/2005	2,097.00
Total: $	**6,291.00**
Average: $	**2,097.00**

Show Report

   • Change the date range from the default settings.

   • Set how the report calculates subtotals.

   • Edit individual transactions within the mini-report.

   • Click **Expand All** to display all information about each transaction.

   • Click **Collapse All** to show only the totals for each payee or category.

5. Click **Close** to close the Transaction Report window.

TIP

As with all graphs, you can double-click on a pie slice or bar to display the next level of detail.

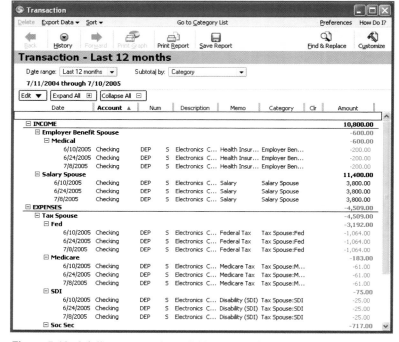

Figure 5-10: *A full report can be quickly created from a mini-report.*

2. Click the graph you want. The standard graph will appear, as shown in Figure 5-11.

3. If you want to customize the graph, click **Customize**.

4. Click **Print Graph** in the menu bar if you want to print the graph.

5. Click **Close** to close the graph.

NOTE

Hold down the SHIFT key and click a pie slice or a bar in a graph if you want to hide it. Quicken will still calculate its value, but the value will not display. You can display the hidden item by creating the graph again.

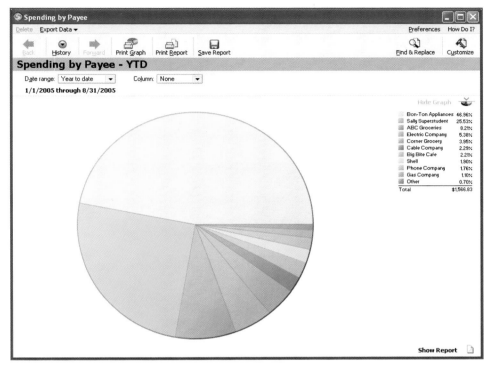

Figure 5-11: *Graphs created in Quicken can be pie graphs or bar graphs.*

Chapter 6

Tracking Your Assets and Liabilities

In the last chapter you learned how to memorize and schedule transactions and were introduced to reports and graphs. In this chapter you use those skills as you work with transactions in the Property & Debt Center. This chapter will teach you how to link your assets with the related liabilities, enter information that affects the value of your assets, track your loans, and record other liabilities or payments. You'll learn how to customize reports, set alerts, and display your net worth. You'll also learn how to create a listing of your other assets, such as furniture and sports equipment, and use that list in Quicken.

6

Work with Asset and Liability Accounts

When you used Quicken Guided Setup (see Chapter 1), you probably set up your house and its accompanying mortgage accounts. It is a good idea to track the asset value in one account and the liability, or amount you owe, in another. While you may not have an asset account for every liability account, review your accounts now to ensure you include all the assets you want to watch. Quicken can track any loan type you may have, as described in Table 6-1.

For most of us, our biggest asset is our home, so much of the information in the following section is focused on that. However, you can make adjustments to any asset in the same way as described here.

Link an Asset to a Liability Account

The Account Setup dialog box, shown in Figure 6-1, walks you through the creation of a new asset or liability account. You can access this dialog box in several ways.

1. Click the **Property & Debt** menu, click **Property & Debt Accounts**, and click **Add Account**.
   –Or–
   Press CTRL+A to open the Account List, and click **Add Account**.

2. If you started by pressing CTRL+A, you'll be asked if this account is held by a financial institution. Answer that question and click **Next**.

LOAN TYPE	DESCRIPTION
Mortgage	A long-term loan, usually secured by real property, such as your house. A mortgage can have a *fixed* or an *adjustable* interest rate. Fixed rate means the amount of interest you pay is set at the beginning and stays at that rate for the life of the mortgage. Adjustable rate means that the rate of interest is adjusted at regular intervals throughout the life of the mortgage. Adjustable-rate mortgages are sometimes called variable-rate or floating-rate mortgages.
Home Equity	This type of loan is secured by the equity in your house. It is sometimes called a *second mortgage*. In some cases, the interest you pay on this type of loan may be tax-deductible. Consult with your tax professional for more information. Home equity loans can also have either fixed or variable interest rates.
Reverse Mortgage	This type of loan allows homeowners with no mortgage to borrow against the equity in their home. This type of loan pays the homeowner regular monthly payments and is paid off when the home is sold. This type of loan is often used by people on a fixed income to provide additional income, such as during retirement.
Vehicle Loan	This type of loan uses a vehicle—such as a boat, automobile, or recreational vehicle—as the *collateral* for the loan. Collateral is property used as security for a loan. The interest is normally not tax-deductible, but check with your tax professional.
Personal Loan	This type of loan usually requires no collateral, and interest is often charged at a higher rate than with the other types of loans.

Table 6-1: **Types of Loans You Can Track in Quicken**

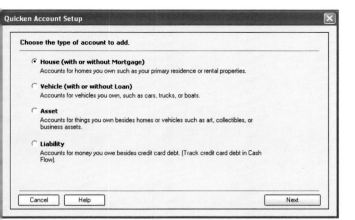

Figure 6-1: *Quicken allows you to set up, link, and track a number of different assets and liabilities.*

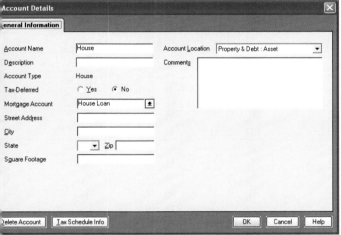

Figure 6-2: *The Account Details dialog box can be used to link asset account with a liability account as well as to enter other information.*

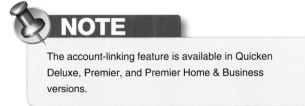

NOTE

The account-linking feature is available in Quicken Deluxe, Premier, and Premier Home & Business versions.

The next dialog box, although different from the one in Figure 6-1, still allows you to choose a type of Property & Debt Account.

3. From the dialog box, select the type of account you are creating:

   - House (With Or Without Mortgage)
   - Vehicle (With Or Without Loan)
   - Asset
   - Liability

If you have not yet created your house or mortgage account, do it now, following the directions in Chapter 3. If you have created your mortgage account but not the asset account, create the asset account now. If you have created both accounts but not yet linked them, you can link them quickly.

1. Click the **Tools** menu and click **Account List**.
   –Or–
   Press CTRL+A to see the Account List.

2. Click the asset account with which you want to work.

3. Click **Edit** in the menu bar. The Account Details dialog box appears, as shown in Figure 6-2.

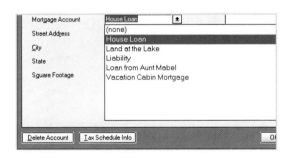

4. Click the **Mortgage Account** down arrow to see a list of liability accounts.

5. Click the relevant liability account, and click **OK**.

Adjust the Value of an Asset

As time passes, you will probably add improvements to your home, thereby increasing its value. Furthermore, in many areas, real-estate market values increase over time. You may want to record this information in your Asset Account register.

RECORD IMPROVEMENTS

An improvement, such as remodeling a bathroom or adding a garage, is called a *capital* improvement and adds to the value of your home. For example, if you

LINKING MULTIPLE LIABILITY ACCOUNTS TO ONE ASSET ACCOUNT

If you have a second mortgage or line of credit secured by your home, you can track this information in Quicken.

1. Press CTRL+A to open the Account List.

2. Click the liability account you want to link with your asset account.

3. Click **Edit** on the menu bar.

4. Click the **Linked Asset Account** down arrow to open a list of assets.

5. Click the asset to which this liability is to be linked.

General Information

Account Name	Loan from Aunt Mabel
Description	
Account Type	Liability
Interest Rate	7.50 %
Linked Asset Account	House

6. Click **OK** to close the Account Details dialog box.

7. Click the asset account you just linked.

8. Click **Edit** to open the Account Details dialog box. Note the Mortgage Account now reads "Multiple," indicating there is more than one liability account associated with this asset. (The word may appear faintly, depending on your monitor settings.)

Mortgage Account	[multiple]

9. Click **OK** to close the dialog box.

10. To unlink a liability account, reverse this process.

---

purchased your home for $180,000 and added a garage for $25,000, the adjusted basis, or cost, of your home is $205,000. For additional information on how capital improvements may affect you, consult your tax professional. To ensure that an improvement is recorded in your asset register:

1. Open the account from which you want to pay for the improvement, for example Checking.

2. Enter the transaction in the normal manner.

3. Select the **House Asset Account** category.

4. The transaction appears in the Checking Account register, and the improvement is automatically added to the value of the house in the House Asset register.

8/15/2005	12586	Garage Contractor			25,000 00	*Deposit*
		[House]	new garage		Enter	Edit

8/15/2005		Garage Contractor		25,000 00	235,000 00
		[Checking Account]			

USE THE UPDATE BALANCE DIALOG BOX

As your real estate assets increase in value and your other assets, such as cars and boats, decrease in value, you may want to adjust the account balances to ensure your financial net worth shows properly in Quicken. To access the Update Balance dialog box:

1. Click the **Property & Deb**t menu, and click **Go To Property & Debt Center**.

2. Double-click the account you want to update. The account register displays.

3. Click **Update Balance** in the register menu bar to open the Update Account Balance dialog box.

Delete	Find	Transfer	Update Balance

4. Enter the new total value of the asset in the Update Balance To field.

5. Enter the adjustment date if it is different from today's date.

6. Click the **Category For Adjustment** down arrow to open a list of categories for this adjustment. Quicken uses "Misc" as the default category. Consult your tax professional for a recommendation if needed.

7. Click **OK** to close the dialog box.

Update Account Balance: House

The last statement ending date: N/A

1. Enter the current balance for this account.

| Update Balance to: | 15,750.00 |
| Adjustment Date: | 9/8/2005 |

2. Choose a category for the balance adjustment.

| Category for Adjustment: | Misc |

OK   Cancel   Help

CAUTION

With any transaction that may have significant tax implications, consult your tax professional for the best way to handle the transaction for your particular situation.

NOTE

Many people use their annual property-tax valuation statement to determine their home's market value.

QUICKFACTS

UNDERSTANDING DEPRECIATION

If you rent out, gain income from, or use an asset in business, your tax advisor may want you to depreciate that asset. *Depreciation* is the amount that a property's value declines because of general wear and tear, heavy use, or becoming outdated. There are several instances when you may want to track depreciation in Quicken:

- You rent out part of your home.

- One or more of your assets is a rental property.

- You rent out your motor home or houseboat.

- Part or all of your home or other asset is used for your business.

In all cases, consult your tax professional for advice on whether depreciation should be recorded in your situation. You should understand both the type of depreciation used—since there are a number of different types—and the amount to enter every year. Once you know the amount to be entered, you can schedule this transaction as described in Chapter 5.

Work with Loans

Whether you used Quicken Guided Setup to set up your loans or manually entered the information regarding your debts (other than credit cards), you may have to change interest rates or otherwise work with your loan information on occasion.

Adjust the Interest Rate on a Loan

From time to time, interest rates on loans may be adjusted by your lender. The rate change may take effect at some future date or it may be effective immediately with the next payment.

CHANGE THE INTEREST RATE IN THE FUTURE

To adjust your loan when the change takes effect with future payments:

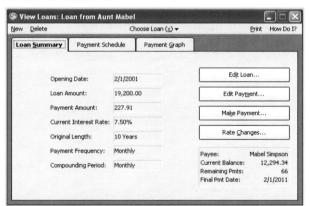

1. Click the **Property & Debt** menu, and click **Loans**.
   –Or–
   Press CTRL+H to open the View Loans dialog box.

2. Click **Choose Loan** in the menu bar to display a list of all of your loans. Click the loan whose rate you want to change.

3. Click **Rate Changes**. The Loan Rate Changes dialog box appears.

In the Insert An Interest Rate Change dialog box, you can also enter the amount of your new payment, instead of letting Quicken calculate it, and Quicken will adjust the loan's length to reflect both the interest rate and the payment.

4. Click **New** to open the Insert An Interest Rate Change dialog box.

5. Type a date in the Effective Date field. Press **TAB** to move to the next field.

6. Type the new interest rate in the Interest Rate field. Press **TAB**, and Quicken calculates the new payment amount without changing the length of the loan.

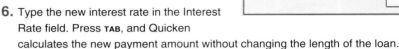

7. Click **OK** or **Close** to close the Insert An Interest Rate Change dialog box, and click **Close** to close the Loan Rate Changes dialog box. Finally, click **Close** to close the View Loans dialog box.

CHANGE THE INTEREST RATE FOR THE NEXT PAYMENT

If your new interest rate is effective with the next payment:

1. Open the **View Loans** dialog box, and select your loan, as described in the first two steps of "Change the Interest Rate in the Future."

2. Click **Edit Payment** to open the Edit Loan Payment dialog box.

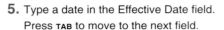

3. Type the new rate in the Current Interest Rate field. Quicken calculates the principal and interest payment for you using the next payment date as the effective date of the change without changing the length of the loan. However, if you change the payment amount (Principal And Interest field), Quicken changes the loan's length to accommodate the new payment.

4. Click **OK** to close the Edit Loan Payment dialog box, and click **Close** to close the View Loans dialog box.

Handle Other Loan Functions

In addition to changing the interest rate, you may need to handle other loan functions, including changing the loan balance, making additional principal payments (including tax and insurance payments), handling interest-only or balloon payments, and printing a loan summary.

CHANGE LOAN BALANCES

Periodically, you may get statements from your lender showing the current balance of a loan or the balance as of a specific date. If you want to change the loan balance in Quicken to match the lender's record:

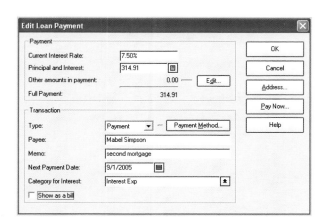

1. Click the **Property & Debt** menu, and click **Loans**.

   –Or–

   Press CTRL+H to display the View Loans dialog box.

2. Click **Choose Loan** and click the loan with which you want to work.

3. Click **Edit Loan** to open the Edit Loan dialog box.

4. Click **Next** in the bottom-right corner.

5. Type the balance shown by the lender in the **Current Balance** field.

6. Click **Done** to close the dialog box, and click **Close** to close the View Loans dialog box.

INCLUDE TAX AND INSURANCE PAYMENTS

Many mortgages, and some home equity loans, include other amounts with each payment, such as property taxes, *PMI* (Private Mortgage Insurance), or homeowners' insurance. The property taxes and insurance payments are then paid by the lender directly to the taxing authority and insurance company. If these amounts are changed, you should reflect that information in your loan payment.

1. Press CTRL+H to open the View Loans dialog box.

2. Click **Choose Loan** and click the loan.

3. Click **Edit Payment** to open the Edit Loan Payment dialog box.

4. Click **Edit** to open the Split Transaction window.

5. Fill in the **Category** and **Amount** fields for each of the fees included in your payment:

   • You may want to use the standard

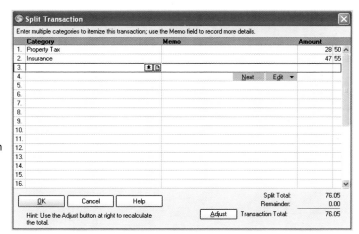

TIP

Some lenders send periodic escrow account statements. If you have entered the escrow amounts of insurance and taxes as split transactions, you can easily compare your records to that of the lender's.

QUICKSTEPS

MAKING ADDITIONAL PRINCIPAL PAYMENTS

Making additional principal payments can reduce the amount of interest you pay over the term of a loan. To record these additional payments:

1. Press CTRL+H to open the View Loans window.

2. Click **Choose Loan** and click the loan with which you want to work.

3. Click **Make Payment** and click **Extra**.

4. Click the **Account To Use** down arrow, and select the account you want.

5. Click the **Type Of Transaction** down arrow, and choose how you want to make the payment.

6. Type a value in the Amount field, click the **Number** down arrow, and select how you will reference the payment.

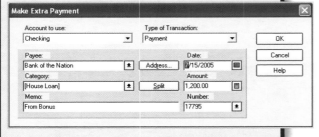

7. Click **OK** to close the dialog box, and click **Close** to close the View Loans dialog box.

The transaction is entered in the relevant checking account and is reflected as an additional principal payment in the liability account register.

Date/	Num	Payee/Category/Memo△	Payment	Clr	Deposit	Balance
7/15/2005	17795	Bank of the Nation	1,200 00			1,846 33
		[House Loan]	from bonus			

Quicken category of Insurance:Home Insurance for the insurance portion of your payment.

- Quicken's standard category for property taxes is Taxes - Property.

6. Click **OK** to close the Split Transaction window, click **OK** once more to close the Edit Loan Payment dialog box, and click **Close** to close the View Loans dialog box.

HANDLE INTEREST-ONLY OR BALLOON PAYMENTS

Some mortgages are interest-only loans, with the full amount of the loan payable at the end of the loan's term. In this way, consumers have a lower monthly payment and can make principal payments whenever they choose. To enter a new loan of this type:

1. Press CTRL+H and click **New**. The Loan Setup Wizard starts.

2. Click **Next**.

3. Click **Borrow Money**, click **Next**, enter an account name, click **Next**, tell Quicken if payments have been made on this loan by clicking **Yes** or **No**, and click **Next** again.

4. Enter the date of the loan and the original balance, and click **Next**.

5. Click **Yes There Is A Balloon Payment**, and click **Next**.

6. Enter the original length of the loan in years, and click **Next**. Enter the same number of years in the **Amortized Length** field, and click **Next**.

7. Click **Standard Period** if you make regular payments—usually monthly, although you can select a different period—and click **Next**.

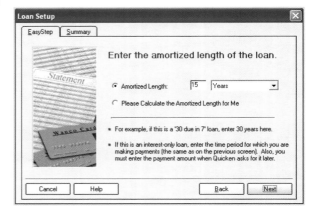

NOTE

Simple interest is interest paid only on the original amount, not on the interest accumulated on the original amount. *Compound interest* is calculated on both the original amount and the accumulated interest.

8. Click the **Compounding Period** down arrow, and select the number from the drop-down list. The default is monthly, but most financial institutions use daily. Click **Next**.

9. Enter the date of the first payment if it is different than a month from today, and click **Next**. Click **Yes** when asked if you know the amount of the first payment, and click **Next**. Type this amount in the Payment Amount field, and click **Next**.

10. Enter the interest rate as a percent (you don't need to include the percent sign), and continue through the wizard by clicking **Next** and then clicking **Done**.

11. Enter the payee in the Set Up Loan Payment dialog box, and click **OK**.

12. Click either **Yes** or **No** when asked if you want to create an Asset Account for this loan. If you click **No**, you will see a summary of your loan. Click **Close** to close the View Loans dialog box.

PRINT A LOAN SUMMARY

The View Loans dialog box allows you to print a summary of each loan, the payment schedule, and a graph that shows the progress of the loan repayment. To access this dialog box:

1. Press CTRL+H to open the View Loans dialog box. Click **Choose Loan** and select the loan you want to print.

2. Click **Print** to open a Windows Print dialog box.

3. Click **Preview** to see how the report will look when it is printed. Figure 6-3 shows an example of this report.

4. Click **Print** to print the report, or click **Close** to close the Print Preview without printing.

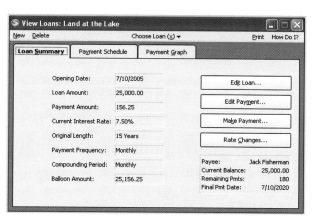

| Print | Prev Page | Next Page | Zoom Out | Help | Close |

Loan Schedule for Account "Land at the Lake"

Pmt	Date	Principa	Interest	Balance
158	9/10/2018	0.00	156.25	25,000.00
159	10/10/2018	0.00	156.25	25,000.00
160	11/10/2018	0.00	156.25	25,000.00
161	12/10/2018	0.00	156.25	25,000.00
162	1/10/2019	0.00	156.25	25,000.00
163	2/10/2019	0.00	156.25	25,000.00
164	3/10/2019	0.00	156.25	25,000.00
165	4/10/2019	0.00	156.25	25,000.00
166	5/10/2019	0.00	156.25	25,000.00
167	6/10/2019	0.00	156.25	25,000.00
168	7/10/2019	0.00	156.25	25,000.00
169	8/10/2019	0.00	156.25	25,000.00
170	9/10/2019	0.00	156.25	25,000.00
171	10/10/2019	0.00	156.25	25,000.00
172	11/10/2019	0.00	156.25	25,000.00
173	12/10/2019	0.00	156.25	25,000.00
174	1/10/2020	0.00	156.25	25,000.00
175	2/10/2020	0.00	156.25	25,000.00
176	3/10/2020	0.00	156.25	25,000.00
177	4/10/2020	0.00	156.25	25,000.00
178	5/10/2020	0.00	156.25	25,000.00
179	6/10/2020	0.00	156.25	25,000.00
180	7/10/2020	25,000.00	156.25	0.00

Opening Date:	7/10/2005
Loan Amount:	25,000.00
Payment Amount:	156.25
Current Interest Rate:	7.50%
Original Length	15 Years
Payment Frequency:	Monthly
Compounding Period	Monthly
Balloon Amount:	25,156.25
Payee:	Jack Fishermar
Current Balance:	25,000.00
Remaining Pmts	180
Final Pmt Date:	7/10/2020

Figure 6-3: **Printing a loan schedule report shows not only the payment schedule, but also a summary of the loan itself.**

Understand Alerts

One of the most powerful features in Quicken Deluxe, Premier, and Premier Home & Business editions is the ability to set up *alerts,* or reminders. While they cannot be printed, alerts remind you to download transactions, pay bills, know when your credit card balance is nearing its limit, know when an account is near its minimum balance, or know when your auto insurance is approaching its renewal date, among other things. With Quicken.com, you can create a Watch

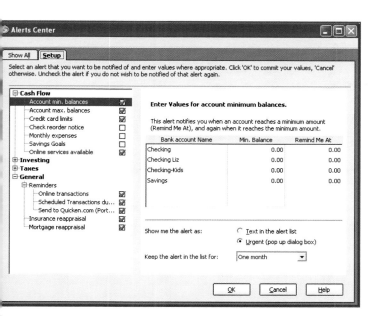

List for securities you want to track. Chapter 7 discusses investments and securities in further detail. There are four major categories of alerts:

- **Cash Flow alerts** let you monitor minimum or maximum balances, credit card limits, monthly expenses, and savings goals, as shown in Figure 6-4. You can even check your financial institutions for new services they offer.

- **Investing alerts** remind you to download quotes and prices, notify you when earnings fail to meet or exceed projections, tell you when mutual funds increase their fees, give you useful information about mutual fund distributions, and identify the holding periods for your securities.

- **Tax alerts** notify you when you have either over- or under-withheld income tax from your paycheck, remind you about upcoming tax dates, and provide useful tax information about personal deductions.

- **General alerts** remind you to download transactions and notify you that scheduled transactions are soon due, that insurance policies are approaching renewal dates, and that a mortgage interest rate may be changing.

*Figure 6-4: **Cash Flow alerts help you manage your finances.***

Set Up Alerts

To set up an alert:

1. Click the **Tools** menu and then click **Set Up Alerts**.
   –Or–
   Click **Quicken Home** and then click **Set Up Alerts** in the Activity Center.

2. If the Setup tab is not already displayed, click it. You should see the window shown in Figure 6-4.

3. Select the type of alert you want to set, and click the plus sign (**+**) to the left of it.

4. Click the check box corresponding to the alert you want. The values that can be entered appear on the right side of the window.

5. Click the individual categories for which you want to receive alerts, and enter the required information.

6. Click either **Text In The Alert List** or **Urgent (Pop Up Dialog Box)** to tell Quicken how you want the alert displayed.

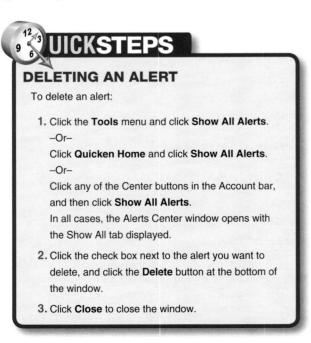

Figure 6-5: *You can set a wide variety of alerts and customize them further by selecting various options.*

7. Click the **Keep The Alert In The List For** down arrow, and choose how long you want the alert to remain in the list, as shown in Figure 6-5.

8. Click **OK** to save the alert and close the window.

Create Custom Reports

In Chapter 5 you learned how to create standard Quicken reports and graphs. The following sections will discuss how to customize reports so that they provide exactly the information you want. You can review your spending, know your net worth, and get ready for taxes. You can save reports, or you can tell Quicken to save new reports automatically. You can even save your reports as PDF files that can be read with Adobe Acrobat Reader on any computer, even if Quicken is not installed.

Customize an Existing Report

The easiest way to make a report your own is to start with an existing report and customize it to meet your needs. We'll start with one report (the Transaction report) and create a report based on what we want to know. Each standard report may have slightly different options.

1. Click **Reports** in the menu bar, and then click **Reports & Graphs Center**.

2. In the left pane of the Reports & Graphs window, click the arrow to the left of **Banking** to display the standard reports available in that area.

3. Click **Transaction**. Year To Date is shown as the time period on which you want the report based.

4. Click **Customize** to open the Customize Transaction dialog box:

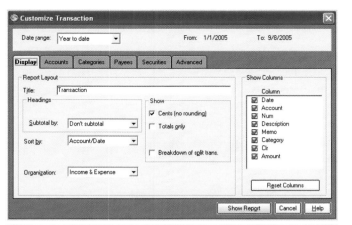

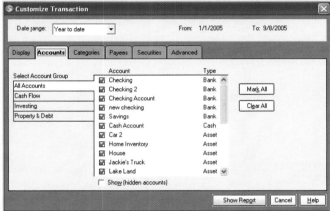

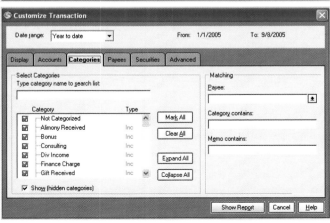

a. Click the **Date Range** down arrow, and choose from a list of preset periods.

b. Click **Custom Dates** from the Date Range list to set your own date range.

5. Click the **Display** tab to tell Quicken how to lay out your report:

a. Click in the **Title** field, and type a new title.

b. Click the **Subtotal By** down arrow, and choose to subtotal by one of several time periods, or by Category, Payee, Account, Class, or Tax Schedule.

c. Click the **Sort By** down arrow, and choose how you want your data sorted.

d. Click the **Organization** down arrow, and choose whether the report is organized with income at the top and expenses at the bottom or with income items interspersed with expense items to show the cash flow at any period of time.

e. Click **Cents (No Rounding)** if you want to see transactions to the nearest penny, or clear this check box to round items to the nearest dollar.

f. Click **Totals Only** if you want only the summary categories displayed. Clear this check box if you want all transactions displayed.

g. Click **Breakdown Of Split Trans.** if you want to show how split transactions were categorized.

h. Click the columns you do not want displayed in the Show Columns area (all columns are displayed by default). To reselect all the columns, click **Reset Columns**.

6. Click the **Accounts** tab to choose the accounts included in the report. You can choose to use all accounts or specify accounts within each Center:

a. Click **Mark All** to choose all accounts.

b. Click **Clear All** to clear all accounts and select the ones you want to use. This is the quickest way to select only one or two accounts.

c. Click **Show (Hidden Accounts)** to include accounts you have chosen to not normally display.

7. Click the **Categories** tab to select the categories included in your report:

a. Click **Mark All** to choose all accounts.

b. Click **Clear All** to clear all accounts and select the ones you want to use.

c. Click **Expand All** if you want details about subcategories included, or click **Collapse All** if you want only the main category information to be displayed.

It may be confusing why you can enter a payee in the Reports & Graphs Customize Transaction Categories tab or enter a category in the Payees tab. The answer is that the Categories tab allows you to select all the categories in the report and to select a single payee in those categories. Step 8 allows you to select all the payees in the report and to select a single category for those payees. In most instances the payee is left blank in the Categories tab and the category is left blank in the Payees tab so you can create a report with both multiple categories and multiple payees.

TIP

Expand the date range if your payee name does not appear and you are sure you have paid this payee.

TIP

If the payee name does not appear, review the list again. You may have misspelled the name the first time you entered it.

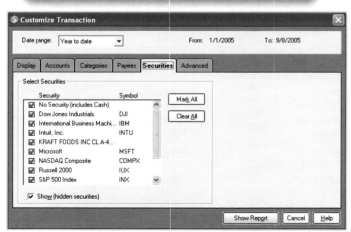

d. Enter the payee's name or choose a name from the drop-down list if you want only transactions with a certain payee displayed.

e. Enter information into the **Category Contains** or **Memo Contains** fields if you want to include only those transactions that contain specific information in the Category and/or Memo fields.

8. Click the **Payees** tab to select the payees to include in the report. Type a payee name or choose one from the list. Click **Clear All** to clear all payee check boxes and select the ones you want.

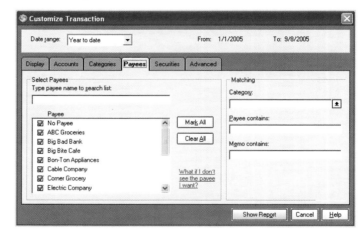

9. Click the **Securities** tab to choose the securities included in the report.

10. Click **Show (Hidden Securities)** to include securities you have chosen not to display in your report, or clear the check box if you do not want them included.

11. Click the **Advanced** tab, shown on the next page, to further refine your report:

a. Click the **Amounts** down arrow, and click a criterion for selecting the amounts you want to include.

b. If you choose a criterion other than All, enter an amount to use with the criterion.

c. Click **Include Unrealized Gains** if you have set up investment accounts and want to include paper gains and losses in your report (see Chapter 8 for more information).

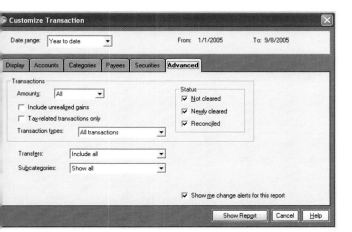

d. Click **Tax-Related Transactions Only** to include only those transactions that relate to income tax.

e. Click the **Transaction Types** down arrow, and choose **All Transactions** (selected by default), **Payments**, **Deposits**, or **Unprinted Checks**.

f. Clear the check boxes in the Status area to limit your report to transactions that have not cleared, newly cleared transactions, or reconciled transactions.

g. After saving this report (see "Save a Customized Report"), if you want to be alerted when changes are made elsewhere in Quicken, such as new categories or new securities that need to be added to the report, make sure **Show Me Change Alerts For This Report** is selected.

12. Click **Show Report** to display the report after you have finished customizing.

13. Click the **Print Report** icon on the tool bar to print the report.

Save a Customized Report

After you have created your custom report, you can save it to your My Saved Reports folder, recall it, revise it, and resave it with either a new name or as a replacement for the original saved report.

To save a customized report when you first create it:

1. Click the **Save Report** icon on the tool bar to open the Save Report dialog box.

2. Type a name in the Report Name field to identify this report, press **TAB**, and type a description if you want. The description will appear in your list of saved reports under the title of the report.

3. Click the **Save In** down arrow, and click the folder in which you want your report stored. If you do not create a separate folder, the report will be displayed on the right side of the Reports & Graphs window under My Saved Reports.

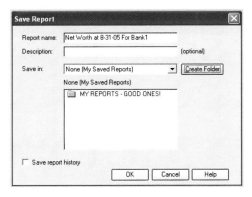

4. Click **Save Report History** if you want to save all versions of this report. By default, Quicken does not save this history.

5. Click **OK** to save the report.

Save Report

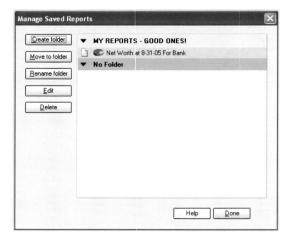

Manage Custom Folders for Saved Reports

You might want to organize your saved reports into different folders so that you can easily retrieve them. To create a folder:

1. Click the **Reports** menu and then click **Reports & Graphs Center**. The Reports & Graphs window opens.

2. Click **Manage Saved Reports** on the bottom of the window, and click **Create Folder**. The Create New Report Folder dialog box appears.

3. Type a new folder name, and click **OK**.

4. In the Manage Saved Reports dialog box, click a folder, click **Rename Folder**, type a new name, and click **OK**

5. Click a report within a folder, or click **No Folder** and click **Edit** to change a report's name or description.

6. Click a report or a folder, and click **Delete** to delete the report or folder.

7. Click a report and click **Move To Folder** to move a report to another folder.

8. Click **Done** when you have finished organizing your saved reports.

Create a Net Worth Report

Your *net worth* is the difference between the value of what you own (your assets) and what you owe (your liabilities). From time to time, you may need to print a report of your net worth, and Quicken makes this easy to do.

1. Click **Reports** in the tool bar. The Reports & Graphs window opens.

2. Click the arrow to the left of **Net Worth & Balances** to display the related reports.

3. Click **Net Worth**.

4. In the **Report Balance As Of** text box, enter the date for which you want the report displayed.

5. Click **Show Report**.

TIP

To include the information from Home Inventory, make sure that you have created an asset account for Home Inventory. For more information, see "Start a Home Inventory" later in this chapter.

6. Click **Print Report** in the Report tool bar to print your report.

7. Click **Customize** to change the date or other items within the report, as described in "Customize an Existing Report" earlier in this chapter.

8. Click **Save Report** to open the Save Report dialog box, as described in "Save a Customized Report."

9. Click **Close** to return to Quicken.

Use Quicken Home Inventory

The Quicken Home Inventory, which is only available in Quicken Deluxe, Premier, and Premier Home & Business editions, allows you to maintain an inventory of your belongings. With this feature you can:

- Maintain an itemized list of your goods for insurance purposes.
- Provide a list of where items are located. This is especially useful if you have a vacation home or boat or even a storage unit.
- Keep a list of your heirs and what you plan to give them.
- Help determine your true net worth.

Set Options for Quicken Home Inventory

To start working with the Quicken Home Inventory:

1. Click the **Property & Debt** menu, and then click **Quicken Home Inventory**. The Quicken Home Inventory window opens displaying a welcome message. Click **Continue**.

2. Click the **Edit** menu and then click **Options**. The Options dialog box appears.

3. Click the **Suggested Item List** tab to see the default settings for your inventory:

   a. Clear the **Use Suggested Values For New Inventory Items** check box if you do not want Quicken to use its database to suggest values for items you choose from its Suggested Item List.

   b. Click **Automatically Set Resale Value To** if you want Quicken to set a resale value at the percentage you enter in the text box. Otherwise, Quicken uses the replacement cost for the item as its resale value.

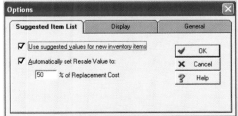

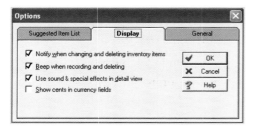

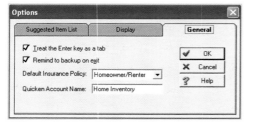

4. Click the **Display** tab to set how the inventory is displayed and sounds.

5. Clear the **Notify When Changing And Deleting Inventory Items** check box to stop a warning prompt from appearing when you change or delete an item.

6. Clear the **Beep When Recording And Deleting** check box to turn off the sound when you record an item.

7. Clear the **Use Sound & Special Effects In Detail View** check box to turn off the sound of a page turning when you click either Prev Item or Next Item.

8. Click the **Show Cents In Currency Fields** check box to include exact amounts. This ensures that when you send the information from Quicken Home Inventory to Quicken, there will be no discrepancies.

9. Click the **General** tab to set the inventory name, type of insurance, and other options.

10. Clear the **Treat The Enter Key As A Tab** check box if you want to use ENTER to close windows or perform other regular Windows tasks. Otherwise, pressing ENTER moves the cursor between fields like pressing the TAB key does.

11. Clear the **Remind To Backup On Exit** check box if you don't want to be reminded to back up your data each time you leave Quicken Home Inventory.

12. Click the **Default Insurance Policy** down arrow, and click which type of policy covers your goods. You can choose **Unassigned** and move items later if you want.

13. Enter the name of the account in the Quicken Account Name field where you want your information sent if you have more than one Quicken file.

14. After you have entered all of your choices, click **OK** to close the dialog box.

Understand Quicken Home Inventory

Quicken Home Inventory comes preset with locations, categories, suggested items, and suggested replacement costs. You determine which way you want to view your possessions—either by location, such as the living room—or by category, such as furnishings. There are several combinations of views available. To see them, click the **View** menu. Depending on the view you are currently in, there may be only one choice available to you:

- If you are in Category view, your only choice is **By Location**.
- If you are in Location view, your only choice is **By Category**.

- If you are in List view, your only choice is **Detail View**.
- If you are in Detail view, your only choice is **List View**.

Each time you enter an item, it is included in the total for that category and location. You can change, delete, or move items between locations and categories.

Start a Home Inventory

To start a Home Inventory, you begin by entering your belongings. You can choose to use the List View to enter each item and use the default values supplied by Quicken. For a more accurate record, use Detail View. As you can see in Figure 6-6, you can track a lot of information about each item.

1. Click the **Property & Debt** menu, and click **Quicken Home Inventory**.

2. Click the **View** menu and click **By Location** if it isn't already selected (it will appear dim if it is already selected). If necessary, click the **View** menu again, and click **Detail View**. The window that opens looks similar to the one pictured in Figure 6-6.

3. Click the **Category** down arrow, and choose the category from the drop-down list.

4. Click the **Location** down arrow, and choose the location from the drop-down list.

5. Change the **Insurance Policy** field if necessary.

6. Click **Description** and enter the name of your item, or choose it from the Suggested Items List on the right side of the window.

7. Press TAB and enter the make and model of this item. Press TAB again and enter the serial number.

8. Press TAB, enter where the item was purchased, press TAB again, and enter the purchase date.

9. Press TAB, enter the original price, and press TAB again. If you chose an item from the Suggested Items List, Quicken will enter a replacement cost and a resale value based on the percentage you entered in the Edit menu Preferences (see "Set Options for Quicken Home Inventory" earlier in this chapter).

10. Click **Receipts & Records** to record what type of receipt you have for this item and where the receipt and other records pertaining to this item are located. Click **OK** to close the Receipts & Records dialog box.

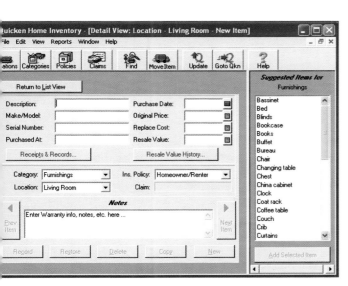

Figure 6-6: The Detail View of Quicken Home Inventory allows you to keep a complete and accurate record of all your possessions.

NOTE

If an item does not appear on the Suggested Items List in one category, check another category.

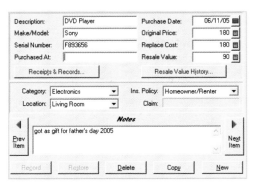

11. Enter any notes pertaining to this item.

12. Click **Record**.

13. Click **Next Item** and repeat steps 3–12 to enter another item.

14. Click **Return To List View** to display all items in this location or category.

Create and Print Reports in Quicken Home Inventory

Quicken Home Inventory provides a number of reports for you to view and print.

1. Click the **Reports** menu and choose the report you want to see. Both Inventory reports can be viewed by category, location, or insurance policy.

2. Click **Inventory Value Summary** to open a summary report, as shown in Figure 6-7.

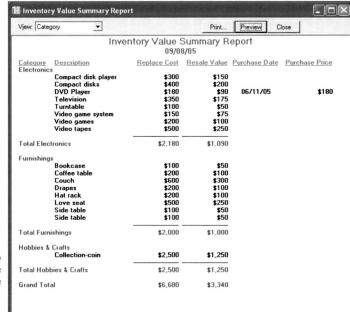

Figure 6-7: Quicken Home Inventory gives you detailed reports of your possessions.

QUICKSTEPS

PROTECTING YOUR INVENTORY DATA WITH PASSWORDS

As you use your Home Inventory, you might want to protect your work by creating a password so that no one can inadvertently access or change your information. You can change or delete this password at any time.

CREATE A PASSWORD IN QUICKEN HOME INVENTORY

1. In the Quicken Home Inventory window, click the **File** menu and click **Password**. The Password dialog box appears.

2. Type your new password in the **Password** field.

3. Press TAB and type the same password in the **Confirm Password** field.

4. Click **OK** to close the dialog box. Make a note of your password, and keep it in a safe place. If you lose the password, you might not be able to get into this file again.

Continued . . .

3. Click the **View** down arrow, and click **Category** to display each item in each category. This type of report shows a subtotal by category and a grand total.

4. Click the **View** down arrow, and click **Location** to display the same information subtotaled by location.

5. Click the **Reports** menu and click **Inventory Detail** to display a detailed report of each inventory item with the same fields displayed as indicated in Detail View (see Figure 6-8).

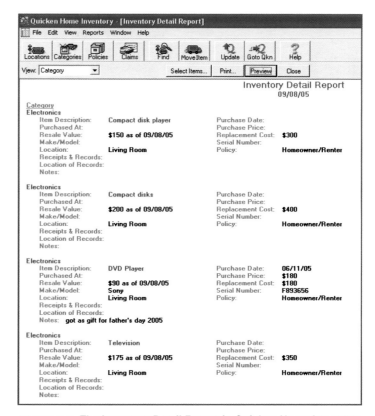

Figure 6-8: *The Inventory Detail Report in Quicken Home Inventory displays complete information about each of your belongings.*

6. Click **Select Items**. The Select Items For Inventory Detail Report dialog box appears.

7. Click **Clear All** to deselect all items and choose the items manually.

8. Click **Select All** (which is selected by default) to display all your inventory items.

9. Click **OK** to close the dialog box.

10. Click **Preview** to display how the report will look when it is printed and how many pages it will be.

11. Click **Next Page** or **Prev Page** to move between the pages.

12. Click **Close** to close the preview.

13. Click **Print** to open the Windows Print dialog box.

14. If needed, select the printer name and change the number of copies.

15. Click **OK** to print the report.

Send Quicken Home Inventory Data to Quicken

You can add your Quicken Home Inventory resale value to a Quicken Asset Account and more accurately reflect your net worth and financial position. From Quicken Home Inventory:

1. Click the **Update** icon ![Update] on the tool bar. A message appears, asking if you want to send your inventory data to the Quicken Asset Account Home Inventory.

2. Click **Yes**. Your resale value data is sent to Quicken.

3. To verify the information is in Quicken, click the **Goto Qkn** icon in the tool bar.

4. Click **Quicken Home** and then click the **Property & Debt Center** to see the accounts there. Your Home Inventory Account should be listed.

Chapter 7

Keeping Your Records Up to Date

What does it mean to reconcile an account? Why should you do it? *Reconciling* is the process of verifying that what is in your Quicken register is the same as what the bank or other financial institution shows in their records. Reconciling, or *balancing*, your checking and other accounts ensures that you have entered any fees and charges, that all deposits have been credited to your account (banks do make errors), and that your records accurately reflect what has happened during the period since you last balanced your account. This chapter will discuss how to reconcile and update checking and savings accounts, credit card statements, and investment accounts from paper statements as well as from online ones. In addition, you'll learn how to set up and maintain records information your family may need in an emergency.

Reconcile Checking and Savings Accounts

You are probably familiar with the checking and savings account statements sent by your bank. They show the balance at the beginning of the month, all of the transactions for the account that occurred since the last statement, any fees charged to your account, and the bank's balance for the account at the end of the month. This section will show you how to reconcile your Quicken checking and savings accounts with your bank's paper statements and online information. It will also discuss how to deal with items that appear on the bank statement that aren't recorded in Quicken, what to do if the account doesn't balance the first time, and how to find discrepancies.

Reconcile with Your Bank's Paper Statement

One of the great features of Quicken is its ability to quickly reconcile or balance your bank's statement to your Quicken account. To reconcile an account with the bank's paper statement:

Statement Summary: Checking

The last statement ending date: N/A

1. Enter the following from your bank statement.
   - Opening Balance: 1,277.22
   - Ending Balance:
   - New Statement Ending Date: 9/15/2005

2. Enter and categorize your interest and bank charges, if any.
   - Service Charge: Date: 9/15/2005
   - Category: Bank Charge
   - Interest Earned: Date: 9/15/2005
   - Category: Interest Inc

   [OK]   [Cancel]   [Help]

1. Click the name of the account you want to reconcile on the Account bar to open its register.

   Quicken Home 🏠

   ▼ **Cash Flow Center**
   ┣ **Checking**   495.75
       Checking 2   -332.23

2. Click **Reconcile** on the register menu bar to open the Statement Summary dialog box. If you see the Reconcile Online Account window, click **Paper Statement** to open the Statement Summary dialog box.

3. Confirm the amount in the **Opening Balance** field. If the statement opening balance is not what Quicken shows, type the statement amount. Press TAB to continue.

4. Type the amount from your bank statement in the **Ending Balance** field, and press TAB.

5. Change the date in the **New Statement Ending Date** field to the date of the bank statement, if the two are different. Press TAB to continue.

6. Enter any service charges shown on the bank statement in the **Service Charge** field, and change the date it was charged. Press TAB.

NOTE

The first time you reconcile a Quicken account, Quicken uses the starting account balance as the opening balance. After you have used Quicken once to reconcile the account, Quicken uses the ending balance from the last time you reconciled as the opening balance.

7. Click in the **Category** field, and enter the category for the service charge. By default, Quicken uses **Bank Charge**.

8. Click in the **Interest Earned** field, and enter the amount of interest shown on the bank statement. Enter the date the bank credited the account in the second **Date** field. Press TAB.

9. Click in the **Category** field, and enter the category for the interest. By default, Quicken uses **Interest Inc** as the category.

10. Click **OK** to close the dialog box and open the Statement Summary window. All of the transactions you have entered into this Quicken account that have not yet been cleared appear in this window, an example of which is shown in Figure 7-1.

11. Click **Clr** (for "cleared") by each deposit and check that appears on the bank statement. After you have selected all the cleared checks and deposits, the difference shown in the bottom-right corner of the window should be zero. If it does, you're done reconciling. If you don't have a zero difference, see "Make Corrections in the Statement Summary Window" later in this chapter.

Cleared Balance:	707.22
Statement Ending Balance:	707.22
Difference:	**0.00**

Cancel | Finish Later | Finished

12. Click **Finished** to open the Reconciliation Complete dialog box.

13. Click **Yes** to create a reconciliation report, or click **No** if you don't want to create one. If you click Yes, the Reconciliation Report Setup dialog box appears.

14. Type a title in the **Report Title** field if you want. If you leave this field blank, Quicken uses the default title "Reconciliation Report."

15. Change the date in the **Show Reconciliation To Bank Balance As Of** field if you want it to be the statement date instead of today's date.

NOTE

"Interest Inc" in Quicken is an abbreviation for "Interest Income."

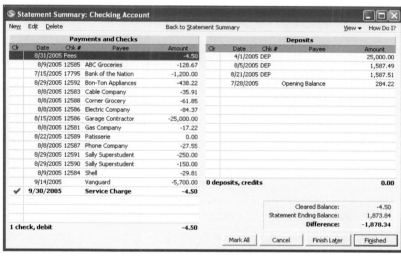

Figure 7-1: The Statement Summary window allows you to quickly reconcile an account.

TIP

If most of the transactions have cleared, click **Mark All** and then click the transactions that haven't cleared to deselect them.

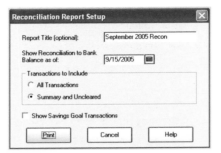

16. Click either **All Transactions** or **Summary And Uncleared** to tell Quicken what to include on the report. The default selection, Summary And Uncleared, makes for a shorter, more concise report.

17. If you have established savings goals and want to include them in the report, click the **Show Savings Goal Transactions** check box. Chapter 9 discusses savings goals and other financial-planning matters in more detail.

18. Click **Print** to open a Windows Print dialog box. Click **Preview** to see how the report will appear when printed, and then click **Print** in the Preview window or click **OK** in the Print dialog box to print the report.

Make Corrections in the Statement Summary Window

If your transactions do not immediately balance, you can make corrections in the Statement Summary window to eventually reconcile the account:

- Click **New** to enter a transaction into the register that appears on the bank statement but that has not been entered into the register. This could be a charge for new checks or money withdrawn using a cash machine or a debit card.

- Select a transaction and click **Edit** to make changes to that transaction in the register. This is great for fixing transpositions or penny errors.

- Select a transaction and click **Delete** to permanently remove a transaction from the register.

- Click **Back To Statement Summary** to go back to the Statement Summary dialog box to make changes to service charges or interest.

- Click **View** to change how Quicken sorts the transactions in this window.

- Click **How Do I?** to display a Help screen.

- Click **Mark All** to mark all of the transactions displayed in the window. If it has already been clicked, **Clear All** is displayed on the menu bar to perform the reverse operation.

- Click **Cancel** to stop the reconciliation. This opens a dialog box that asks if you want to save your work or close the window without saving it. Click **Yes** to close the window without saving your work.

- Click **Finish Later** to save what you have done so far. When you return to the register, you will notice that any transactions you have selected now display a "c" in the Clr column.

QUICKFACTS

RECONCILING FOR THE FIRST TIME

Before you reconcile a Quicken account for the first time, you may have to enter checks or deposits that occurred before you started using Quicken. When you entered the beginning balance of your account from last month's ending bank statement, the bank's balance did not include outstanding checks or deposits. Before you reconcile, enter any of those checks or deposits that had not cleared the bank as of last month's statement, even though you made the transaction before the opening date of your account. That way, these transactions will be available to you during the reconciliation process.

When you have finished the reconciliation, the "c" turns into an "R," and, if you have set the preferences to their default setting, the entire transaction will be gray.

- Click **Finished** to complete the reconciliation and open the Reconciliation Complete dialog box.

Deal with Unrecorded Items

Items may appear on your bank statement that do not appear in Quicken. Some examples can be automatic withdrawals, such as payments for your safety-deposit box, or withdrawals from the cash machine you forgot to record. To enter an item from the Statement Summary window:

1. Click **New** on the menu bar to open the account register.

2. Enter the date on which the transaction occurred. The default is today's date, but you probably want to use the actual transaction date.

3. Enter the type of transaction in the **Num** field, and then fill in the **Payee**, **Category**, and **Amount** fields.

4. Click **Enter** and then click **Return To Reconcile** to return to the Statement Summary window.

FIND STATEMENT DISCREPANCIES

Several things need to be considered when trying to find a discrepancy between a bank statement and your Quicken account register:

- Ensure you are working with the right account. It's easy to click the wrong name if you have several accounts.

- Verify that the Deposits, Credits total and the Checks, Debits total displayed at the bottom of the Statement Summary window match the totals shown on the bank statement.

- Check the **Difference** amount in the bottom-right corner of the window. If the difference is evenly divisible by nine, you may have transposed an entry. For example, if the difference is $.63, you may have entered a check into Quicken as $29.18 and written the actual check for $29.81.

- If the difference is not a transposition, you may have neglected to enter a transaction, or you entered a deposit as a check or vice versa. If the difference does not equal a check amount on either your bank statement or your register, look in both for a transaction equaling half the amount of the difference. You may have entered a deposit as a payment or vice versa.

Cleared Balance:	1,859.89
Statement Ending Balance:	1,859.26
Difference:	**0.63**

| Cancel | Finish Later | Finished |

USING A QUICKEN ADJUSTMENT

If you do not want to locate a discrepancy between the bank and your Quicken register, Quicken will enter an adjusting entry for you.

1. Click **Finished** in the Statement Summary window. The Adjust Balance dialog box appears.

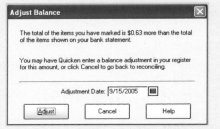

2. Click in the **Adjustment Date** field, and enter the date of the adjustment. This can be the date of the paper statement or today's date, whichever makes more sense to you. Click **Adjust**.

3. A Reconciliation Complete dialog box appears. Click **Yes** if you want to create a reconciliation report; click **No** if you do not. If you click No, the dialog box closes and you are returned to the register.

4. Locate the balance adjustment that Quicken just created, and, if you want, change the category by clicking in the **Category** field and entering a new one. Click **Enter** to save the change.

- Determine if the difference is positive or negative. If the difference is negative, the bank shows more money than your register does. The bank may have a deposit you haven't entered, or you may have cleared checks the bank hasn't received. If the difference is positive, the bank shows less money than your register does. You may have neglected to enter a fee or an automatic withdrawal in your register.

- Watch for pennies. If your handwriting is not clearly legible, the automated machinery used by the bank for clearing checks may not read the amount correctly, for example, it might mistake an eight as a three.

- Take a time out. If you've been looking at your account for some time and can't locate the discrepancy, walk away for a few minutes. Often when you come back after a break, the difference seems to appear as if by magic.

Reconcile Online

Before you reconcile online, ensure that all of your transactions have been downloaded and that you have reviewed and accepted them. When you update your Quicken register, the transactions can be automatically reconciled (see the QuickSteps "Activating Automatic Reconciliation"). There are two methods for reconciling online:

- You can update several times during a month and then reconcile to the paper statement at the end of the month.

- You can reconcile each time you download transactions.

Whichever method you use, stick to that method.

To perform the online reconciliation after you have downloaded and accepted all of the transactions:

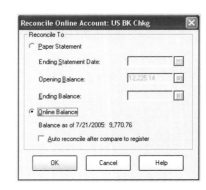

1. Open the register of the account with which you want to work.

2. Click **Reconcile** to open the Reconcile Online Account dialog box.

3. Click **Online Balance**. This option lets you reconcile to the balance that was last downloaded for this account.

CAUTION

Working back and forth between reconciling online and with a paper statement can be confusing. Transactions that appear on your paper bank statement may not appear in the Statement Summary window since Quicken has already reconciled them.

QUICKSTEPS

ACTIVATING AUTOMATIC RECONCILIATION

When you have activated the downloading of transactions from your bank accounts, you can use a Quicken feature that makes reconciling automatic each time you download.

1. Open the register of the account you want to use.

2. Click **Reconcile** on the tool bar.

3. Click **Online Balance**.

4. Click **Auto Reconcile After Compare To Register**.

The setting takes effect after the next time you go online. Quicken will automatically reconcile the downloaded transactions after you have accepted them.

4. Click **OK** to open the Statement Summary window. Items you have already accepted are selected by default.

5. Verify any unselected transactions that are more than a few days old. If a transaction is on your register and is not included with your downloaded transactions, you may have made an error entering that transaction into your Quicken register or the transaction may have been lost.

6. Complete the reconciliation process by clicking **Finished**.

Reconcile Credit Card Statements

Reconciling your credit card statement is similar to reconciling your checking or savings account statement, especially if you enter your credit card purchases as you make them. If you wait until the credit card statement arrives to enter the charges and categorize them, however, the process takes a bit longer.

RECONCILE A PAPER CREDIT CARD STATEMENT

To reconcile your credit card account to a paper statement:

1. Click the **Cash Flow** menu, click **Cash Flow Accounts**, and click the account with which you want to work.
   –Or–
   Click the name of the account on the Account bar to open the register.

2. Click **Reconcile** to open the Credit Card Statement Summary dialog box.

3. Enter the total from the statement in the **Charges, Cash Advances** field.

4. Click in the **Payments, Credits** field, and enter the total from the statement.

5. Click in the **Ending Balance** field, and enter the balance due on the statement.

6. Click in the **New Statement Ending Date** field, and enter the ending date of the statement.

7. Click in the **Finance Charges** field, and enter the amount of finance charges, if any. Click in the **Date** field, and change the date of the charges from the default of today's date if needed.

8. Click in the **Category field,** and either choose a category from the drop-down list or type the category for the finance charges.

9. Click **OK**. The Credit Card Statement Summary window opens.

TIP

When you pay your credit card or other bills, take the envelopes directly to the post office rather than leaving them in the mailbox. This ensures that anyone stealing mail from the boxes cannot get your information.

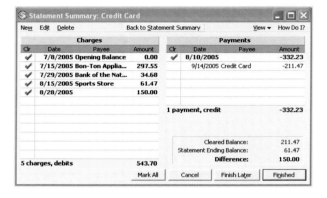

TIP

If you want to keep track of your credit card spending by category, you will need to enter each transaction, both charges and credits, separately so that you can categorize them.

10. Proceed as described in "Reconcile with Your Bank's Paper Statement" earlier in the chapter.

11. If zero appears in the Difference field, click **Finished** to open the Make Credit Card Payment dialog box. You are asked if you want to make a payment on the balance now. If so:

   a. Click **Bank Account** to choose the account from which to write the check.

   b. Choose the method of preparing the check, and click **Yes**.

   c. If you click **No**, the window closes and you are returned to the register.

   d. If you click **Printed Check**, a check facsimile opens for you to fill in. The default category is the Credit Card Account.

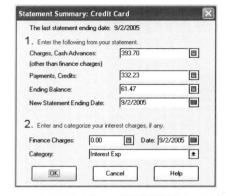

   e. If you click **Hand Written Check**, the check is entered into the register and pauses for you to enter the check number.

RECONCILE A CREDIT CARD ONLINE

As with reconciling bank accounts, if your credit card company offers it, downloading and reconciling transactions directly into your credit card register is the most efficient way to reconcile your account. However, if you want to keep track of your spending by category, you must remember to enter the category for each downloaded transaction. The process for performing an online reconciliation of your credit card account is the same as described in "Reconcile Online" earlier in the chapter.

FINDING AND RESOLVING CREDIT CARD ERRORS

Using Quicken to reconcile your credit card statements may help you find errors in your account. To ensure there are no errors on your statement and that your account is protected:

- Check each item on the statement as soon as you get it.

- Ensure that each charge is the amount you expected.

- Know the date on which your statement usually arrives. Set an alert in Quicken to remember that date. If your statement has not arrived, call the credit card company to advise them the statement has not been delivered.

- If the credit card company provides online access to your account, go online on a regular basis to ensure that each charge to your account is valid.

RESOLVE CREDIT CARD ERRORS

If you do find an error, or if you have a dispute with a seller, take the following steps:

- Call the seller that charged you to see if the issue can be resolved between the two of you. Document the call; the name of the seller's agent; and the date, time, and nature of the problem.

- Call the credit card company to tell them of the problem. Document the call as to date, time, and the name of the person with whom you spoke.

Continued . . .

MAKE CREDIT CARD STATEMENT ADJUSTMENTS

Sometimes, you just don't want to take the time to find all the discrepancies in a credit card register. Perhaps you've just started entering transactions and some of the beginning balances aren't right. Quicken can help you fix these problems.

1. When you have completed the reconciliation as far as you want, click **Finished** in the Statement Summary window. The Adjusting Register To Agree With Statement dialog box appears.

Adjusting Register to Agree with Statement

In order to bring your records into balance with the statement, Quicken is about to make the following entries in your register.

Opening balance difference
56.46   Category (optional): Misc

Register missing one or more charges
10.71   Category (optional): Misc

Adjust   Cancel   Help

2. In the Opening Balance Difference area, if there is one in your dialog box, click in the **Category** field and change the category from the default Misc.

3. In the Register Missing One Or More Payments area, if there is one in your dialog box, click in the **Category** field and change the category.

4. In the Register Missing One Or More Charges area, if there is one in your dialog box, click in the **Category** field and change the category.

5. Click **Adjust** to have the entries recorded in the credit card account register.

6. If you want to apportion each entry between several categories, make no changes to the categories in the Adjusting Register To Agree With Statement dialog box. When you return to the register, locate each adjustment and select the first one with which you want to work:

- Click **Split** to open the Split Transaction window, and assign the categories you choose.

- Select the other adjustments you want to change, and assign categories to them.

Reconcile Investment Accounts

You use the same process to reconcile an investment account as you do with a checking account, except you have to balance to both a cash balance and a share balance. If your financial institution offers it, the easiest way to reconcile each

- Write a letter to the credit card company explaining the same information. The Fair Credit Billing Act requires that you notify your credit card company in writing. Include any supporting information. This must be done within 60 days of the statement date.

- The credit card company has two billing cycles, or 90 days—whichever is less—to determine if the charge was in error. They are required to notify you in writing of their determination. If the charge was correct but there is still a dispute, write the credit card company again. They are not allowed to charge interest or require payment until the issue has been resolved.

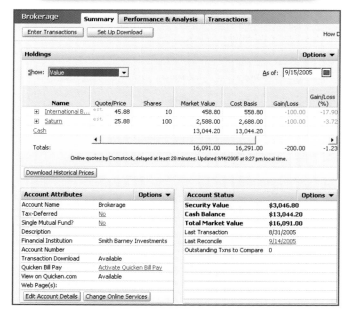

Figure 7-2: **The Summary section of your Activity Center shows the holdings, account status, account attributes, and investing activity of this account.**

account is to sign up for their download services. That way, you can download each transaction directly from your broker and use Quicken's Compare To Portfolio feature to monitor the account.

Reconcile an Investment Account to a Paper Statement

The process of reconciling an investment account is the same as described in "Reconcile with Your Bank's Paper Statement" earlier in the chapter. To reconcile an investment account to a paper statement:

1. Click **Investing Center** in the Account bar. Click the account you want to reconcile.

2. Click the **Summary** tab to open the Activity Center, shown in Figure 7-2.

3. Click the **Options** down arrow on the right of the Account Status title bar, and click **Reconcile This Account**.
   –Or–
   Click the **Transactions** tab, click the **Investing** menu, click **Investing Activities**, and then click **Reconcile An Account**.
   In either case, the Statement Summary dialog box appears.

4. Click in the **Starting Cash Balance** field, and enter the beginning balance amount from your statement.

5. Click in the **Ending Cash Balance** field, and enter the amount from your statement.

6. Click in the **Statement Ending Date** field, and type the date.

7. Click **OK**. The Statement Summary window opens. This is similar to the Statement Summary window for your checking account.
   The only difference is that instead of Checks and Deposits you see Decreases and Increases to the account.

UPDATING PRICES MANUALLY FROM A PAPER STATEMENT

After you have reconciled an investment account, Quicken gives you the opportunity to update the prices of your securities directly from your statement. After you have finished the reconciliation and returned to the Investing Center:

1. Click the **Investing Center** heading in the Accounts bar, and then click the **Portfolio** tab.

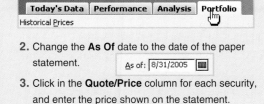

2. Change the **As Of** date to the date of the paper statement.

   As of: 8/31/2005

3. Click in the **Quote/Price** column for each security, and enter the price shown on the statement.

Name	Quote/Price
📁 Brokerage	
⊞ International Busine...	45.88

---

8. Click each transaction to note that it has cleared.

9. Click **Finished** to complete the reconciliation.

Reconcile a Single Mutual Fund Account

Since single mutual fund accounts have no cash balances, you reconcile only the share balances. There are two ways of updating this type of account: with and without transaction detail.

USING A STATEMENT THAT SHOWS TRANSACTION DETAIL

If your mutual fund statement includes the transaction detail:

1. Click **Investing Center** in the Account bar, and click the account with which you want to work.

2. Click **Enter Transactions** to open the Buy - Shares Bought dialog box, which is displayed in Figure 7-3.

   | Single Mutual Fund | Summary |
   | Enter Transactions | Set Up Download |

3. Enter each transaction listed on your statement. Click **Enter/New** to move to a new transaction. Click **Enter/Done** when you have entered all of the transactions shown on the statement.

4. Click **Options** in the Account Status title bar, and click **Reconcile This Account**.

5. Follow the procedure in "Reconcile an Investment Account to a Paper Statement" earlier in the chapter.

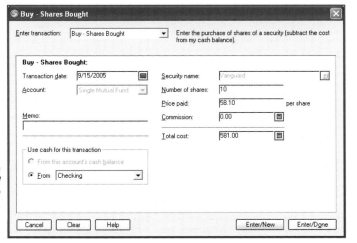

Figure 7-3: **The Buy - Shares Bought dialog box is used to enter transactions into your investment account.**

7

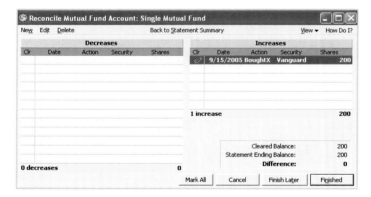

USING A STATEMENT WITHOUT TRANSACTION DOLLAR DETAIL

Some brokerage and mutual fund statements only show transactions in terms of shares and not the dollars relating to those shares. To reconcile that type of statement:

1. Click the account with which you want to work.

2. Click **Options** in the Account Status menu bar, and click **Reconcile This Account**. The Reconcile Mutual Fund Account dialog box appears.

3. Enter the starting share balance and ending share balance from the statement in the relevant fields.

4. Enter the statement ending date.

5. Click **OK**. The Reconcile Mutual Fund Account window opens.

6. Click each transaction that appears in the window. Note that the balance is displayed in number of shares rather than in dollars. The ending balance in the Reconcile Mutual Fund Account window should be the same as the ending balance on the statement.

7. Click **Finished** when you have reconciled the account. The Reconciliation Complete dialog box appears. Click **OK** to close the dialog box.

Update 401(k) Accounts

401(k) accounts are tracked a bit differently than other investment accounts. You can track actual shares or dollar amounts. If your financial institution offers it, you can even download your transaction details. You can also manually enter

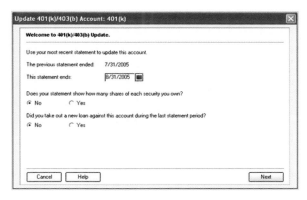

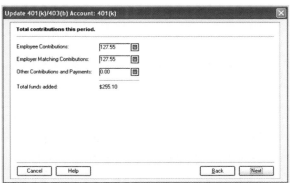

the information from a paper statement or use the 401(k) Update Wizard. The easiest method to use is the download option; however, the 401(k) Update Wizard lets you track the performance of funds in your 401(k).

USE THE 401(K) UPDATE WIZARD

1. Click the **Investing** menu, click **Investing Activities**, and click **Track 401(k)**.

2. Click **Update An Existing 401(K) Account**, and then click **OK**.

3. Select the 401(k) account with which you want to work, and click **OK**. The 401(k) Update Wizard starts.

4. Enter the date of the statement in the **This Statement Ends** field.

5. Click the **No** option in response to the question Does Your Statement Show How Many Shares Of Each Security You Own?, and then click **Yes**.

6. Click either **No** or **Yes** in response to the question Did You Take Out A New Loan Against This Account During The Last Statement Period?, and then click **Next**.

7. Enter the amount in the **Employee Contributions** field as shown on the statement.

8. Enter the amount in the **Employer Matching Contributions** field as shown on the statement.

9. If needed, click in the **Other Contributions And Payments** field, and enter those amounts from the statement. Quicken adds all of these transactions, which should match your paper statement.

10. Click **Next**. The **Total Withdrawals This Period** dialog box appears.

11. Enter the amount in the **Your Withdrawals, Not Including Loans** field from the statement.

12. Enter the amount in the **Federal Tax Withheld** field if it is shown on the statement.

13. Enter the amount in the **State Tax Withheld**, **Penalty Withheld**, and **Other Withdrawals And Fees** fields from the statement. Quicken shows the total, which should match the statement. Click **Next**.

14. If you have a loan on the account, the Loan Repayments dialog box appears. Enter the amount of principal and interest paid as shown on the statement, and then click **Next**.

15. The name of each security held in the account is displayed in the next dialog box. Click **Add New Security** if there is a security on the statement that does not appear on this list. Otherwise, click **Next**.

16. Click either **No** or **Yes** in response to the question Did You Move Any Money From One Security To Another?

17. If you clicked Yes, enter the number of transfers on the statement in **How Many Transfers Appear On Your Statement?** field. Click **Next**.

18. Enter the value in the **Market Value** field from the statement for each security in the account. Click **Next**.

19. Verify that the amount in the **Total Market Value** field shown on the statement matches the 401(k)/403(b) Update Summary page.

20. Click **Done**.

Reconcile Property & Debt Accounts

Property & Debt Center accounts can be reconciled or updated in much the same way as accounts in the other Centers. If you choose to update an asset account based on current market value, you can use documentation such as a property tax statement or valuation summary from a commercial appraisal. As you acquire and enter new items in your Home Inventory, that asset will be updated automatically when you transfer the information into Quicken. You may get monthly statements from a financial institution showing loan balances and loan payments due so that these accounts can be updated. While you can update these accounts without documentation, it is usually best to wait until you have some written proof of your change before you make it.

Update an Asset or Liability Account

You use the same process to reconcile either an asset or a liability account.

1. Click **Property & Debt** in the Account bar.

2. Click **Options** on the right of the Property & Debt Accounts title bar.

3. Click **Reconcile An Account**. The Choose Reconcile Account dialog box appears.

4. Click the **Account** down arrow, and choose the asset or liability account to reconcile. Click **OK** when you have made your selection.

5. In the Update Account Balance dialog box, click in the **Update Balance To** field, and enter the balance from the statement or other documentation.

6. Click in the **Adjustment Date** field, and enter the date of the documentation.

7. Click the **Category For Adjustment** down arrow, and choose the category in which the adjustment will be entered. You might choose **Interest Exp** to reflect additional interest being added to a loan.

8. Click **OK** to return to the Activity Center. The adjustment has been added to the account.

Watch for Escrow Discrepancies

If your financial institution pays real estate taxes or insurance premiums from the payments you send them each month, you may get an escrow statement from them each year. If you have set up your mortgage loan account using the Split Transaction window and have been tracking the portion of each payment that goes to insurance and the portion that goes to real estate taxes, as well as the portion that goes to principal and interest, it is an easy task to reconcile the escrow statement you receive.

1. Click the **Reports** menu, click **Banking**, click **Transaction**, and click **Customize** on the far right of the tool bar. The Customize Transaction dialog box appears.

2. Click the **Date Range** down arrow, and click the date range of the escrow statement. Click the **Display** tab if it is not already selected.

3. Click the **Subtotal By** down arrow, and click **Category** from the list, as shown in Figure 7-4.

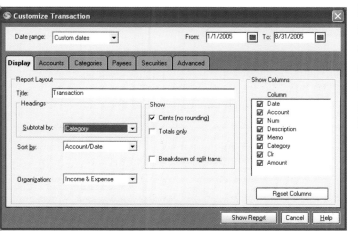

*Figure 7-4: **The Customize Transaction dialog box can help you reconcile an escrow statement.***

USING THE FIND AND REPLACE DIALOG BOX

When you need to locate a number of transactions for one payee, one category, or one amount, Quicken has a useful Find utility.

1. Click the **Edit** menu, click **Find & Replace**, and click **Find/Replace**. The Find And Replace dialog box appears.

2. Click the **Look In** down arrow, and click the field or fields where Quicken is to look for the data.

3. Click the **Match If** down arrow, and click the type of match.

4. Click in the **Find** text box, and enter the information for which you want to search.

5. Click **Find All**. A list of all matching transactions is displayed in the Found list, as shown in Figure 7-5.

6. Click **Show Matches In Split** if you want Quicken to include information shown in the Split Transactions window.

7. Click **Mark All** to select all items on the list, or choose only the transactions you want to change.

8. Click the **Replace** down arrow, and choose a field whose contents you want to replace.

9. Click in the **With** text box, and type the replacement text, or choose it from the drop-down list, and then click **Replace** to change the transactions.

10. Click **Done** to close the dialog box.

4. Click the **Accounts** tab, click **Clear All**, and click the account from which you pay this loan.

5. Click the **Categories** tab, click **Clear All**, and click the categories that are on the escrow statement. Click the **Payee** down arrow to select the payee.

6. Click **OK** or **Show Report** to return to or open the report, respectively. If you want to save this report, click **Save** in the Save Report dialog box that appears. Otherwise, click **Don't Save**. If you click Save, you will be prompted to name the report and designate the Center into which it should be saved.

7. Match the totals on the report to your paper escrow statement, and make any changes to the loan account.

8. Click **OK** to close the Customize Transaction dialog box, and click **Close** in the Transaction window.

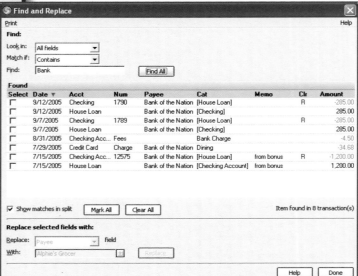

Figure 7-5: **The Find And Replace dialog box allows you to quickly locate and modify transactions.**

Prepare for Emergencies

Just as you are building a complete set of financial records with Quicken, it is a good idea to have a thorough set of family-related information should it be needed in an emergency. In the Deluxe, Premier, and Premier Home & Business editions, Quicken provides an Emergency Records Organizer to keep important personal and legal information in the same place as your financial data.

With the Emergency Records Organizer you can:

- Organize all information about you and your family that might be needed during a time of crisis.

- Create reports about this information by an entire topic or using selected areas of the Organizer.

- Print customized reports for family members or others, such as legal or medical professionals.

- Record insurance policy numbers, coverage, and policy locations; Social Security numbers of family members; medical information, such as shots or allergies; and even wishes for funeral arrangements.

Use the Emergency Records Organizer

To enter information in the Emergency Records Organizer:

1. Click the **Property & Debt** menu, and then click **Emergency Records Organizer**. The Emergency Records Organizer Introduction window opens.

2. Click the **Create/Update Records** tab.

3. Click the **Select An Area** down arrow, and click one of the 11 areas in which to enter information.

4. Click an option under **Select A Topic**. The records pane on the right will display text boxes to enter information pertaining to that topic. Figure 7-6 gives an example of the first record under the Physicians/Dentists topic of the Adults' Emergency Info.

5. Enter the relevant information in each field. Press **TAB** to move between fields.

6. Click **Save** to save the record when finished.

7. Click **New Record** to add another record in this topic.

CAUTION

When you first open the Emergency Records Organizer, all of the accounts you currently have set up are included in the Topic List. No new accounts can be added to this list. However, as you add new accounts, you can use the generic Other Accounts or add the new record to an existing account.

The Notes area can hold up to 199 characters, including spaces.

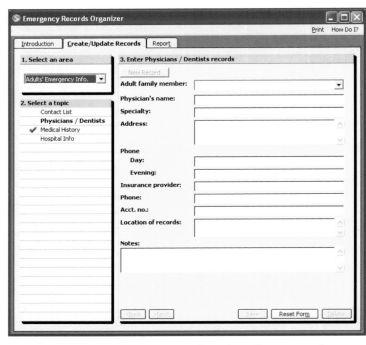

Figure 7-6: *The Emergency Records Organizer allows you to have a wide variety of personal, legal, and emergency information in one location.*

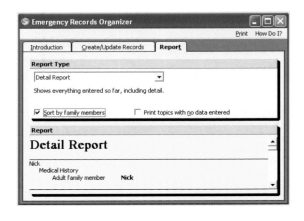

Create Reports in the Emergency Records Organizer

One of the best uses of the Emergency Records Organizer is to create reports that may be needed by various professionals in case of an emergency.

1. With the Emergency Records Organizer displayed, click the **Report** tab, click the **Report Type** down arrow, and choose which report you want.

> Emergency Report
> Caretaker Report
> Survivor's Report
> Summary of Records Entered Report
> Detail Report

2. Click **Sort By Family Members** to include all information about each family member separately. Otherwise, it will be displayed by area.

3. Click **Print Topics With No Data Entered** to show that data has not been entered about this topic as yet.

4. Click **Print** to print the report. The report goes directly to the printer. If you need more than one copy, you must click Print for each copy.

5. Click **Close** to exit the Emergency Records Organizer.

Protect Your Data

As you can see, the information in the Emergency Records Organizer should be protected. Quicken suggests several ways to do this, each method offering a different level of protection.

- Basic security can be provided by making a copy of your Quicken data on a CD or floppy disk and storing that media in a secure location, which might be a bank safety-deposit box.

- Moderate security can be gained by assigning a password to protect your entire Quicken data file.

To create such a password:

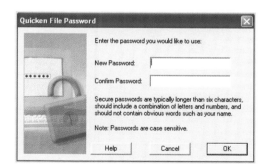

1. Click the **File** menu.

2. Click **Passwords** and click **File**. The Quicken File Password dialog box appears.

3. Type your new password in the **New Password** field. Press TAB.

4. Confirm your password by typing it again in the **Confirm Password** field.

5. Click **OK** to close the dialog box.

The highest level of security for this information is obtained as follows:

1. Create a new Quicken data file that will contain only the Emergency Records Organizer information by clicking the **File** menu and clicking **New**.

2. Choose **New Quicken File** and click **OK**. Type a name for the file in the **File Name** field, and click **OK**.

3. To assign a password to this file, copy or back up the file to a CD or floppy disk. Make two copies as additional insurance in case one floppy disk or CD becomes unusable.

4. Delete the data file from your hard disk.

Chapter 8
Managing Your Investments

Your investments help shape your financial future. Whether you are saving for a new home, your children's education, or your own retirement, Quicken can help you with your investments in many ways. You can obtain a quick online quote for a specific security or learn the historical value of your portfolio. You can use Quicken to monitor pricing on securities you already own or are thinking about purchasing. You can download information from your broker, analyze your asset allocation, estimate your capital gains, or use other sophisticated analysis tools included with Quicken. Whatever your financial position today, Quicken can help you strengthen it for tomorrow. The Investing Center not only gives you access to all of your investment accounts, it also provides links for downloading transactions, online quotes, and other investment services. You can set alerts

8

and establish a Watch List, track the performance of both individual securities and your mutual funds, and get an analysis of your entire portfolio. The Investing Center displays three tabs (four if you are using Quicken Premier or Premier Home & Business edition). Each tab contains *different views* of your information in the form of graphs, charts, and tables, some of which are customizable.

Understand the Today's Data Tab

The Today's Data tab provides an Internet link so you can download quotes, a way to set alerts for your investment accounts, information about your individual investment and retirement accounts, the list of securities you have told Quicken to watch for you, links to investing services, and the option to update all of your accounts in one step. To open the Investing Center:

> Click **Investing Center** in the Account bar. Click the **Today's Data** tab.
>
> –Or–
>
> Click the **Investing** menu and click **Go To Investing Center**.

The Investing Center opens with the Today's Data tab displayed, as shown in Figure 8-1.

Download Quotes

Quicken provides the means to download the most current *quotes*, or prices, for all of the securities in your portfolio if you have an Internet connection. (A quote is the highest price being offered by a buyer or the lowest price being asked by a seller for a security at a given point in time.) To download quotes from the Today's Data tab:

1. Click the [Download Quotes] button in the upper-left corner of the Investing Center.

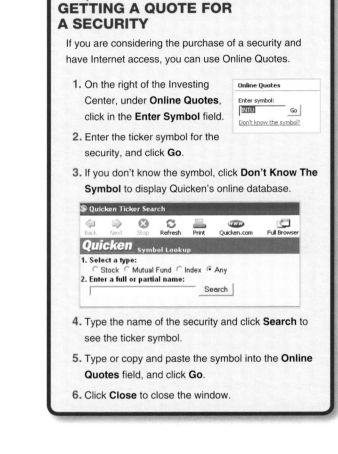

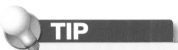

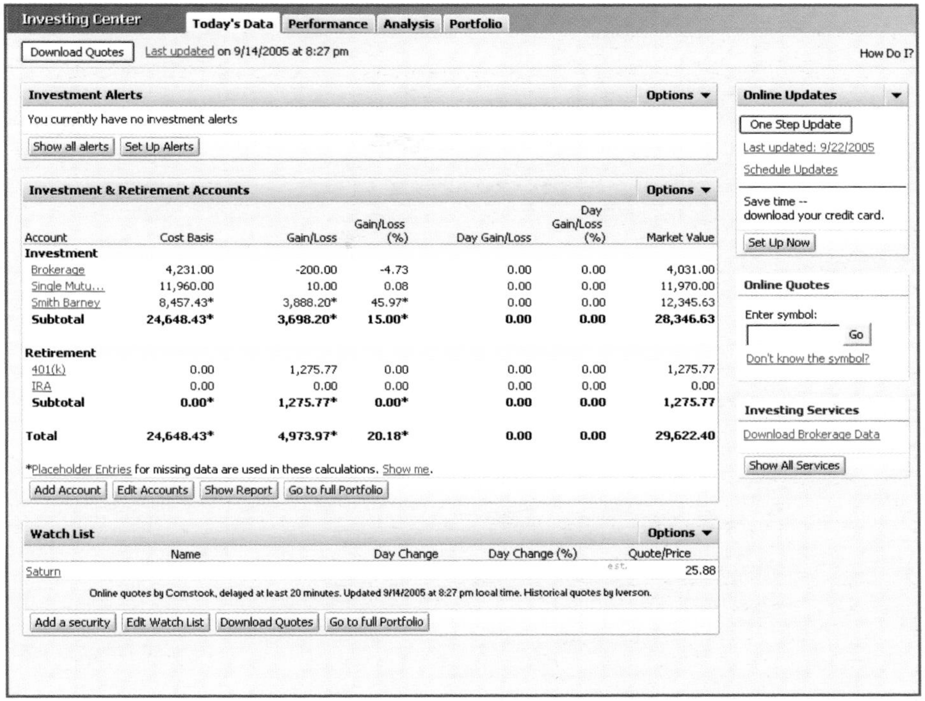

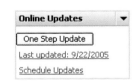

Figure 8-1: ***The Today's Data tab offers many tools with which you can manage your investments.***

TIP

Ensure that the ticker symbol is displayed for each security because that is what Quicken uses to get the quote. To look up a symbol using Quicken's online database, click **Don't Know The Symbol** in the Links bar on the right, enter the company name, and click **Search**.

–Or–

Click the **One Step Update** button on the right side of the Activity Center.

–Or–

Click **Download Quotes** in the Watch List area of the Activity Center.

2. You must have Internet access to connect. Once you are connected, the quotes for your selected securities are downloaded to your computer.
3. If you are having trouble connecting and downloading, click **Help** to display Quicken Help.

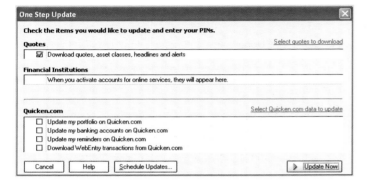

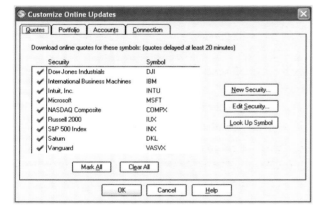

Set Up Quicken.com

When you registered Quicken, you may have created a Quicken.com account. With this account, you can keep an eye on your Quicken data from any computer with Internet access. You can even update your account information from your Quicken.com account, including alerts, and can schedule transactions using the WebEntry data form from any location with a Web browser. To use Quicken.com for your investment information:

1. From either the Quicken home page or the Investing Center, click **One Step Update** to open the One Step Update dialog box.

2. In the upper-right corner of the One Step Update dialog box, click **Select Quotes To Download**.

3. Click the **Quotes** tab and select the securities for which you want to download quotes as described later in the QuickSteps "Managing One Step Update."

4. Click the **Portfolio** tab and then:

   • Click to select each investment account you want included. A green check mark appears.

   • Click **Track My Watch List On Quicken.com** if you want to see Watch List information on your Quicken.com account. (See the QuickSteps "Working with Your Watch List" later in this chapter.)

   • Click **Send My Shares** to track the value of your portfolio and any tax implications.

   • Click **Send Only My Symbols** to download only the current price of your securities.

5. Click the **Accounts** tab and select the cash flow, asset, and liability accounts you want to see using Quicken.com.

6. Click the **Connection** tab to select how online updates will be run:

- Click **Quicken Usage Study** to help Quicken improve the program.
- Click **Run One Step Update When Starting Quicken** to quickly update your accounts when you first start Quicken.
- Click **Quicken.com Login** to change your member ID and password the next time you run One Step Update.

7. Click **OK** to close the Customize Online Updates dialog box, and then click **Close** to close the One Step Update dialog box.

Use Quicken WebEntry

If you have registered with Quicken.com, you can use WebEntry to enter transactions in the accounts you set up in "Set Up Quicken.com."

1. Open your Internet browser, connect to the Internet, and go to www.quicken.com.

2. Click **Investing Center-Portfolio**. The sign-in screen is displayed.

3. Enter your member ID and password, and then click **Sign In**. The Investing Center home page is displayed.

4. Scroll to the bottom of the page, and, opposite Quicken, click **Quicken Web Entry** to display the WebEntry data form, as shown in Figure 8-2.

5. Type the name of the account in the Quicken Account field or, if it appears, click the **Quicken Account** down arrow and select the Quicken account you want to use.

6. Click the **Type** down arrow, and click either **Payment** or **Deposit**.

7. Click in the **Date** field, and type the date of the transaction.

8. Click in the **Payee** field, and type the payee name. This can be the name of the company or the person paying you as well as the recipient of a payment you made.

9. Click in the **Amount** field, and type the amount of the transaction.

10. Click in the **Check #** field (if this is a payment), and type the check number. This is optional if you are entering a deposit, although it is a good idea for tracking purposes.

11. Type a category in the Category field or, if it appears, click the **Category** down arrow to choose a category.

12. Click in the **Memo** field, and enter any description or other information if necessary.

13. Click **Enter Transaction** to save the transaction for the next time you download to your Quicken account.

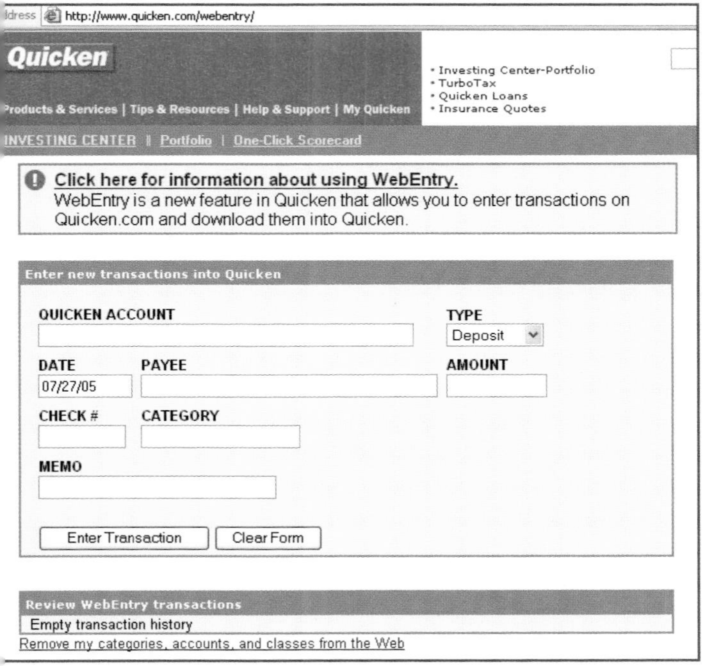

Figure 8-2: The WebEntry data form allows you to enter transactions from any computer with Internet access.

QUICKSTEPS

MANAGING ONE STEP UPDATE

The One Step Update utility allows you to download your quotes at the same time you update information from your financial institutions. Additionally, you can send information regarding your portfolio and bank accounts to Quicken.com so that you can keep them up-to-date from any computer.

1. Click the **Online** menu and click **One Step Update**. The One Step Update dialog box appears.

2. Click **Download Quotes, Asset Classes, Headlines And Alerts** to instruct Quicken to download the most current quotes for your securities, along with headlines and alerts.

3. Click **Select Quotes To Download** to open the Customize Online Updates dialog box.

4. Click the **Quotes** tab to display a list of all the securities you have entered as part of your investment accounts.

5. Click **Mark All** to include all of the listed securities when you download quotes; or click **Clear All** and click to the left of each security for which you want a quote to select it.

6. Click **OK** to close the Customize Online Updates dialog box, and click **Close** to close the One Step Update dialog box.

NOTE

For security purposes, only the Category List, Account List, and Class List (if any) are sent to Quicken.com. No other information, such as account numbers or descriptions, is transmitted. If you want to delete this information, click **Remove My Categories, Accounts And Classes From The Web**.

---

14. Click **Clear Form** to delete what you just entered.

15. Download the transaction to Quicken:

   a. From the Quicken home page, under Online Updates on the right, click **One Step Update** to open the One Step Update dialog box.

   b. If necessary, click **Download WebEntry Transactions** under Quicken.com.

   c. Click **Update Now**. The Online Update Summary dialog box appears. Review the contents, making sure your transactions are there, and then click **Done**. Downloaded transactions appear at the bottom of the register for the account to which they relate.

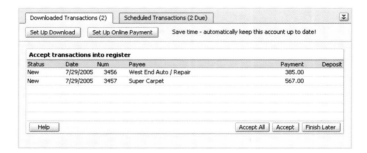

   d. Accept each transaction individually by selecting it and clicking the **Accept** button on the line; or you can accept all your transactions at once by clicking **Accept All**.

16. Click **Sign Out From Quicken.com** to sign out. This is especially important if you are using a computer accessible to the public.

Work with Investment Alerts

You can set three different alerts for your investments.

1. Click the **Investing Center** in the Account bar to open the Investing Center.

2. Click the **Today's Data** tab, and then click **Set Up Alerts** under the Investment Alerts section. The Alerts Center dialog box appears.

3. If it is not already open, click the **Setup** tab, and then click the plus sign to the left of **Investing** in the left column to open its subsidiary options.

4. Click **Price And Volume** to ask Quicken to notify you if a price goes over or under a value or a percentage you set. You can also direct Quicken to advise you of any announcements or "industry buzz" about the security, as shown in Figure 8-3.

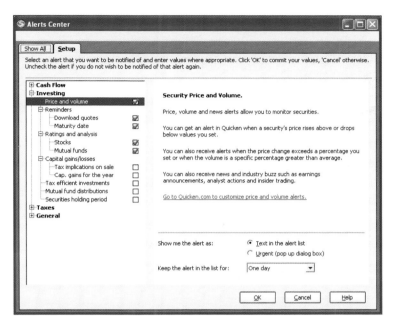

Figure 8-3: The Investment Alerts dialog box lets you set a variety of alerts to keep track of your investments.

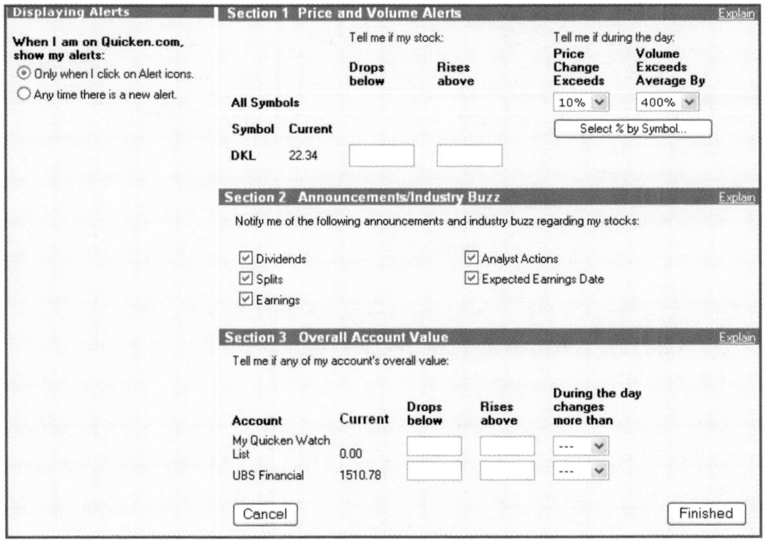

Figure 8-4: The Alerts Setup dialog box at Quicken.com allows you to schedule alerts for many changes in your investments.

5. Click the **Go To Quicken.com To Customize Price And Volume Alerts** link. If necessary, enter your Quicken.com member ID and password, and click **Continue**. The Alerts web page is displayed, as shown in Figure 8-4.

6. For an individual security, click in the **Drops Below** text box and enter the amount at which you want to receive an alert when the price of the security drops below that amount. Click in the **Rises Above** text box and enter the amount at which you want to receive an alert when the price of the security rises above that amount.

7. To obtain an alert if any of your securities' prices changes by more than a percentage you specify, or if the volume of trading of any of your securities goes over the volume you specify during a one-day trading period, click the **Price Change Exceeds** down arrow, and select a percentage, and/or click the **Volume Exceeds Average By** down arrow, and select a percentage.

8. In Section 2, click the **Dividends**, **Splits**, **Earnings**, **Analyst Actions**, or **Expected Earnings Date** check boxes to be advised of any announcements regarding this security.

9. In Section 3, click in the **Drops Below** field, and enter an amount; or click in the **Rises Above** field, and enter an amount; or click the **During The Day Changes More Than** down arrow, and select a percentage to receive an alert of a change in your account's overall value.

10. Click **Finished** to open the Standard Portfolio window in Quicken.com. Scroll to the bottom of the Standard Portfolio window, and, opposite Investing Center, click **Sign Out** to end the session. A message appears, indicating that you have signed out.

11. Click **Close** to end the Quicken.com session and close your browser. You are returned to the Online Update Summary dialog box. Click **Done** to close the dialog box. You are returned to the Today's Data tab.

12. Click **Set Up Alerts** to open the Alerts Center and set additional alerts. Click the **Setup** tab and, under Reminders, if it isn't already selected, click **Download Quotes** to create an alert reminding you to download quotes from Quicken.com and update your portfolio.

13. If it isn't already selected, click **Maturity Date** to be reminded of the maturity date of a CD.

14. Click **OK** to close the dialog box.

Manage Your Security List

Once you have entered your investment accounts, you may want to work with the individual securities in your accounts. When you created your investment accounts and told Quicken which securities were included in those accounts, Quicken created a list of these accounts in its data file. To access your Security List:

1. Click the **Investing** menu and click **Security List**.

–Or–

Press CTRL+Y.

The Security List dialog box appears. From this list, you can add, edit, hide, and delete specific securities or add securities to your *Watch List*. (The Watch List is a special snapshot in the Investing Center that allows you to track the performance of securities you own or may purchase on a daily basis. See the QuickSteps "Working with Your Watch List" later in this chapter.)

2. To add a new security to your Security List, click **New**. The Add Security To Quicken dialog box appears:

a. Click in the **Ticker Symbol** field, and type the ticker symbol for this security. If you don't know the symbol and have Internet access, enter the company name and click **Look Up**.

b. Click **Include This Security On My Watch List** if you want to monitor its daily performance.

c. Click **Next** to continue. The Quicken One Step Update window opens briefly, and information about this security is downloaded into Quicken.

d. A summary window displays the name of your security, its ticker symbol, security type, asset class, and whether you have chosen to include this security on your Watch List. If the information is correct, click **Done**. The new security is displayed on your Security List in alphabetical order by name.

3. To edit an existing security, click the security name to select it, and then click **Edit**. The Edit Security Details dialog box appears:

Edit Security Details

Name: Vanguard
Symbol: VASVX [Look Up...]
Type: Mutual Fund ▼

Asset Class
○ Single Domestic Bonds ▼
○ Mixture [Define]
☐ Download Asset Class Information
(This will replace your current asset class information.)

☐ Tax Free   ☑ Use Average Cost
Back Load: 0%

☐ Matched with online security   [Other Info]

[OK] [Cancel] [Help]

CAUTION

It is better to use the Look Up button to change the symbol of a security rather than typing it yourself in the Symbol field to ensure you have correctly entered the new symbol.

CAUTION

It is usually better to hide a security than to delete it. Before you delete a security, you must first find and delete all transactions related to that security.

a. Click in the **Name** field, and change the security name.

b. Click in the **Symbol** field, and change the ticker symbol.

c. Click the **Type** down arrow, and change the security type.

d. In the Asset Class area, click **Single** and then click the down arrow to choose a single asset class. Click **Mixture** if the security is made up of several different classes. Click the **Define** button to manually enter the percentage of each asset class in the Asset Class Mixture dialog box. Click **OK** to close the Asset Class Mixture dialog box.

e. Click **Download Asset Class Information** to download relevant information next time you download quotes or use One Step Update.

f. Click the **Other Info** button to open the Additional Security Information dialog box, and enter the information you want to maintain. Click **OK** when you are done.

g. Click **OK** to close the Edit Security Details dialog box.

4. To permanently delete a security, click the security and click **Delete**. A warning message appears, telling you that you are about to permanently delete a security. Click **OK** if you want to continue.

5. To hide a security so that its information is available but not included in totals or reports, click its name and then click **Hide**. To include hidden securities in the Security List, click **Options** and then click **View Hidden Securities**. To restore a hidden security, click it and click **Hide again**.

6. Click **Choose Market Indexes** to display a list of market indexes, which you can include as part of your Security List and your Watch List. By including these indicators, you can compare their short-term performance to those of your securities:

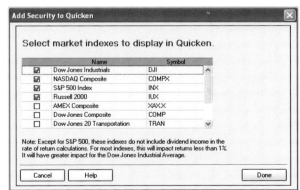

Add Security to Quicken

Select market indexes to display in Quicken.

	Name	Symbol
☑	Dow Jones Industrials	DJI
☑	NASDAQ Composite	COMPX
☑	S&P 500 Index	INX
☑	Russell 2000	IUX
☐	AMEX Composite	XAX.X
☐	Dow Jones Composite	COMP
☐	Dow Jones 20 Transportation	TRAN

Note: Except for S&P 500, these indexes do not include dividend income in the rate of return calculations. For most indexes, this will impact returns less than 1%. It will have greater impact for the Dow Jones Industrial Average.

[Cancel] [Help]   [Done]

a. Click to the left of each index you want to include. A small green check mark is displayed.

b. Click **Done** to close the dialog box.

Continued . . .

QUICKSTEPS

WORKING WITH YOUR WATCH LIST

The Watch List in the Today's Data tab provides a convenient way to see the short-term performance of securities you currently hold and securities you may want to purchase in the future and compare them to various market indicators. From the Watch List you can add a new security to your Security List, edit the Watch List, download quotes, see your entire portfolio, research a stock or mutual fund with your Quicken.com account, set up a price alert, and display ticker symbols rather than names in the Watch List. To display the Watch List:

Watch List				Options ▼
Name	Day Change	Day Change (%)		Quote/Price
International Business Machines			est.	45.88
Intuit, Inc.			est.	47.93
KRAFT FOODS INC CL A-401K			est.	1
Saturn			est.	25.88

Online quotes by Comstock, delayed at least 20 minutes. Updated 9/22/2005 at 11:46 am local time. Historical quotes by Iverson.

[Add a security] [Edit Watch List] [Download Quotes] [Go to full Portfolio]

1. Click **Investing Center** in the Account bar, and click the **Today's Data** tab.

2. Scroll to the bottom of the Watch List, and click **Add A Security** to open the Add Security To Quicken dialog box.

3. Enter a ticker symbol or a company name for the new security, click **Look Up** for the security you want to track, and then click **Next**.

4. Confirm that the information that appears is for the correct company, and then click **Next**. A dialog box appears, notifying you that the new security has been added to Quicken.

5. If you want to add another security, click **Yes**, click **Next**, and repeat steps 3–4. When you are finished, click **Done** to return to the Today's Data tab in the Investing Center.

Continued . . .

7. Click the name of the security, and click **Report** to create a report about that security.

8. Click **Print** to print the Security List.

9. Click **Close** to close the Security List.

Work with the Analysis Tab

The Analysis tab allows you to break down your portfolio by account, asset class, or security. You can then analyze its performance with several useful analysis tools, including the Asset Allocation Guide, the Portfolio Analyzer, and the Capital Gains Estimator. If you are using Quicken Premier or Premier Home & Business edition, the Morningstar Mutual Fund Ratings appear in the Activity Center.

Choose Accounts to Analyze

Depending on the version of Quicken you are using, you will see three or four ways to analyze your portfolio in the Analysis tab, as well as several links to analysis tools. The choices at the top of the Analysis tab for determining the accounts on which to do the analysis are:

- Click **All** to view information for all of your investment accounts.
- Click **Investment** or **Retirement** to include only the investment or retirement accounts.
- Click **Multiple Accounts** to select the accounts with which you want to work.

  a. Click the drop-down list box to open the Customize dialog box with a list of your investing accounts. Select the check box to the left of each account you want to include, or click **Mark All** to include all accounts. Click **Clear All** to clear all check boxes and select individual accounts.

  b. Click **Show (Hidden Accounts)** to include them in the analysis.

  c. Click **OK** to close the Customize dialog box.

6. At the bottom of the Watch List, click **Edit Watch List** to display the Security List. Click the security you want to work with, and then click **Edit** in the menu bar; or click the **Watch** check box to include or exclude the security or market index in the Watch List. Click **Close** to close the Security List.

7. Click **Download Quotes** to download the latest quotes for your holdings. The last date and time you downloaded appears as a note just above the Download Quotes and other buttons at the bottom of the Today's Data tab.

8. At the bottom of the Watch List, click **Go To Full Portfolio** to display the Portfolio tab. See the discussion in "Work with the Portfolio Tab" later in this chapter. Click the **Today's Data** tab to return to it.

9. In the Watch List title bar, click **Options** and click **Research A Stock Or Mutual Fund** to use your Quicken.com account to research a specific security. You are prompted for your user name and password and are then directed to enter the ticker symbol for the stock or mutual fund you want to research. The Quicken Security Evaluator window opens. Review the research findings on six different pages. When you're finished, click **Sign Out** to return to the Watch List.

10. Click **Options** and click **Show Symbols In Name Column** to display ticker symbols for your watched securities rather than the names.

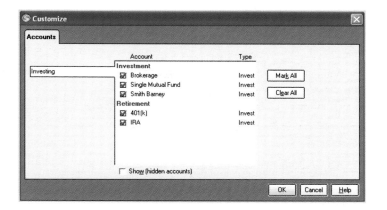

- Click **Choose Securities** to select individual securities to analyze. This also opens the Customize dialog box, but it now lists all your securities. Use the same steps as with the Multiple Accounts option.

Allocate Your Assets

Quicken provides an Asset Allocation Guide to help you structure your portfolio. In the Asset Allocation area of the Analysis tab, you see a graph that shows your current allocation and a second graph that shows your target allocation. To work with the allocation of your assets:

1. Click **Show Allocation Guide** at the bottom of the Asset Allocation area.

   –Or–

   Click **Asset Allocation Guide** in the Analysis Tools links section on the right side of the window.

   Either way, the Asset Allocation Guide displays the How Can Quicken Help With Asset Allocation page. Click **Print** to print a page of the Guide. Figure 8-5 shows the first page. If you have downloaded quotes or other information from your brokerage firm or Quicken.com, this page displays your current asset allocation. If you don't see your asset allocation, click the **Replace It With An Example** or **Set Up Quicken So You Can** link.

2. Click **What Are Asset Classes And Why Should I Use Them?** to display a discussion of asset classes.

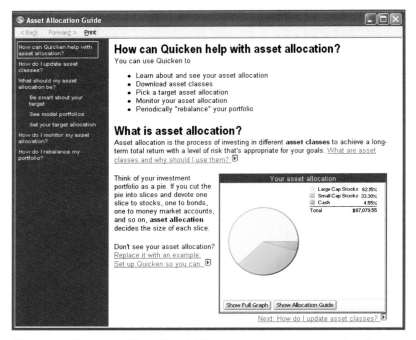

NOTE

Several firms rate mutual funds on their performance and risk. Morningstar is one of the highest regarded and is included with Quicken. There are three time periods in each Morningstar assessment: 3 years, 5 years, and 10 years (a mutual fund must have at least three years' worth of history to be included). Each fund is categorized by special classes developed by Morningstar. The risk portion is computed by calculating the fund's monthly return to the return on a Treasury bill. The result is then compared to other similar funds, and the rating shows how risky a fund is compared to the others. Each fund is rated on a basis of five stars, with five being the best and one being the lowest.

Figure 8-5: *The Asset Allocation Guide shows you how to determine if your securities meet your risk and return objectives.*

3. On the left side of the Asset Allocation Guide, click **How Do I Update Asset Classes** to display the next page.

   –Or–

   On the How Can Quicken Help With Asset Allocation page under the graph, click **Next: How Do I Update Asset Classes**.

4. Click **Go Online And Update Asset Classes** to open the Download Security Asset Classes dialog box.

   a. Click to the left of each security name for which you want the asset class downloaded, or click **Mark All** to choose each security in the list.

   b. Click **Update Now** to update your asset classes. After the transmission window has closed, the Online Updates Summary window may display what was

NOTE

The asset allocation graph that appears in the Asset Allocation Guide is identical to the asset allocation graph that appears in the Asset Allocation area of the Analysis tab.

downloaded. If you don't need to see this summary each time, click **Don't Show This Summary Again Unless There Is An Error**. Otherwise, click **Done** to return to the Analysis tab.

5. Click **Show Allocation Guide** to return to the How Do I Update Asset Classes page.

6. Click **Common Questions About Downloading Asset Classes** to display a list of frequently asked questions.

7. Click **Back: How Do I Update Asset Classes** to return to that page.

8. Click **Next: What Should My Asset Allocation Be** to continue. On this page of the guide, two sample asset allocation graphs are displayed: a current allocation and a target allocation, as shown in Figure 8-6.

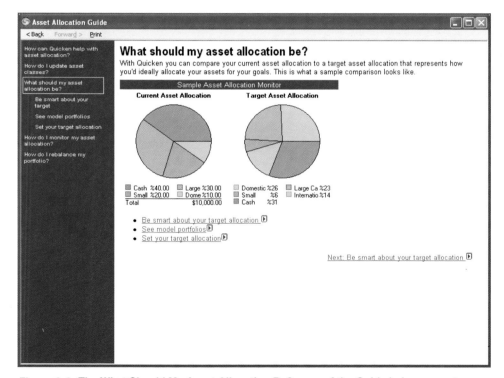

*Figure 8-6: **The What Should My Asset Allocation Be? page of the Guide helps you set your allocation.***

9. Click **Be Smart About Your Target Allocation**, or click **See Model Portfolios** to read advice about your allocation.

10. After you have read the material, click **Set Your Target Allocation**.

11. Click **Set**. The Set Target Asset Allocation dialog box appears.

12. Click **Percentage** for each of the various asset classes to enter the percentage you want to achieve. Click **OK** when finished.

13. If this is the first time you've allocated your assets, click **How Do I Rebalance My Portfolio**. *Rebalancing* means moving money between investments so that your total investments are allocated in the best way for you to achieve your goals, as shown in Figure 8-7. Goal setting and planning is discussed in Chapter 9. Follow the directions and links on the page.

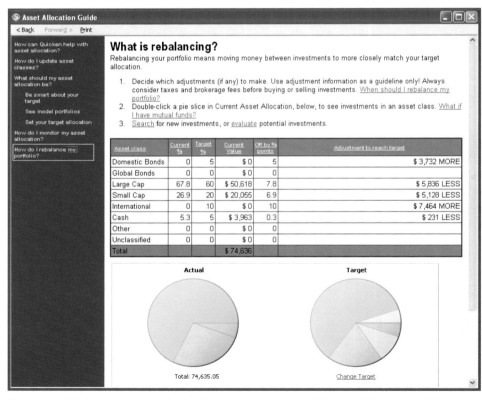

*Figure 8-7: **It's important to periodically rebalance your portfolio to achieve your objectives.***

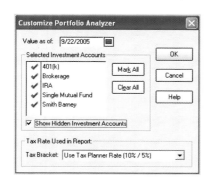

14. Click **How Do I Monitor My Asset Allocation** to understand how this is done.

15. Click **Close** to close the Guide.

Use the Portfolio Analyzer

The Portfolio Analyzer helps you review the risks and performance of your holdings. You can customize which accounts are being analyzed.

1. Click **Portfolio Analyzer** under Analysis Tools in the links on the right of the Analysis tab.

2. Click **Customize** in the menu bar to open the Customize Portfolio Analyzer dialog box. If not all of your investments appear in the list, click **Show (Hidden Accounts)**.

  a. Click to the left of each account to select it for analysis, or click **Mark All** to choose all of the accounts on the list.

  b. Click the **Tax Bracket** down arrow to select the tax rate used in the report. (See Chapter 10 for a complete discussion of tax planning.)

  c. Click **OK** to close the dialog box.

3. Click **Performance** on the left to display a discussion of your holdings' performance. This can include a graphic presentation of your returns, your five best and five worst performers, tips on what to look for, and actions you can take to improve performance. Figure 8-8 shows the top part of the Portfolio Analyzer.

4. Click **Holdings** to go directly to the graphic representation and accompanying tips on your holdings.

5. Click **Asset Allocation** to view the allocation graphs, tips on asset allocation, and actions you can take to better meet your goals.

6. Click **Risk Profile** to view a risk graph, tips on what to look for when considering risk, and actions you can take to limit your risks.

7. Click **Tax Implications** to view the potential capital-gains tax implications of your holdings, along with tips and actions you can take based on those implications.

8. Click **Close** to close the Portfolio Analyzer.

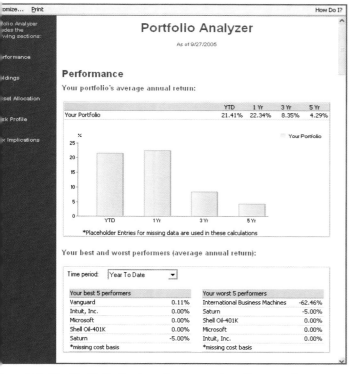

Figure 8-8: The Portfolio Analyzer has several sections, each one designed to help you with your financial investments.

Estimate Capital Gains

The Capital Gains Estimator helps you determine how much tax you might have to pay if you sell a security.

1. Click **Capital Gains Estimator** under Analysis Tools in the links on the right of the Analysis tab.

2. Click **Let's Get Started** at the bottom of the Welcome message to start the wizard.

3. You can create up to three scenarios for comparison. Click one of the scenarios and then click **Next** to continue.

4. Click to the left of the account name you want to include in the scenario. Click **Next**.

5. Click a federal tax rate, or click the **Use Tax Planner Rates** option to use the federal tax rate Quicken calculates from the income numbers you have entered in the Tax Planner (see Chapter 10). For example, 10 percent for short-term gains (first number) and 5 percent for long-term gains (second number), as shown in Figure 8-9.

6. If your state has a state income tax, enter your state rate or rates. Click **Next**.

7. Click the **Use Tax Planner Values** option for any capital loss carryovers, or click **Enter Different Values**, and enter the values. Click **Next**.

8. Follow the instructions on the page. Enter the amount of money you want to make.

9. Click the goal you want to achieve, such as Maximize After Tax Return, or Balance My Year-To-Date Capital Gains. The default is **Maximize After Tax Returns And Minimize Fees**.

10. Click **Search** to have Quicken find the best way to meet your goal. When the Search dialog box has reached 100%, click **View Results**. The What Should I Sell dialog box may appear and notify you that Quicken could not complete the scenario as you requested. Click **OK** and click **Settings**. The Search Settings dialog box appears:

    a. Click in the **% Of Your Target Goal** text box and enter a percent of your target goal. Ten is the default percentage.

    b. Click in the **Seconds** text box, and enter the maximum number of seconds you want Quicken to try to meet your goal.

    c. Click in the **Optimal Solutions** text box, and enter the maximum number of possible solutions.

    d. Click **Stop As Soon As The First Acceptable Answer Is Found** to have Quicken end the search when any answer is found matching your criteria.

NOTE

Your recommended Tax Planner percentages may be different from those shown in Figure 8-9 depending on your income.

Capital Gains Estimator

Tax Planner   Report   Print ▾   Options ▾   How Do I?

Introduction
  Welcome

Select Tax Rates

Choose the tax rates you think best represent your situation.

The Tax Planner has calculated your Federal tax situation to be:

Set Up
  Saved
  Scenarios

  Select Accounts

  Tax Rates

  Capital Loss
  Carryovers

YTD Gain/Loss: $16
Short term: $0   Long term: $16
Estimated Federal Tax Refund: $6,716

Estimator
  What Should I
  Sell?

  What If
  Scenarios

Federal Tax Rates (Short/Long-term %):

  ⦿ Use Tax Planner Rates (28% / 15%)   [Recommended]
  ○ 10% / 5%
  ○ 15% / 5%
  ○ 25% / 15%
  ○ 28% / 15%
  ○ 33% / 15%
  ○ 35% / 15%
  ○ Custom: [0]   % / [0]

Scenarios
  Scenario A

  Scenario B

  Scenario C

State Tax Rates (Short/Long-term %):

Enter your state tax rates to apply to this scenario of the Capital Gains
Estimator. (This is optional):

□ State Tax Rate [0]   % / [0]   %   How do I find my State Tax
Rate?

◀ Previous   Next ▶

*Figure 8-9: The Select
Tax Rates page allows
you to tell Quicken how
to handle the tax liability
on your capital gains.*

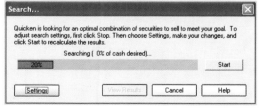

Search...   ✕

Quicken is looking for an optimal combination of securities to sell to meet your goal. To
adjust search settings, first click Stop. Then choose Settings, make your changes, and
click Start to recalculate the results.

Searching (0% of cash desired)...

[20%]   Start

[Settings]   View Results   Cancel   Help

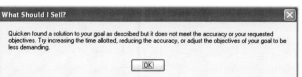

What Should I Sell?   ✕

Quicken found a solution to your goal as described but it does not meet the accuracy or your requested
objectives. Try increasing the time allotted, reducing the accuracy, or adjust the objectives of your goal to be
less demanding.

[OK]

e. Click **Quick Search** to choose one best method, or click **Exhaustive Search** to
have Quicken merge a number of searches to give you a result.

f. Click **OK** to return to the Search dialog box, and click **Start**.

11. After the search is complete, you may see a message stating that Quicken was
not able to complete the task. Otherwise, click **View Results** to display the Capital
Gains Estimator.

12. In the Current Holdings area, click to the left of the name of the security you want to
sell. A green check mark appears.

13. In the Step 2 area, click in the **Shares To Sell** column opposite the stock you want
to sell, and enter the number of shares you will be selling (see Figure 8-10).

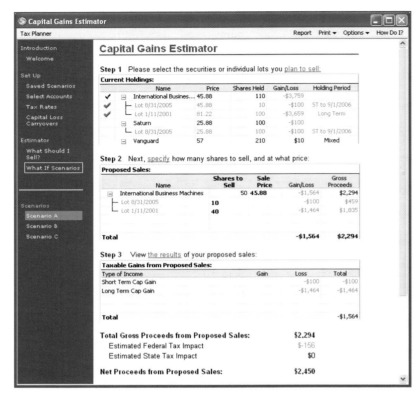

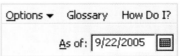

Figure 8-10: *The Capital Gains Estimator lets you decide which shares to sell to reach your objectives.*

14. In the Step 3 area, view the potential taxable gains from your proposed sales. Read the bottom of the page to see detailed information about the proposed sale.

15. Click **Close** to return to the Analysis tab.

Work with the Portfolio Tab

The Portfolio tab in the Investing Center displays all of your investment information. By customizing the way you see this information, you can make educated decisions about the performance of each investment. To view your portfolio, press **CTRL+U**.

Understand Portfolio Terms

You can include several different columns of information in a custom view of your portfolio. To learn what the column headings mean:

1. Click **Glossary** in the menu bar. The Help screen is displayed.

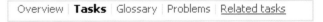

2. At the top of the Help screen, click **Glossary** again if it isn't already selected.

3. Click **Show Investment Terms Only**.

4. Click the first letter of the word you want to look up, and then scroll to the term you want to find, and click it to read the definition.

Customize Your Portfolio View

Quicken has nine standard views for the portfolio, and you can customize up to nine others. All of the views can use any

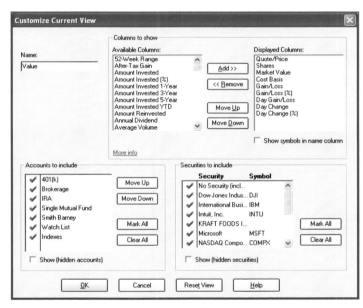

Figure 8-11: ***The Customize Current View dialog box allows you to tailor how you view your portfolio.***

of a number of column headings. Before you create a customized view, make sure you download both the latest quotes and historical prices. To customize a view in your portfolio:

1. In the Investing Center Portfolio tab, click the **Show** down arrow to select the view you want to customize.

2. Click **Customize View** to open the Customize Current View dialog box (see Figure 8-11). The name of the current selected view is displayed in the Name field. Type a new name for this view if you want.

3. In the Accounts To Include list, click to the left of the accounts to select the ones you want to use. Click **Show (Hidden Accounts)** to include hidden accounts.

4. By default, your accounts are displayed alphabetically. If you want to change this, click an account and then click **Move Up** or **Move Down** to change that account's position in the list.

5. To choose all of the accounts in the list, click **Mark All**.

6. In the Securities To Include list, click to the left of the securities that you want to show. Click **Show (Hidden Securities)** to include hidden securities. You cannot change the order in which securities are displayed; they are always displayed in alphabetical order.

7. The columns that appear by default for this view are shown in the Displayed Columns list. To remove a column, click its name and then click **Remove**. The column heading moves from the Displayed Columns list to the Available Columns list.

8. Click a column in the Available Columns list, and click **Add** to include it in the Displayed Columns List.

9. Click a column heading and click **Move Up** or **Move Down** to change its position in the list.

10. Click **Show Symbols In Name Column** to display the ticker symbol rather than the name of your security.

11. Click **Reset View** if you want to return to the original default settings.

12. Click **Done** when you are finished.

SETTING OPTIONS IN YOUR PORTFOLIO VIEW

The Portfolio tab in your Investing Center allows you to set options for each view you display. From your Portfolio tab:

1. Click **Options** in the menu bar, and then click **Preferences**. The Portfolio View Options dialog box appears.

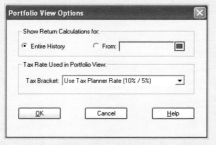

2. Click **Entire History** to include all transactions for your securities. This is the default setting. The alternative is to click **From** to enter a beginning date from which to display the information. The ending date is always today's date.

3. Click the **Tax Bracket** down arrow to choose a tax rate. The tax rate for short-term gains is shown first, and the rate for long-term gains is shown second. For example, (15%/5%) indicates that short-term gains are calculated at a 15-percent tax rate and that long-term gains are calculated at a 5-percent tax rate.

4. Click **OK** to close the dialog box.

NOTE

In order to be included in the graph, market indexes must be included on your Security List.

Explore the Performance Tab

If you use Quicken Premier or Premier Home & Business editions, Quicken provides additional analysis tools in the Performance tab.

Use the Growth Of $10,000 Utility

Quicken uses a utility called the Growth Of $10,000 that you can use to see how your portfolio compares to the main market indexes. This utility shows the value of $10,000 invested in your selected accounts compared with the same $10,000 invested in one or more of the market indexes over the same time period, as shown in Figure 8-12. To use and customize this utility:

1. Click the **Investing** menu and click **Go To Investing Center**.

2. Click the **Performance** tab and, if needed, scroll down to Growth Of $10,000.

3. At the top of the Investing Center, opposite Show Accounts, click one of the options—**All**, **Investment**, **Retirement**, or **Multiple Accounts**—to tell Quicken which accounts to include in the graphs in this tab.

4. Click **Choose Securities**. The Customize dialog box appears. Select the securities you want to compare in the graph:

   a. Click **Mark All** to choose all the securities on your Security List, or click **Clear All** to clear all selections and choose just a few.

   b. Click **OK** to close the dialog box and return to the graph.

5. If it is available, click **Enable Market Indexes** at the bottom of the graph to download market index information.

   Click **Download Historical Prices**. The Get Historical Prices dialog box appears:

   a. Click the **Get Prices For The Last** down arrow, and click **Month**, **Year**, **Two Years**, or **Five Years**, depending on the time period for which you want to download prices.

   b. Select the securities for which you want to download prices.

   c. Click **Update Now** to download the information. When the information has been downloaded, the summary screen is displayed.

   d. Click **Done** to return to the graph.

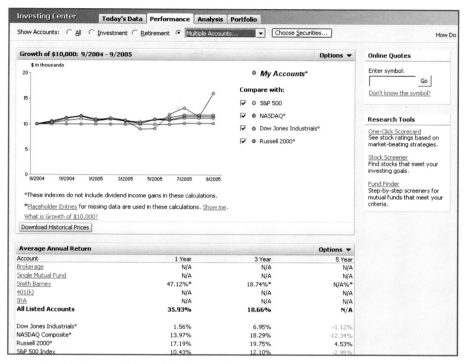

Figure 8-12: **The Growth Of $10,000 analysis tool compares your securities with the performance of several market indexes.**

TIP

After you have downloaded all of the historical information, you can click the names of market indices to select and deselect them for comparison.

QUICKSTEPS

CUSTOMIZING THE DATE RANGE

The default view for the Growth Of $10,000 snapshot is the last 12 months; however, you can customize the date range.

1. Click the **Investing** menu and click **Go To Investing Center**.

2. Click the **Performance** tab.

3. Click **Options** on the right of the menu bar, and then click **Customize This Graph**. The Customize dialog box appears.

4. Click the **Date Range** down arrow to see the list of possibilities, or click **Custom Dates** to determine your own dates.

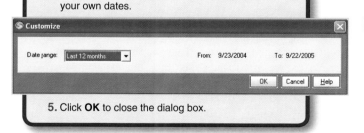

5. Click **OK** to close the dialog box.

Filter the Average Annual Return Analysis

The second analysis tool on the Performance tab of your Investing Center is the Average Annual Return. This shows the return on your investments as an annualized figure. To filter and customize this:

1. At the top of the Investing Center, opposite Show Accounts, click **All**, **Investment**, **Retirement**, **Multiple Accounts**, or **Choose Securities** to determine which accounts or securities to include. (See "Use the Growth Of $10,000 Utility" earlier in the chapter.)

2. Click **Options** and click **Show Security Performance**. The Security Performance dialog box appears:

   a. Click **Customize View** to open the Customize Current View dialog box. Follow the instructions in "Customize Your Portfolio View" earlier in the chapter.

   b. Click in the **As Of** field to enter the date for which you want to see the data. The default is today's date.

   c. Click **Close** when you are finished.

3. Click **Options** and click **Show Security Performance Comparison** to work with the Security Performance dialog box. You can customize this view as well. Click **Close** when you are finished.

Use the Performance Research Tools

Quicken includes several additional research tools in its Premier and Premier Home & Business editions, including Fund Finder, Stock Screener, and One-Click Scorecard. You will need Internet access to use these. For all three:

Research Tools

One-Click Scorecard
See stock ratings based on market-beating strategies.

Stock Screener
Find stocks that meet your investing goals.

Fund Finder
Step-by-step screeners for mutual funds that meet your criteria.

1. Click the **Investing** menu and click **Go To Investing Center**.

2. Click the **Performance** tab.

USE THE FUND FINDER

The Fund Finder allows you to search for a mutual fund with the performance and characteristics that meet your objectives.

1. Click **Fund Finder** under Research Tools on the right side of the Performance tab. The Overview dialog box appears. The default selection on all choices is **Any**. Figure 8-13 shows part of the Overview dialog box.

2. Click the **Category** down arrow to see a list of funds. You may have to scroll down to see the entire list.

3. Click the **Fund Family** down arrow to select a specific fund family.

4. Click the **Rank In Category** down arrow to choose a fund's ranking in its category. Your choices range from Any to 10%.

5. Click the **Manager Tenure** down arrow to select how long of a time period a manager must have managed a fund.

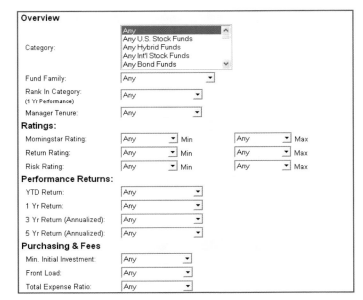

Figure 8-13: **The Overview dialog box in the Fund Finder allows you to search for funds that meet your criteria.**

WORKING WITH A SINGLE INVESTMENT ACCOUNT

The information available to you in the Investing Center for a specific account is similar to the information you can see in the Investing Center tabs.

1. In the Account bar, click the name of an investment account to select it. The Activity Center opens displaying three tabs.

2. Click the **Summary** tab to view the holdings in that account, its attributes, status, and the investing activity. Figure 8-14 displays the single investment account options.

3. Click the **Performance & Analysis** tab to view several graphs representing the performance, allocation, and cost for that account.

4. Click the **Transactions** tab to view, add, or edit specific transactions in that account.

5. Click **Options** in each section to customize it.

6. Continue through the Overview screen, making relevant selections and leaving the others with the default selection Any.

7. Click **Find Funds** to see a list of available funds that meet your criteria.

8. Click **Close** to return to the Portfolio tab.

Figure 8-14: **You can also view a single investment account's performance.**

USE STOCK SCREENER

The Stock Screener allows you to go online to research specific securities, provided you have Internet access. From the Performance tab in the Investing Center:

1. Click **Stock Screener** on the right of the Activity Center to open the Stock Screener window.

CAUTION

Make signing out of Quicken.com a habit even when you're using your home computer. This way, you won't forget to sign out when using a public computer.

2. Click in the **Enter Symbol** text box, and enter the ticker symbol of the stock you want to research.
3. Click **Go** to open a window displaying the relevant information.
4. Click **Close** to return to the Investing Center.

WORK WITH THE ONE-CLICK SCORECARD

If you have registered with Quicken.com, you have yet another research tool available to you. After connecting to the Internet, from the Performance tab in the Investing Center:

1. Click **One-Click Scorecard** on the right of the Activity Center.
2. The Quicken.com Sign In dialog box may appear. If so, enter your member ID and password, and click **Sign In**. The One-Click Scorecard window opens, shown in Figure 8-15.
3. Click in the **Enter Symbol(s)** text box, and enter the ticker symbol of the security you want to research.
4. Click **Go** to see the report. Quicken creates a report showing the opinion of three different industry experts about this security.
5. From the report window you can:
   - Click **Add To Your Watchlist** to include this security in your Quicken Watch List.
   - Click **Printer-Friendly Version** to open a report without the graphics that can be printed more easily.
   - Click **Choose An Investing Strategy** to view information from one of three experts.
   - Scroll down to view the grades and the reason for each grade in eight different categories.
6. Click **Sign Out** at the bottom of the window to open the Signed Out dialog box.
7. Click **Close** to return to Quicken.

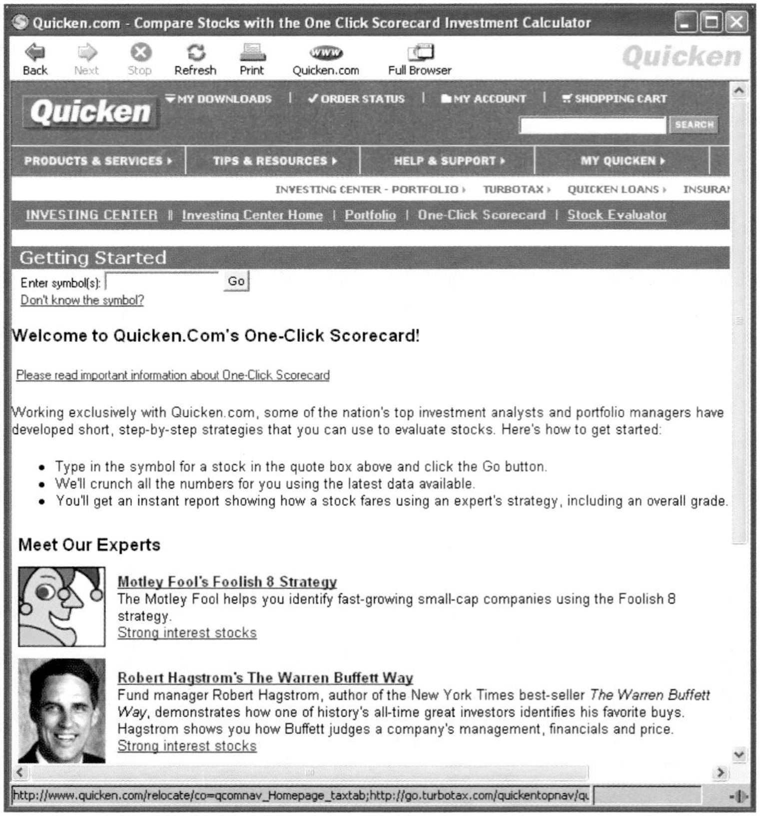

Figure 8-15: ***Quicken's One-Click Scorecard provides extensive research from three different sources.***

Chapter 9

Making Plans for Your Future

Why should you plan for your financial future? It has been said that anyone who fails to plan, plans to fail. College for your children, a house of your own, a once-in-a-lifetime cruise, retirement, a debt-free lifestyle, and a vacation cabin are all major financial events. Will you have the money to fund them? By using the Life Event Planners in Quicken, you can create a road map that will help you achieve your goals. In this chapter you will learn how to create plans in Quicken using assumptions. You will learn how to use the various planners and how to create a budget or spending plan that will help you reach your goals. In addition, you will see the various professional planning tools available in Quicken.

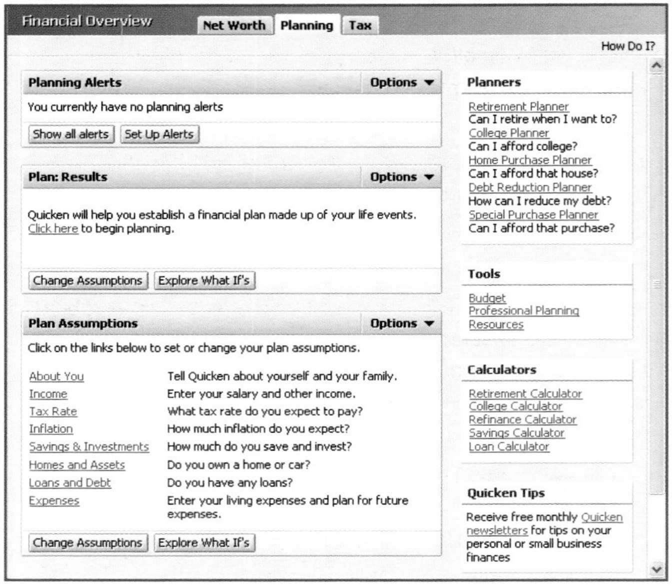

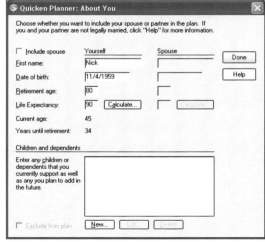

Figure 9-1: *The Planning tab in the Financial Overview Activity Center helps you create a plan to achieve your financial goals.*

Figure 9-2: *The Quicken Planner: About You dialog box is used to enter age-related information for you and your spouse.*

Work with Assumptions

All of the planners in Quicken are based on a set of assumptions that you create. You can change or add to these assumptions at any time. Quicken uses the data you have already entered to help you with your long-term plans, but if you have not yet entered all your data, you can enter it while you are creating your plans.

Understand How to Plan with Quicken

You begin by telling Quicken some information about yourself. Then, you continue by including information about your income, tax rate, savings, investments, other assets, any debt, and living expenses. Quicken uses this information—along with the financial data you have already entered and a large database of financial resources—to help you create a plan. Within the Financial Overview Activity Center are three tabs: Net Worth, Planning, and Tax. This chapter will discuss the Planning tab (see Figure 9-1). Taxes deserve a chapter of their own and are covered in Chapter 10.

Enter Information About Yourself

All good plans start with information. This one is no exception. To begin your plan:

1. Click the **Planning** menu and click **Go To Planning Center**. The Financial Overview Center is displayed.
   –Or–
   Click **Financial Overview** at the bottom of the Account bar.

2. Click the **Planning** tab.

3. If necessary, scroll down until you see Plan Assumptions. Click **About You** in the Plan Assumptions section to open the Quicken Planner: About You dialog box (see Figure 9-2).

4. Click **Include Spouse** if you want to include your spouse in the assumptions.

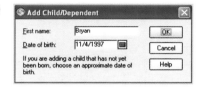

5. Click in the **First Name** field under Yourself, and type your first name. If you are including your spouse, click in the **First Name** field under Spouse, and type your spouse's first name.

6. Click in the **Date Of Birth** field under Yourself, and type your date of birth. If necessary, do the same thing under Spouse.

7. Click in the **Retirement Age** field for yourself and your spouse, and type the relevant ages.

8. Click the **Calculate** button under Yourself. The Calculate Life Expectancy dialog box appears. Click in each of the fields and select or type your response. When you are finished, click **OK** to close the dialog box and return to the Quicken Planner: About You dialog box. If you are including your spouse in this dialog box, follow the same procedure for your spouse.

9. Click **New** at the bottom of the dialog box. The Add Child/Dependent dialog box appears. Type the name and date of birth of each child, and click **OK**. This information can include children you plan to have that are not yet born.

10. Click the name of a dependent, and click **Exclude From Plan** if you don't want Quicken to include dependents in the financial assumptions.

11. Click **Done** when you have entered all of your information and are ready to return to the Planning tab Activity Center.

The Plan Assumptions section now displays your name, your spouse's name if you included one, the ages at which you and your spouse plan to retire, and the number of dependents you chose to include in your plan.

TIP

You can include or exclude a spouse at any time when making your assumptions.

CAUTION

If you support a parent or other family member who was born before 1930, you must enter all four digits in the year, for example, 1929. Otherwise, Quicken will use 2029 as the date of birth.

Enter Income Information and Your Tax Rate

The next item in the Plan Assumptions section pertains to information about your income. This includes regular salaries; self-employment income; retirement benefits; and other income, such as child support or alimony.

ENTER SALARIES AND SELF-EMPLOYED INCOME

1. Click **Financial Overview** in the Account bar, and, if needed, click the **Planning** tab.
2. Scroll down, if necessary, to **Plan Assumptions**, and click **Income**. The Quicken Planner: Income dialog box appears.
3. Click the **Salary** tab to enter salary information for yourself and your spouse if you are including a spouse in your planning assumptions.
4. Click **New** in the middle of the dialog box under Salary. The Add Salary dialog box appears. Click in each field and select or type the required information. When you are done click **OK** to return to the Quicken Planner: Income dialog box. The information you entered for the starting and ending dates for this salary appear in the Adjustments To Salary section.

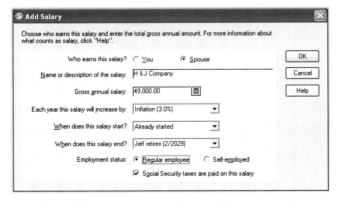

5. If you have other adjustments to your salary, such as a promotion or an expected bonus, click **New**. The Add Salary Adjustment dialog box appears. Choose the options and enter the information that is correct for you. When you have finished, click **OK** to return to the Quicken Planner: Income dialog box.
6. If you need to enter another salary, repeat steps 4 and 5.
7. If you don't want to enter retirement and/or other income information, click **Done**.

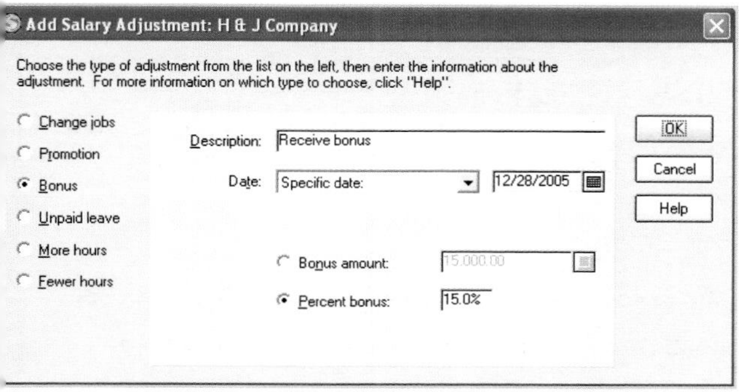

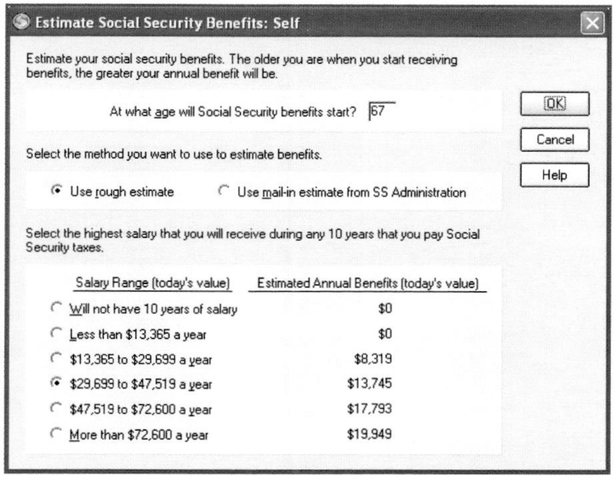

Figure 9-3: **When using the rough-estimate option to determine your future benefits, Quicken displays several salary and benefit ranges using today's values.**

TIP

Use the **Reduced Benefit Amount** text box, and type 100% if you don't want your plan to rely on Social Security benefits at all.

USE THE RETIREMENT BENEFITS TAB

If you have a retirement plan through your employer or want to include Social Security benefit information in your plan, use the Retirement Benefits tab in the Quicken Planner: Income dialog box (see "Enter Salaries and Self-Employed Income" to open this dialog box).

1. Click the **Retirement Benefits** tab to enter information about retirement income.

2. Click **Social Security Starting Age** to enter the age at which you expect to start collecting Social Security benefits. If you don't know, click the **Estimate** button. The Estimate Social Security Benefits dialog box appears:

   a. Click in the **At What Age Will Social Security Benefits Start** field, and type the age. See the QuickFacts "Understanding Your Social Security Retirement Age" earlier in this chapter for more information.

   b. Click either **Use Rough Estimate** or **Use Mail-In Estimate From SS Administration**. If you choose the Use Rough Estimate option, Quicken displays a list of salary ranges and their corresponding estimated annual benefits, as shown in Figure 9-3. If you choose the Use Mail-In Estimate From SS Administration option, you are prompted to enter the amount from your mailed estimate that corresponds to the age you entered in At What Age Will Social Security Benefits Start.

   c. Click OK to close the Estimate Social Security Benefits dialog box and return to the Quicken Planner: Income dialog box. The amount from either the Quicken rough estimate or the amount you entered from the mailed estimate appears in the Annual Benefit area.

3. If you think Social Security benefits will be reduced in the coming years, click **Yes** in response to Reduce The Estimated Benefit Amount, and enter a percentage by which you think the benefits will be reduced. This amount is displayed below the Annual Benefit amount.

4. If you or your spouse will be receiving any pension benefits in the future, click **New** under Pension Benefits. The Add Pension dialog box appears. Click in each of the fields and select or type the requested information. When you are finished, click **OK** to close the dialog box and return to the Quicken Planner: Income Retirement Benefits tab.

5. To enter another pension benefit, repeat step 4.

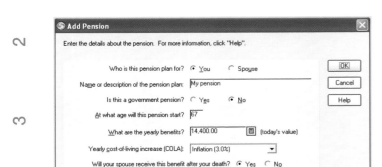

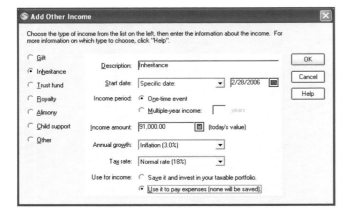

Figure 9-4: *Other income can be a one-time event or can span several years.*

6. Select a pension benefit and click **Edit** to change that benefit, or click **Delete** to remove it from your list. If you want to exclude a specific pension benefit from your plan, select it from the list, and click **Exclude From Plan**.

7. When you are done, click either the **Other Income** tab to enter additional, non-investment income or click **Done** to return to the Planning tab Activity Center.

ENTER OTHER INCOME

The Other Income tab in the Quicken Planner: Income dialog box is for gifts, inheritances, royalties, and other miscellaneous income you expect to receive. (See "Enter Salaries and Self-Employed Income" to open the Quicken Planner: Income dialog box.)

1. Click the **Other Income** tab, and then click **New**. The Add Other Income dialog box appears.

2. Click the option from the list on the left that corresponds to the type of income you want to include, as shown in Figure 9-4.

3. Click in the **Description** field, and type the relevant information. If you have chosen one of the specific types of income from the list on the left, this name appears in the field.

4. Click in the **Start Date** field, and enter a date, or click the down arrow to choose one from the list.

5. Click either **One-Time Event** or **Multiple-Year Income** to indicate the income period for this income. If you choose Multiple-Year Income, enter the number of years you will receive this income.

6. Click in the **Income Amount** field, and enter the amount of income you will receive per year (if it is for multiple years) or in total (if it is a one-time event).

7. Click the **Annual Growth** down arrow, and choose how to describe this income's annual growth. Alternatively, you can accept the default **Inflation (3.0%)**.

8. Click the **Tax Rate** down arrow, and choose the tax rate for this income. Alternatively, you can accept the default **Normal Rate (18%)**.

9. Opposite Use For Income, click **Save It And Invest In Your Taxable Portfolio** if this income is to be invested, or click **Use It To Pay Expenses (None Will Be Saved)**.

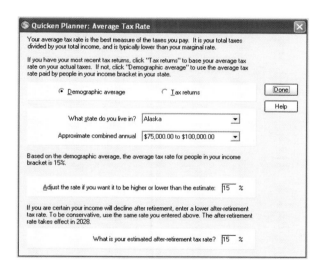

10. Click **OK** to close the Add Other Income dialog box and return to the Quicken Planner: Income dialog box.

11. Click **Done** to close the Quicken Planner: Income dialog box and return to the Planning tab Activity Center.

DETERMINE YOUR TAX RATE

Quicken takes your tax liability into account when helping you create your plan. To tell Quicken what rate to use:

1. Click **Financial Overview** near the bottom of the Account bar.

2. Click the **Planning** tab.

3. Scroll, if necessary, to the **Plan Assumptions** section, and click **Tax Rate**. The Quicken Planner: Average Tax Rate dialog box appears.

4. Click **Demographic Average** if you want Quicken to calculate your average tax rate based on the average rate of people in your income category in your state.

   a. Click the **What State Do You Live In** down arrow, and click the name of your state.

   b. Click the **Approximate Combined Annual** down arrow, and chick the approximate annual income for you and your spouse.

5. Alternatively, click **Tax Returns** if you want to enter information from your most recent tax return. A different set of questions appear:

   a. Enter the Total Income (From Form 1040).

   b. Enter the Total Federal Taxes (From Form 1040).

   c. If your state has a state income tax, enter the Total State Taxes (From Your State Tax Form).

6. The average tax rate for your income bracket in your state appears in the **Adjust The Rate If You Want It To Be Higher Or Lower Than The Estimate** field. Enter any change in the estimated tax rate you want Quicken to use.

7. This same rate appears in the **What Is Your Estimated After-Retirement Tax Rate** field. Enter any change you want Quicken to use.

8. Click **Done** when you have entered all of the information to return to the Planning tab of the Financial Overview Activity center.

QUICKSTEPS

ESTIMATING INFLATION FOR YOUR PLAN

Quicken uses an average inflation rate of 3 percent. *Inflation* is a rise in the price of goods or services when consumer spending increases and supplies or services decreases. For the last 50 years, inflation in the United States has ranged from 0 to 23 percent, with an average of 2–3 percent per year. As you make your assumptions in Quicken, you may choose to be conservative and increase the default inflation rate of 3 percent or be more optimistic and decrease the rate. To change the rate of inflation used by Quicken:

1. Click **Financial Overview** in the Account bar.

2. Click the **Planning** tab.

3. Scroll to the **Plan Assumptions** section, if necessary, and click **Inflation**. The Quicken Planner: Estimated Inflation dialog box appears.

4. Click in the **What Inflation Rate Do You Want To Use In Your Plan** field, and type the number you want to use.

5. Click **Done** to close the dialog box.

Consider Savings, Investments, and Rate of Return

Quicken can use the information you entered for your checking, savings, and investment accounts in its assumptions for planning. You can choose to have Quicken include or exclude any account from its computations, designate the use for each account, and indicate what contributions will be made to these accounts in the future.

INCLUDE CHECKING AND SAVINGS ACCOUNTS

To tell Quicken how to use your checking and savings accounts:

1. Click the **Planning** menu and click **Go To Planning Center**.

2. In the Financial Overview Activity Center, click the **Planning** tab.

3. Scroll to the Plan Assumptions section, if necessary, and click **Savings & Investments**. The Quicken Planner: Savings And Investments dialog box appears.

4. Click the **Savings** tab to display a list of your checking and savings accounts. If you have not yet entered all of your accounts, now is a good time. Click the **New** button to add a new account, and follow the directions in Chapter 3.

5. Click an account and click **Exclude From Plan** to exclude that account from the plan. Click **Show Excluded Accounts** if you want them to be displayed in the list even if they are not included in the plan.

6. Click **Details** to open the Account Details: Savings dialog box:

   a. Click the **Account Will Be Used For** down arrow, and select the account you want to use. If you have used any of the specific planners, such as the Home Purchase Planner or the Retirement Planner, you will have that choice included; otherwise, your only choice is the default **General Expenses**.

   | General expenses |
   | Expense for House |
   | College expense for Bradley |
   | College expense for Melissa |
   | phd |
   | College expense for Pat |

   b. Click **OK** to return to the Quicken Planner: Savings And Investments dialog box.

Add Contribution: Savings

Select whether this contribution is a percentage of salary or a yearly amount.

The contribution is: ○ a percentage of: [spouse's salary ▼]

○ an amount that increases each year by:

[Inflation (3.0%) ▼]

[Cancel] [Help]   [Next]

7. If either you or your spouse regularly put money in any of these bank accounts, click **New** underneath Contributions To Savings. The Add Contribution: Savings dialog box appears:

a. Click the **A Percentage Of** option, and then click the down arrow to choose a contribution of a percentage of your salary, your spouse's salary, or a combination of the two.

b. Alternatively, click the **An Amount That Increases Each Year By** option, and enter the standard inflation rate that you entered earlier (or use the default inflation rate of 3%), or choose a rate from the drop-down list. If you choose Custom Rate Of, a percentage field displays. Enter the custom rate by which you want to increase your contribution annually.

c. Click **Next** to continue.

d. Click **The Contribution Amount Is**, and enter the annual amount contributed to this bank account.

e. Click **Starting On** and enter a specific date, or click the down arrow to choose one from the list. If you choose Specific Date, you must enter the date.

f. If this is a one-time contribution, click **One-Time Contribution**. Otherwise, click **Regular Contribution, Ending**, and choose a date from the drop-down list or enter a specific date.

g. Click **Done** to return to the Quicken Planner: Savings And Investments dialog box.

INCLUDE INVESTMENT ACCOUNTS

The Investments tab shows all of the investment accounts you have entered. You can include or exclude any of these accounts from your plan and tell Quicken about regular contributions you make to any of them.

● Click the **Investments** tab and follow the procedure in "Include Checking and Savings Accounts" earlier in this chapter.

Work with Homes and Other Assets

You can include your home and other assets in your plan, both those you currently own and those you plan on purchasing.

ENTERING YOUR EXPECTED RATE OF RETURN

The *rate of return* is how much you get back each year on your investments expressed as a percentage. For example, if you make $200 on a $2,000 investment, your rate of return is 10 percent ($2,000 divided by $200). You can use different rates for taxable and tax-deferred investments. Before retirement, your investments must grow enough to ensure that you have funds available to you even when you are not earning a salary. After retirement, your funds must grow to keep pace with inflation and fund your living expenses. To enter your estimated rate of return on your investments:

1. Click **Financial Overview** in the Account bar.

2. Click the **Planning** tab.

3. If necessary, scroll to display the Plan Assumptions section. Click **Savings & Investments**.

4. Click the **Return** tab.

5. Click **Use Separate Rates Of Return For Taxable And Tax-Deferred Accounts** if applicable.

6. Click in the **Rate Of Return** field under Before Retirement, and enter the return you expect on your investments before you retire.

Continued . . .

INCLUDE CURRENT ASSETS

To work with the Homes And Assets Planner:

1. Click **Financial Overview** in the Account bar.

2. If necessary, scroll down to the **Plan Assumptions** section, and click **Homes and Assets**. The Quicken Planner: Homes And Assets dialog box appears.

3. Click the **Asset Accounts** tab to display a list of the accounts you have created so far in Quicken, including homes, vehicles, real estate, and so on. The list shows a description of the asset, its purchase date, a planned sale date (if any), and its current value, as shown in Figure 9-5.

4. Click **New** to add a new account, follow the directions in Chapter 3, and return to the Quicken Planner: Homes And Assets dialog box.

5. Select an asset and click **Exclude From Plan** if you want Quicken to ignore this asset in your plan.

6. Click an asset to see if there are loans, expenses, or income associated with this asset.

7. Click **Sale Info** to open the Asset Account Sale Information dialog box. Click in each of the fields and select or type the requested information, clicking **Next** as needed.

8. Click **Done** to return to the Quicken Planner: Homes And Assets dialog box.

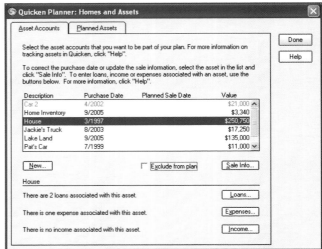

*Figure 9-5: **The Asset Accounts** tab lists all of the asset accounts you have entered into Quicken.*

ENTERING YOUR EXPECTED RATE OF RETURN

(*Continued*)

7. Click in the **Rate Of Return** field under After Retirement, and enter your expected after-retirement return.

8. In the **How Much Of Your Taxable Return Will Be Subject To Taxes Each Year** field, enter an appropriate percentage. In most cases, all of the return may be taxable. Check with your financial professional to learn what you should enter.

9. Click **Done** to return to the Planning tab.

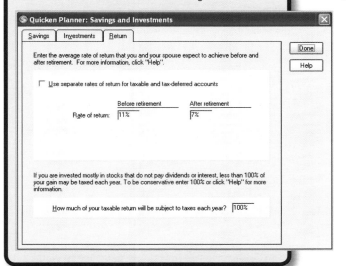

CONSIDER LOANS ON ASSETS

If you intend to add, pay off, or change a loan using one of your assets as collateral:

1. Click the name of the asset, and then click the **Loans** button to open the Quicken Planner: Loans dialog box.

2. Click the **Loan Accounts** tab to display the current loans associated with this asset.

3. Select a loan and click **Exclude From Plan** if you want to exclude that loan from your plan.

4. Click the **Planned Loans** tab (see Figure 9-6) and click **New**. The Planned Loan dialog box appears. Click in each of the fields and select or type the information that is correct for your loan. Click **Done** to return to the Loans dialog box.

5. Click **Done** to return to the Quicken Planner: Homes And Assets dialog box.

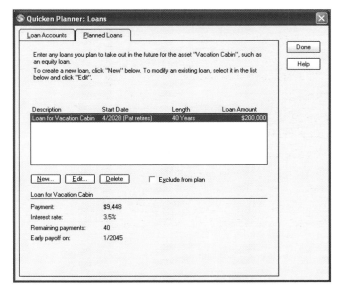

*Figure 9-6: **The Planned Loans tab asks for information about future indebtedness.***

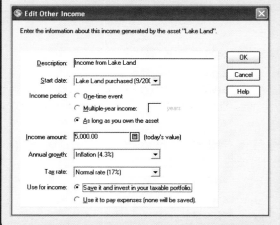

QUICKSTEPS

ASSOCIATING INCOME WITH AN ASSET IN YOUR PLAN

Part of your future retirement may come from income you earn by renting an asset you own, such as a motor home, boat, cabin, or real property. You can include this information in your Quicken Planner: Homes And Assets dialog box.

1. Click **Financial Overview** in the Account bar.

2. Scroll down, if necessary, to **Plan Assumptions**. Click **Homes And Assets** to open the Quicken Planner: Home And Assets dialog box.

3. Click the name of the asset from which you earn income, and click **Income** at the bottom of the dialog box.

4. Click **New** to open the Edit Other Income dialog box. Click in each of the fields and select or type the information that is requested.

5. Click **OK** to close the dialog box.

ENTER EXPENSES ASSOCIATED WITH AN ASSET

Many assets have expenses associated with them that must be included in the plan. You can include them here with their associated asset or include them later, as described in the "Figure Your Living Expenses" section of this chapter. To include expenses with their associated asset:

1. Click the asset in the list of asset accounts in the Asset Accounts tab of the Quicken Planner: Homes And Assets dialog box.

2. Click the **Expenses** button toward the bottom of the dialog box. The Quicken Planner: Asset Expenses dialog box appears.

3. Click in the **How Much Tax Do You Pay On This Asset** field, and enter the tax amount, if any, that you pay. If the asset you selected is a house, a message will appear, mentioning property taxes and providing a formula to figure the amount.

4. If there are other expenses, such as homeowner association fees, moorage fees, maintenance fees, or gardening expenses, click **New**. The Add Asset Expense dialog box appears. Click in each of the fields and select or type the information that is appropriate for this expense, clicking **Next** as needed and clicking **OK** to return from any subsidiary dialog box you open.

5. Click **Done** to return to the Quicken Planner: Asset Expenses dialog box. Click **Done** again to return to the Quicken Planner: Homes And Assets dialog box.

INCLUDE PLANNED ASSETS

You can include in your planning the acquisition of additional assets, such as a new home, a new weekend property, a new business or income property, and so on.

1. From the Quicken Planner: Homes And Assets dialog box (see "Include Current Assets"), click the **Planned Assets** tab.

2. Click **New** to open the Add Planned Asset dialog box. Click in each of the fields and select or type the information that is requested, clicking **Next** as needed.

3. Click **Done** to return to the Quicken Planner: Homes And Assets dialog box. See the sections, "Include Current Assets," "Consider Loans on Assets," and "Enter Expenses Associated with an Asset" earlier in this chapter, as well as the QuickSteps "Associating Income with an Asset in Your Plan" to perform the same functions with planned assets as with current assets.

4. Click **Done** to close the Quicken Planner: Homes And Assets dialog box.

Use the Loans And Debt Planner

To have a comprehensive plan, you need to include your liabilities (loans and debt), as well as your assets.

1. From the Quicken Home Activity Center, click **Financial Overview** at the bottom of the Account bar, and click the **Planning** tab. Scroll to the **Plan Assumptions** section, and click **Loans And Debt** to open the Loans And Debt Planner.

2. Click the **Loan Accounts** tab to display a list of all the loans you have entered. You can select loans and exclude them from your plan, change the payoff date, and add new loans.

3. Click the **Planned Loans** tab to display a list of any loans you plan to take out in the future. You may have entered these loans in the Quicken Planner: Homes And Assets section. You can edit, delete, and exclude these loans from the plan, as well as add new ones.

4. Click the **Debt** tab. A message appears, stating that you have not yet used Quicken's Debt Reduction Planner. See "Use the Debt Reduction Planner" later in this chapter.

5. Click **Done** to close this dialog box.

Figure Your Living Expenses

Expenses are a critical part of your plan. To figure what your expenses will be:

1. Click **Financial Overview** in the Account bar. Scroll to **Plan Assumptions** (if necessary).

2. Click **Expenses** to open the Quicken Planner: Expenses dialog box.

3. Click the **Living Expenses** tab. You are prompted to enter your regular living expenses, such as food, transportation, rent, medical insurance payments, and utility bills. Quicken offers you two methods of entering these items: by Rough Estimate or by Category Detail.

4. Click **Rough Estimate** to let Quicken base an annual estimate of your expenses based on the transactions in your registers.

5. Click **Yearly Living Expenses** and, if needed, modify the amount.

6. Click in the **What Percent Of Surplus Cash Do You Want To Sweep To Savings** field, and enter a percentage if you feel you will be spending less than your income. The most conservative amount to select is 0%.

CAUTION

Ensure that any loans are included in the Loan Accounts section of the Plan Assumptions and that all credit card or other consumer debt is included in the Expenses section.

CAUTION

Do not include amounts in your living expenses that are entered elsewhere. Conversely, do not forget to include credit card and loan payments you make regularly.

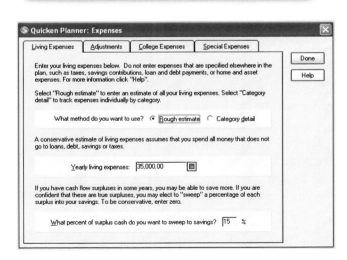

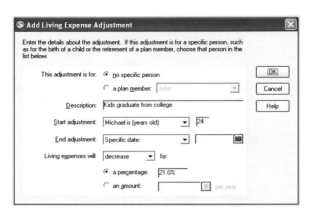

Add Living Expense Adjustment

Enter the details about the adjustment. If this adjustment is for a specific person, such as for the birth of a child or the retirement of a plan member, choose that person in the list below.

This adjustment is for: ● no specific person

○ a plan member: John

Description: Kids graduate from college

Start adjustment: Michael is (years old): 24

End adjustment: Specific date:

Living expenses will: decrease by:

● a percentage: 21.0%

○ an amount: per year

OK / Cancel / Help

ENTER ADJUSTMENTS

The Adjustments tab is used to enter major changes to your living expenses. This could be a layoff from work, a new baby, or an illness.

1. Click the **Adjustments** tab and click **New**. The Add Living Expense Adjustment dialog box appears.

2. Click **No Specific Person** if this is a general adjustment, such as rent from an extra room in your garage. Click **A Plan Member** and choose the member from the drop-down list if it affects one of the persons in your plan. The members are you, your spouse, and any dependents you listed as being included in the plan.

3. Click in the **Description** field, and type a description of the event.

4. Click in the **Start Adjustment** field, and either enter a specific date or choose one from the drop-down list.

5. Click in the **End Adjustment** field, and either enter a specific date or choose one from the drop-down list.

6. Click the **Living Expenses Will** down arrow, click either **Increase** or **Decrease**, click either **A Percentage** or **An Amount**, and enter the amount.

7. Click **OK** to close the dialog box.

WORK WITH COLLEGE EXPENSES

If your plan must fund college tuition and other related expenses:

1. Click the **College Expenses** tab, and click **New**. The first Add College Expense dialog box appears.

2. Click the **This Expense Is For** down arrow, and choose the family member who is going to college. Any member of the plan may be chosen.

3. Click in the **Description** field, and enter a description for this expense.

4. Click the **Start College** down arrow, and select a date from the drop-down list or enter a specific date. If you choose the When *name* Is (Years Old) option, enter the age at which this person will start college.

5. Click in the **Years In College** field, and enter the number of years for which you will be responsible for this expense.

6. Click **Next** and enter the remainder of the information in the dialog boxes that appear, the first of which is shown on the next page, by clicking in each of the fields and selecting or typing the information that is requested, clicking **Next** as needed.

Add College Expense

Enter the college costs you expect to pay in the fields provided.

To get estimated college costs, click on the links provided under College Costs.

Tuition & fees:	26,000.00	🔳
☐ Out-of-state fees:	0.00	🔳
☑ Room & board:	0.00	🔳
☑ Books & supplies:	0.00	🔳
☑ Other costs:	0.00	🔳
Total annual costs:	$26,000	

[Cancel] [Help] [Back] [Next]

---

7. Click **Done** to close the dialog box and return to the Quicken Planner: Expenses dialog box. If you have entered all the expense assumptions you want, click **Done** again to close the Quicken Planner: Expenses dialog box.

Understand the Plan Results

After you have entered all of your assumptions, the result of your hard work is displayed in graphical format in the Plan: Results section of the Planning tab. The graph shows if your plan is working and how much money you will have in retirement. A list of major events is displayed under the graph, as shown in Figure 9-7.

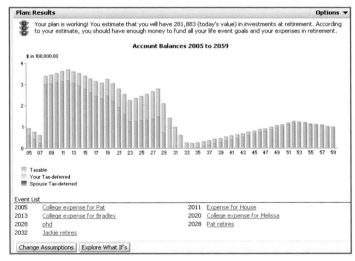

Plan: Results — Options ▼

Your plan is working! You estimate that you will have 281,883 (today's value) in investments at retirement. According to your estimate, you should have enough money to fund all your life event goals and your expenses in retirement.

Account Balances 2005 to 2059

$ in 100,000.00

☐ Taxable
☐ Your Tax-deferred
■ Spouse Tax-deferred

Event List
2005	College expense for Pat	2011	Expense for House
2013	College expense for Bradley	2020	College expense for Melissa
2028	phd	2028	Pat retires
2032	Jackie retires		

[Change Assumptions] [Explore What If's]

*Figure 9-7: **Your Plan Results tell you if your financial plan will work.***

1. Click **Options** in the upper-right corner of the Plan: Results section of the Planning tab in the Financial Overview Activity Center to see how you can change the graph.

2. Click **Show Amounts In Future Value** to display the graph in future (inflated) dollars. Click **Show Amounts In Today's Value** to change it back.

3. Click **Review Or Change Plan Assumptions** to open the Plan Assumptions dialog box. Each assumption you entered is displayed with its result. Scroll through the

---

dialog box, or click an area on the left to ensure you entered everything correctly. If you did not, click **Edit** in the title of each section to open the relevant dialog box and change the information. You can also access this dialog box by clicking the **Change Assumptions** button underneath the Event List in the Plan: Results section of the Planning tab. Click **Close** to return to the Planning tab.

4. Again, click **Options** in the Plan: Results title bar, and click **What If I Did Something Different** to open the What If dialog box. This allows you to temporarily change any assumption by clicking the assumption area on the left and see the result. If you like the change, keep it; if not, close the dialog box without saving your changes. You can also open this dialog box by clicking the **Explore What If's** button to the right of the Change Assumptions button at the bottom of the Plan: Results section. Click **Close** to return to the Planning tab.

Use the Planners

Planners

Retirement Planner
Can I retire when I want to?
College Planner
Can I afford college?
Home Purchase Planner
Can I afford that house?
Debt Reduction Planner
How can I reduce my debt?
Special Purchase Planner
Can I afford that purchase?

On the right side of the Planning tab Activity Center are five links to planners for specific goals designed for Quicken by the Financial Planning Association. Each link displays a thorough interview that enables you to take a comprehensive look at each goal. Using the information you entered in the Plan Assumptions section, these planners provide additional questions for you to think about, links to resources on the Internet, and a complete list of your information in an easy-to-understand format, and then reviews each part of your plan for potential problems.

You can use these planners to enter information rather than use the Plan Assumptions dialog boxes or to make changes to the data you entered in those assumptions. Perhaps the most important planner in this group is the Debt Reduction Planner. It is difficult to create financial stability when you owe a large amount of debt.

Use the Debt Reduction Planner

With more credit card debt per person in the United States than ever in history, many people's debt load is overwhelming. Quicken's Debt Reduction Planner can help you pay less interest and take control of your debt before you are snowed under. To use the Debt Reduction Planner:

1. Click the **Planning** menu and click **Debt Reduction Planner**.

   –Or–

   Click **Debt Reduction Planner** on the right side of the Planning tab Activity Center under Planners. Either way, the Debt Reduction Planner is displayed.

2. Click the **Start** tab if it isn't already displayed. You are instructed to insert your Quicken CD into the CD-ROM drive before you continue with the Planner.

3. Insert your Quicken CD into the CD-ROM drive, click **Close** in the Install Quicken dialog box, and click **Next** in the Debt Reduction dialog box to continue. The first time you use the Debt Reduction Planner, a short video explaining the Debt Reduction Planner plays for 41 seconds. Click **Next** to continue.

WORK WITH THE DEBTS TAB

The Debts tab lists all of the loans and credit card debt you have entered into Quicken, the interest rate for each liability, and the current balance.

1. Click **Add** to add any debt you have not yet entered into Quicken. The Edit Debt Reduction dialog box appears. Click in each of the fields and select or type the information that is requested.

2. Click **OK**. If there is no Quicken account associated with this loan, a dialog box appears and asks if you would like Quicken to set up an account for the debt. Click **Yes** to set up an account. Follow the procedure outlined in Chapter 3.

3. If you need to change or remove any of your listed loans, click the loan and click **Edit** or **Remove**. If you are editing a loan, repeat steps 1–3. If you are removing a loan, click **Yes** to confirm that you want to permanently remove the debt from the plan.

4. After you have entered any new loans or changed any existing loans, click **Next**. The subsequent Debt Reduction Planner page shows how much you owe and your total monthly payment. At the bottom of the page, Quicken displays when you will be debt-free and how much interest you will have paid for your total outstanding debts.

Debt Reduction

Start | Debts | Order | Savings | Budget | Plan

How much do I owe?

The list shows your debts and the total amount you owe.
1. Review the debts in the list.
2. Update, add, or remove debts from the list.

Debt Name	Type	Balance	Rate
Credit Card	Credit Card	141.36	11.99%
Land at the Lake	Home Equity	125.00	7.5%
Loan from Aunt Mabel	Personal	12,294.34	7.5%
Loan From John	Personal	6,098.94	7.25%
House Loan	Mortgage	88,143.11	6.13%
Vacation Cabin Loan	Other	124,505.31	2.5%
Totals	**(6 debts)**	**231,308.06**	

Add
Edit
Remove
Update Debts

Cancel | Help | Back | Next

REVIEW THE ORDER TAB

The Order tab displays the optimum plan to get you debt-free in the shortest amount of time and paying the least amount of interest. From the second Debts tab:

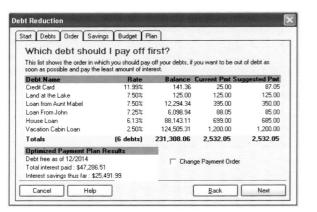

1. Click **Next** to open the **Order** tab. A message explains how Quicken determines the order in which debts should be paid off.

2. Click **Next** to display the order in which Quicken suggests you pay off your debt. At the bottom of the page, the Optimized Payment Plan Results are displayed, showing the new debt-free date, the total interest that would be paid, and the total savings in interest if this new plan is followed.

3. If you do not agree with Quicken, click **Change Payment Order** and then click **Next** to manually change the order in which the debts are paid. Select a debt and click either the **Move Up** or **Move Down** button to change the order. As you make the changes, the results are displayed on the left side of the page.

4. Click **Reset To Optimized Order** to return to Quicken's order. Click **Next** to open the Savings tab. The first time you run the Debt Reduction Planner, another video discusses using a one-time payment from your savings or investment account to reduce your debt.

USE THE SAVINGS TAB

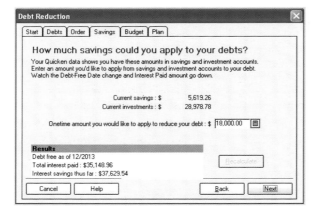

In the Savings tab, you are given the opportunity to see how making a one-time payment from your savings or investment accounts or both could reduce both your interest payments and the length of time it would take to become debt-free.

1. Click in the **Onetime Amount You Would Like To Apply To Reduce Your Debt** field, and enter a dollar amount to apply towards your debt.

2. Click **Recalculate** to see what result this payment would have. The results are displayed in the bottom-left area of the page.

3. Click **Next** to see another video discussing the budgeting process and open the Budget tab.

USING WHAT IFS

As you spend time creating plans for your financial future, Quicken provides a utility that allows you to quickly see the result of a possibility or a different path. The What If Scenarios allow you to change assumptions or make changes in each of the four different goal types: College, Home Purchase, Retirement, and Special Expense. You can save the new scenario or close the What If dialog box without saving your changes. Figure 9-8 illustrates a What If dialog box. To open the What If dialog box:

1. Click the **Planning** menu and click **What If Event Scenarios**.

2. Click the **Choose A Goal Type** down arrow, and select one of the four options. Each option has a different set of What Ifs with which you can work.

3. Click the **What If** option. A Quicken Planner dialog box appears.

4. Click the area that might change.

5. Click **Close** to close the dialog box. The result of this change is displayed in the Plan Result graph at the top of the What If dialog box.

6. Click **Reset What If** to revert to your original settings or assumptions.

7. Click **Save What If As Plan** to keep the change you entered.

8. Click **Close Without Saving** to return to the Planning tab Activity Center.

CUT EXPENSES IN THE BUDGET TAB AND SEE YOUR PLAN

The Budget tab displays how much you spend monthly, the top four discretionary categories. Each category displays the average amount you spend each month and allows you to enter an amount you can cut back.

1. Click in the **Amount To Cut Back** text box for each category, and enter how much you can decrease your spending in this category. The total amount that you will have available to apply to your debt each month is displayed at the bottom of the four categories.

2. Click **Recalculate** to see the result of your changes.

3. Click **Next**. The Plan tab is displayed and shows your Debt Reduction Plan.

4. Click **Print This Action Plan** to print the plan.

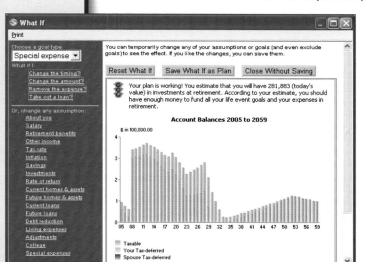

Figure 9-8: The What If dialog box allows you to see the financial effect of a possible event.

5. Click **Next** to open a dialog box that instructs Quicken to track this new plan.

6. Click **Alert Me If I Fall Behind** to create an alert for this plan.

7. Click **Set Up Scheduled Transactions For My Monthly Payments** to create scheduled transactions.

8. Click **Next** to see a graph that tracks how soon you will be debt-free. Click **Done** to display the graph on the entire screen.

9. Click **Update Debt Balances** in the menu bar of the Debt Reduction dialog box to update any balances not being tracked in Quicken.

10. Click **Payment Schedule** in the menu bar to see a detailed payment schedule. Click **Print** to print the new schedule, and click **Done** to close the dialog box.

11. Click **New Plan** in the menu bar of the Debt Reduction dialog box to redo your Debt Reduction Plan. A message appears, warning you that any new data will replace

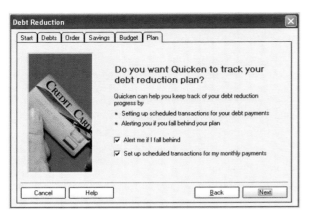

Calculators

Retirement Calculator
College Calculator
Refinance Calculator
Savings Calculator
Loan Calculator

the data in your current plan. Click **Yes** to create a new plan and open the Debt Reduction Planner once again. Click **No** to close the message.

12. Click **Close** to close the Debt Reduction window.

Use the Calculators, Budgets, and Other Tools

Quicken provides several additional sets of tools to help you achieve your financial goals. The Calculators provide a quick look at your financial situation for a particular event without having to enter all the data in Plan Assumptions. The Budget tool helps you create a budget manually or helps you guide Quicken to set it up automatically. The Professional Planning Resources link explains the various types of financial professionals to whom you can turn and, if one of your dreams is running your own business, Quicken has a tool to help you create a business plan for that as well.

Get Quick Answers with Calculators

The five Quicken Calculators—Retirement, College, Refinance, Savings, and Loan—help you to quickly calculate your current position without having to enter all of your assumptions. Each Calculator has different questions but performs in the same manner. We will use the Retirement Calculator as an example.

The Retirement Calculator lets you quickly see where you stand in your retirement preparations, as shown in Figure 9-9. To use it:

1. Click **Financial Overview** in the Account bar, and click the **Planning** tab.

2. Click **Retirement Calculator** on the right side of the Planning tab Activity Center.

3. Click in each of the fields, and select or type the information that is requested.

4. Click **Done** when you have finished.

192   Quicken 2006 QuickSteps   *Making Plans for Your Future*

CHOOSING A FINANCIAL SERVICE PROFESSIONAL

Financial professionals range from stock brokers to accountants to insurance agents. Each professional performs a specific service to help you achieve your goals. Quicken includes a detailed educational tool explaining the different roles.

1. Click **Financial Overview** in the Account bar, and click the **Planning** tab.

2. Click **Professional Planning Resources** under the Tools section on the right side of the Planning tab Activity Center. The Professional Planning Resources guide is displayed.

3. Click **Types Of Financial Service Professionals** in the left column to review each type.

4. Click **How A Professional Planner Can Help** to see some of the reasons you should consider when consulting such a professional.

5. Click **Compensation** to see how their fees are structured, and click **Questions To Ask** to display a list that may help you find the right professional for you.

6. Click **About The FPA** to learn what the Financial Professionals Association offers its clients, and click **Search Online For A CFP Professional** to find a certified financial planner (CFP) in your area.

7. Click **Prepare Your Personal Planner Summary** to create a list of information to give to a professional planner so he or she can be more informed about your needs and goals. Each section of this guide helps you find the person who meets your requirements.

8. Click **Print** in the menu bar to print the summary to take to your meeting with a professional.

9. Click **Close** to close the Professional Planning guide.

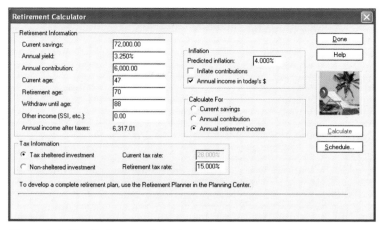

*Figure 9-9: **The Retirement Calculator allows you to quickly see retirement information for you or your spouse.***

Create a Budget

A budget is simply a formal spending plan. Whether you scribble it on the back of an envelope or create color-coded charts and graphs, a budget helps you understand where your money comes from and where it goes. Quicken provides a tool you can use to create a budget simply and quickly using the data you have already entered. There are two steps in budgeting: setting it up and then fine-tuning the income, expense, and savings information.

SET UP A BUDGET

To start your budget in Quicken:

1. Click **Financial Overview** in the Account bar, and click the **Planning** tab.

2. Click **Budget** in the Tools section on the right side of the Planning tab Activity Center. The Budget window opens.

3. Click the **Setup** tab to begin.

4. If you want Quicken to use your data to create an initial budget you can modify, click **Automatic**. If you want a blank budget template into which you can enter information, click **Manual**. Then, click **Create Budget**.

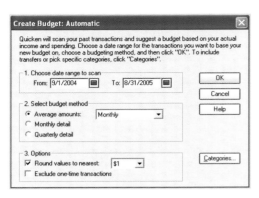

5. If you chose Automatic, the Create Budget: Automatic dialog box appears.

6. In the Choose Date Range To Scan area, enter a date range from which Quicken will create your budget.

7. In the Select Budget Method area, click the **Average Amounts** option, click the corresponding down arrow, and choose from a list of time periods for computing averages.

8. Click **Monthly Detail** or **Quarterly Detail** to have Quicken use these amounts rather than the averages.

9. In the Options area, click the **Round Values To Nearest** check box, click the corresponding down arrow, and choose the detail for rounding averages.

10. Click **Exclude One-Time Transactions** to eliminate these transactions from the calculation.

11. Click the **Categories** button to include or exclude accounts or categories from the calculations.

12. Click **OK** to create the budget. A message appears stating the budget has been created and that you are to use the tabs at the top of the Budget window to proceed.

13. Click **OK** to close the message box. The Budget window opens with the Income tab displayed.

FINE-TUNE THE BUDGET'S DETAILS

The Income, Expense, and Savings tabs in the Budget window display details pertaining to your budget based on the assumptions you chose in the previous procedure. If you want to make changes:

1. In the Income tab, click one of the categories and/or accounts, and then click one of the options on the right—**Average Amount**, **Monthly Detail**, or **Quarterly Detail**—to change the original method.

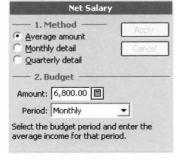

2. Click **Apply** to use this method.

3. Click **Amount** and enter another amount. Click the **Period** down arrow, and choose a time period. Click **Apply** to apply your changes.

4. Click the **Expense** tab and enter the method and/or amounts for each category. Click **Apply** to enter the changes, or click **Cancel** to delete the changes and accept the amounts shown by Quicken.

5. Click **Analyze** to see what the actual amounts were for a selected category during the last year.

6. Click in the **Notify Me When My Spending In This Category Exceeds** field, and enter a dollar amount or a percentage to create an alert.

7. Click the **Savings** tab to view and change your regular savings deposits, and click **Summary** to see your budget in both numerical and graphic format.

8. In all three tabs (Income, Expense, and Savings) you can add a new item to the budget. Click **Choose Categories** in the bottom-left area of the window, click the category or categories you want to add, and click **OK**. Then select the category you just added, click in the **Amount** text box on the right, enter an amount, and click **Apply**.

9. Click **Close** to close the Budget window.

Work with Your Budget

After you have taken the time to create your budget, you may change its focus to create reports, print the reports, and create graphs from the results.

1. Click the **Planning** menu and click **Budget**. The Budget window opens.

2. Click **Options** and click **Save Budget** to save your budget after you have created it.

3. Click **Options** again and select one of the three available budget views:

   - **Separate View** shows each set of categories—Income, Expense, and Savings—as separate tabs so that you can focus on one budget area at a time.

   - **Income/Expense View** includes income transfers and categories as part of the Income tab and expense transfers as part of the Expense tab.

   - **Combined View** includes all categories and transfers on one tab, the Budget tab, so that you can see all categories in one list.

4. Click **Reports** in the Budget menu bar, and select one of the three report options, each of which can be customized to meet your requirements:

   - **Budget Report** creates a standard report based on parameters you set.

   - **Monthly Budget Report** creates a report by month rather than by annual amounts.

   - **Monthly Budget Graph** graphically portrays how much over or under each item is compared to the budget for the time period you stipulate.

9

Chapter 10
Getting Ready for Tax Time

Tax preparation can be stressful and frustrating. You have to locate and organize your financial records, read complex publications, and fill out difficult-to-read forms. In many cases, it means writing a check to the federal and/or state government taxing authority and worrying about how much more you will owe next year. Quicken can lessen the burden. With its planning and organizational features, it can help you be ready well before the tax due date. Quicken also has a Tax Planner, a tool that helps you determine which deductions you can take, and another tool to help you decide how much withholding you should claim. You can access additional tools online through the links provided in the Tax tab of the Financial Overview Activity Center. With Quicken, April 15 can be just another day in your smooth financial life.

Use the Tax Planner

The basis for all of your tax information can be entered into the Tax Planner. The Planner helps you evaluate your income tax position. It bases its estimates on numbers you give it, on the data you've entered into Quicken, or on last year's TurboTax return. It covers such areas as your employment income, interest, and dividends you earn; deductions and exemptions; withholding; and other taxes or credits for which you may be liable. Figure 10-1 shows an example of the Tax Planner Summary worksheet. If you entered information using Guided Setup, the Tax Planner starts with that information; however, you can change it at any time.

Figure 10-1: The Tax Planner Summary worksheet displays information from Quicken, TurboTax, or that you enter yourself.

Enter the Tax Planner Options

If you did not use Quicken Guided Setup to enter the information about yourself, the Tax Planner uses the Quicken default settings. These settings appear in the upper-left area of the Tax Planner.

To change these settings:

1. Click the **Tax** menu and click **Tax Planner**. The Tax Planner is displayed.

2. If the Tax Planner options are not displayed in the right pane, click **Year** in the left pane to display them. While you can click the **Year** down arrow to choose another year for which to plan, there are only a few instances in which you want and can do it, such as the first quarter of a year in which you may still be working with the previous year. The default is the current year.

3. If you change the year, a message box appears. Click your answer, and then click **OK** to close the dialog box.

4. Click the **Filing Status** down arrow to change your income tax filing status from the default, **Married Filing Jointly**, to your status. If you are not sure of your status, consult your tax professional.

5. Click the **Scenario** down arrow to create a new scenario. You can create up to three scenarios in the Tax Planner. For example, if you are thinking of starting a small

NOTE

Most of the tasks performed with the Tax Planner and the other Quicken tax-related tools are easily done with *worksheets* in which Quicken fills in numbers it knows about, you enter other numbers or correct the ones Quicken automatically entered, and then Quicken summarizes these amounts and does the necessary calculations.

NOTE

The Tax Planner is only available in Quicken Deluxe, Premier, and Premier Home & Business editions.

business, you could enter information about your projected income in a second scenario to see how it would affect your tax situation.

6. Click **Next**. The How Can Quicken Help With Tax Planning page is displayed. If you see the Tax Planner Summary instead, which means that the Tax Planner has been used in the past, click **How Can Quicken Help With Tax Planning** in the left pane.

7. Click **More Details** to learn more about the Planner. This opens a Help window displaying information about using the Tax Planner. When you are finished, click **Close** to return to the Tax Planner.

8. Click **Let's Get Started** to display the Tax Planner Summary.

Enter Income into the Tax Planner

Start the Planner by entering your income information.

1. If the Tax Planner isn't already displayed, click the **Tax** menu, click **Tax Planner**, and click **Wages** on the left or click **Wages And Salaries** in the Tax Planner Summary. The Wages worksheet is displayed.

Wages	
Wages and Salaries - Self	32,000
Wages and Salaries - Self (Other)	0
Wages and Salaries - Spouse	15,000
Wages and Salaries - Spouse (Other)	0
Total Wages	47,000
Remaining Tax Due	**2,946**

2. Click in the **Wages And Salaries – Self** text box. Enter the amount of wages or salary you expect to earn for the year. After you enter the information, your projected tax due or refund due is computed and displayed.

3. Click in the **Wages and Salaries – Self (Other)** text box, and enter the taxable amounts from Employee Stock Purchase Plan (ESPP) shares or from the sale of nonqualified-employee stock options. Check with your tax professional to see if either of these options applies to you.

4. Click in the **Wages And Salaries – Spouse** text box, and enter your spouse's wages.

5. Click in the **Wages And Salaries – Spouse (Other)** text box, and enter any ESPP taxable amounts. The total wages for the both of you is displayed in the Total Wages field.

6. Click **Next** to continue to the Interest And Dividend Income worksheet.

USING THE TAX LINE IN CATEGORIES

You have the option to include tax information when entering a new category.

1. Click the **Tools** menu and click **Category List**.

2. Click **New** in the bottom-left area of the window to enter a new category, or select an existing category and click **Edit**.

3. Click the **Tax Line Item** down arrow to display a list of possible tax-line items. These items are arranged by IRS form number and schedule letter. Check with your tax professional if you have questions about the meaning of each tax line. Click the name of the tax item.

Edit Category	
Name:	Finance Charge
Description:	Finance Charge Income
Group:	

Type
- Income
- Expense
- Subcategory of

Tax
Tax line item:
Schedule C:Other business income

☑ Tax-related ● Standard line item list ○ Extended line item list

Miscellaneous income related to the business that is not included in gross receipts (e.g., recovery of bad debts, scrap sales, interest on notes or accounts receivable). Interest earned on business bank accounts is included on

4. Click **Extended Line Item List** if the item you need does not appear on the standard line item list.

5. Click the **Tax-Related** check box.

6. Click **OK** to close the Edit Category dialog box.

Enter Interest, Dividend, and Business Income

If you have received forms from your financial institutions, such as 1099-INTs or partnership K-1s, use the information shown on these forms. Otherwise, enter estimates in this area.

1. If the Tax Planner isn't already open, click the **Tax** menu, click **Tax Planner**, and click **Interest/Dividend Inc** in the left pane.

2. Click in the **Taxable Interest Income** text box, and enter the amount of taxable interest you will receive for the year from savings or money market accounts.

3. Click in the **Dividends** text box, and enter all the amounts reported on K-1 forms from mutual funds, stocks, partnerships, estates, trusts, or S corporations. If you have not yet received a K-1 form, estimate the amount that you received.

4. Click **Next** to display the Business Income worksheet.

5. If you have a small business, use this worksheet to enter the information from your Schedule C (see Figure 10-2) or from a profit-and-loss statement.

6. Click in the **Revenue – Self** text box, and enter the total revenue for your business. Click in the **Revenue Spouse** text box, and enter the revenue for your spouse's business.

7. Click in the **Cost Of Goods Sold** text box, and enter the costs of the items you sold for each business. After you have entered the cost of goods sold, the gross margin appears. The gross margin is the total revenue less the total cost of goods sold.

8. If you have associated any expense category with a Tax Schedule C line, that amount will appear in the Other Allowable Expenses field. Click in the **Other**

Business Income or Loss - Schedule C

	SELF	SPOUSE
Revenue	850	0
Cost of Goods Sold	225	0
Gross Margin	625	0
Meals/Entertainment Expense	195	0
Deductible Meals/Entertainment	97	0
Other Allowable Expenses	485	0
Total Expenses	582	0
Exp. for Business Use of Home	0	0
Business Income or Loss	43	0
Remaining Tax Due		2,946

Flagged items do not appear to be complete. Click on them to examine how Quicken has determined this value.

Figure 10-2: If you operate a small business, enter the data from a financial statement.

CAUTION

There are some very specific rules about using your home or part of it for your business. Consult your tax professional for more information.

NOTE

You may receive information from your broker that some of your investments have *unrealized* capital gains. That means that an investment hasn't been sold yet but would give you a profit if you did sell it.

CAUTION

When you use the Capital Gains And Losses worksheet, make sure you understand which type of gain or loss, short-term or long-term, you are entering. In this, as in all areas, it is important that you consult with your tax professional.

NOTE

Unrecaptured depreciation is a special type of gain that may apply when you sell real property you have previously depreciated, as you might with a home office or a day-care center in your home. Consult your tax professional if you feel this might apply to you.

Allowable Expenses text box to change the amount. After you have entered the amount for these expenses, Quicken calculates your total expenses.

9. Click in the **Exp. For Business Use Of Home** text box, and enter the amount you allot for the business use of your home. The total business income or loss amount is displayed for each business, as well as the total remaining tax due.

10. Click **Next** to display the Capital Gains And Losses worksheet.

Enter Capital Gains

Before you can enter information into the Capital Gains And Losses worksheet, you must know whether a gain is a short-term or a long-term gain. See the QuickFacts "Determining the Type of Capital Gain" later in this chapter. A capital gain is the difference between the price for which you have sold an asset and the price you paid for it. You *realize*, or achieve, a capital gain when you sell an investment for more than you paid for it. You may owe federal income tax (and in some cases, state income tax) on that capital gain. Capital gains are earned on many types of investments, including mutual funds, bonds, stocks, homes, and businesses. If you sell an investment for less than you paid for it, you have a *capital loss*.

1. If the Tax Planner isn't already open, click the **Tax** menu, click **Tax Planner**, and click **Capital Gains** in the left pane.

2. Click in the **Short-Term Gains And Losses** text box, and enter the result you get when you subtract your short-term losses from any short-term gains.

3. Click in the **Unrecaptured Depreciation Gains** text box, and enter any unrecaptured depreciation you have.

4. Click in the **Long-Term 28% Gains And Losses** text box, and enter the gains or losses you have that fall into this tax category.

5. Click in the **Long-Term Gains And Losses** text box, and enter the amount of your long-term gains or losses.

6. Click in the **Loss Carryovers From Prior Years Short Term** and **Long Term** text boxes, and enter any losses from previous years that you had to carry over to this year.

7. Click **Next** to display the Other Income Or Losses worksheet.

Work with Other Income or Losses

The Other Income Or Losses worksheet allows you to enter information that affects your tax situation but that is not covered in other areas of the Tax Planner. These items include taxable state income tax refunds, alimony, taxable Social Security benefits, and so on. As with all items in the Tax Planner, review your entries and discuss them with your tax professional.

1. If the Tax Planner isn't already open, click the **Tax** menu, click **Tax Planner**, and click **Other Income** in the left pane. Figure 10-3 displays a typical Other Income Or Losses worksheet.

Other Income or Losses	
Taxable Refund of State/Local Income Tax	29
Alimony Received	0
Taxable IRA/Pension Distributions	0
Sched E Income - Rents, Royalties and Partnerships	0
Sched F Income - Farm	0
Unemployment Compensation	990
Taxable Social Security Benefits	0
Social Security RRA Income	0
Other Income, Gains or Losses	0
Total Other Income or Losses	1,019
Remaining Tax Due	**3,099**

Flagged items do not appear to be complete. Click on them to examine how Quicken has determined this value.

2. Click in the **Taxable Refund Of State/Local Income Tax** text box, and enter any refund of state or local taxes that you deducted as an itemized deduction on your federal tax return.

3. Click in the **Alimony Received** text box, and enter the total amount of alimony received by either you or your spouse for the year.

Figure 10-3: Enter other income, such as alimony, into the Other Income Or Losses worksheet in your Tax Planner.

4. Click in the **Taxable IRA/Pension Distributions** text box, and enter any amounts shown on a Form 1099-R. These items can be complex. Check with your tax professional or consult IRS Publications 575 and 590.

5. Click the **Sched E Income – Rents, Royalties, And Partnerships** link. A corresponding worksheet is displayed:

   a. Click in the **Rents** text box, and enter any rental income you have received.

   b. Click in the **Royalties** and **Partnership Income/Loss** text boxes, and enter the relevant amounts. Quicken will calculate your total income from these items.

   c. Click in the **Depreciation** text box, and enter the total depreciation you claim on these items. Click in the **Expenses** text box, and enter any expenses relating to your rent income. Quicken calculates your net income or loss and displays it at the bottom of the worksheet.

   d. Click **Previous** to return to the Other Income Or Losses worksheet.

6. Click the **Sched F Income – Farm** link. The Farm Income worksheet is displayed.

   a. Click in the **Sales** text box, and enter the total sales from farming.

   b. Click in the **Supplemental Payments** and **Other Income** text boxes, and enter the relevant amounts. Quicken calculates the total income and displays it.

   c. Click in the **Expenses** text box, and enter the total expenses that pertain to farming. Quicken calculates the net income or loss from farming.

   d. Click **Previous** twice to return to the Other Income Or Losses worksheet.

7. Click in the **Unemployment Compensation** text box, and enter the amount of unemployment benefits you received (or will receive) for this year.

8. Click in the **Taxable Social Security Benefits** or **Social Security RRA Income** text boxes, and enter the relevant amount.

9. Click in the **Other Income, Gains, Or Losses** text box, and enter money you won as a prize or award, jury duty stipends, or other such one-time income. You may receive a 1099 or other documentation showing the total taxable amount.

10. Click **Next** three times or click **Adjustments** in the left pane to display the Adjustments To Income worksheet.

Work with Income Adjustments and Deductions

After entering all your income, you need to consider those items that reduce your income before taxes. These are primarily income adjustments, deductions, exemptions, and tax credits.

ENTER ADJUSTMENT TO INCOME

Adjustments to income are those items that, while not deductible, reduce your income. They include Individual Retirement Account (IRA) contributions, health insurance paid by self-employed persons, Keogh or SEP contributions, alimony you have paid, moving expenses, and other adjustments.

1. If the Tax Planner isn't already open, click the **Tax** menu, click **Tax Planner**, and click **Adjustments** in the left pane.

NOTE

The Tax Planner does not determine which, if any, of your Social Security or RRA income is taxable. The instruction booklet that comes with your 1040 form has a worksheet to help you determine how much, if any, is taxable. You can also consult your tax professional.

Adjustments to Income

Allowable IRA Deduction (Not all IRA Contributions are Deductible)	2,500
One-Half of Self-Employment-Tax	0
Allowable S.E. Health Insurance Deduction	0
Keogh/SEP Deduction	250
Penalty on Early Withdrawal of Savings	0
Alimony Paid	0
Moving Expenses	0
Other Adjustments	0
Total Adjustments	2,750

2. Click in each text box, and enter the relevant amounts if any of these items pertain to you.

3. Click **Next** to display the Standard And Itemized Deductions worksheet.

ENTER STANDARD AND ITEMIZED DEDUCTIONS

According to the IRS, most people take the standard deduction to reduce their income tax bill. However, if you pay high mortgage interest payments or have large medical bills, itemizing your deductions might reduce your tax liability even more. Quicken provides a Deduction Finder to help you with this. See "Use the Deduction Finder" later in this chapter.

1. If the Tax Planner isn't already open, click the **Tax** menu, click **Tax Planner**, and click **Deductions** in the left pane.

2. Click in the **Medical And Dental Expense** field to enter all of your medical and dental expenses for the year. Quicken will compute the amount of your deduction, if you can take one, and display it in the Allowable Medical Deduction area. If you cannot take a deduction, the Allowable Medical Deduction area shows zero.

3. If your state or locality has an income tax, click **State & Local Income Tax** to display the State And Local Income Tax worksheet. If there are figures already filled in from the paycheck detail you entered and you believe that it is correct, you can skip to step 4. Otherwise:

   a. Click in the **Withholdings To Date** text box, and enter the state or local withholding amounts for you and your spouse through your last paychecks. This information should appear on your pay stubs.

   b. Click in the **Next Pay Date** text box, and enter the date on which you will receive your next paychecks.

State and Local Income Tax		
Projected Withholdings	SELF	SPOUSE
Withholdings To Date	950	0
Next Pay Date	10/15/05	10/15/05
Pay Period	Every 2 weeks	Every 2 weeks
Withholding per Pay Period	15	0
Projected Future Withholding	90	0
Projected Total Withholding	1,040	0
Projected Total Withholdings for Self and Spouse		1,040
Estimated Taxes Paid to Date plus Projected Payments Through Year-End		0
Tax Payments this Year for Last Year's State Tax		0
Total Tax Payments to Date plus Projected Withholding Through Year-End		1,040

   c. Click the **Pay Period** down arrow, and choose how often each of you is paid.

   d. Click in the **Withholding Per Pay Period** text box, and enter the amount of state or local taxes withheld from your paychecks.

QUICKFACTS

DEDUCTING STATE SALES TAX

The American Jobs Creation Bill of 2004 allows taxpayers to deduct state and local sales tax from their tax returns if they itemize their deductions. However, you should consider the following:

• To take the deduction, you must itemize deductions.

• If you live in a state that collects income tax, you must choose to deduct either the state (or local) income tax you paid or the sales tax deduction—you cannot deduct both.

• You can add up the sales tax you paid from your cash register and credit card receipts to determine your deduction. This requires that you keep these receipts with your income tax records for the year.

• Alternatively, you can use the appropriate amount from the sales tax tables created by the IRS. These tables are included in your Form 1040 packet and are also available online at the IRS web site.

Exemptions

Number of Exemptions	
Self and Spouse	2
Dependents	2
Total Exemptions	4
Exemption deduction	12,800

---

e. Click in the **Estimated Taxes Paid To Date Plus Projected Payments Through Year-End** text box, and enter how much tax you have paid to the IRS or how much has been withheld to date as the basis for state and local taxes.

f. Click in the **Tax Payments This Year For Last Year's State Tax** text box, and enter any amounts you have paid in state income tax during this calendar year.

g. Quicken calculates what your total payments for state and local income taxes will be.

h. Click **Previous** to return to the Standard And Itemized Deductions worksheet.

4. Click in the **Real Estate And Other Taxes** text box, and enter the amount of real estate taxes you have paid or will pay for the current year.

5. Click in the **Deductible Investment Interest** text box, and enter the relevant amount.

6. Click in the **Mortgage & Other Deductible Interest** text box, and enter your mortgage interest as shown on the Form 1098 you received from your mortgage company.

7. Click in the **Charitable Contributions** text box, and enter the amount of money you have given to charity for the current year. The Tax Planner will adjust your deduction to comply with IRS regulations.

8. Click in the **Deductible Casualty Losses** text box, and enter any losses in this category. To understand what you can deduct, consult your tax professional.

9. Click in the **Misc. Deductions** and **Misc. Deductions (No Limit)** text boxes, and enter any qualifying deductions. Quicken will calculate your total itemized deductions.

10. In the Standard Deduction column, click any check box that pertains to your situation. The amount of your standard deduction appears in the Deduction field. If your itemized deductions are larger than your standard deduction, the larger amount appears in the Larger Of Itemized Or Standard Deduction field.

11. Click **Next** twice to display the Exemptions worksheet.

12. If you have entered the number of members in your family in Quicken Guided Setup, the information about your situation is already displayed. If you did not use Guided Setup, enter the relevant information and click **Next** to display the Other Taxes And Credits worksheet. The information you entered earlier regarding your self-employment

income is already included on this worksheet. If your tax professional tells you that you are subject to the alternative minimum tax, enter any relevant information; otherwise, click **Next** to display the Federal Withholdings worksheet.

Update Your Federal Withholdings

The Withholdings worksheet may already display information you have entered, either from your paycheck setup or on earlier worksheets of the Tax Planner. If not, enter the information as needed.

In the center of the worksheet, the Tax Payment Summary displays your projected tax and your projected withholdings from the Total Withholdings To Date amount. Your estimated tax due or refund due has been calculated by Quicken, as shown in Figure 10-4.

NOTE

The Tax Withholding Estimator helps you determine how much to withhold from your paycheck. See "Use the Tax Withholding Estimator" later in this chapter for more information.

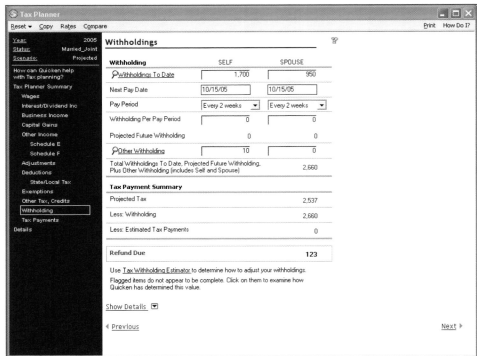

Figure 10-4: The Withholdings worksheet displays your projected withholdings as well as your current tax or refund due.

The Tax Planner may include Turbo Tax data from prior years if you imported that data into your Quicken folder.

You may also be eligible for tax credits, such as the Lifetime Learning Credit or the Earned Income Credit. Check with your tax professional or look for IRS Publication 17 at www.irs.gov.

Figure 10-5: After you have entered all of your information, the Tax Planner Summary worksheet displays the results.

Click **Tax Planner Summary** in the left margin to see the result of your entries into the Tax Planner. Figure 10-5 shows a sample Tax Planner Summary.

Work with the Tax Tab

The Tax tab of the Financial Overview Activity Center provides an overview of your tax standing at any time during the year. It shows all of your tax alerts, the tax calendar, all of your taxable income for the year, any tax-related expenses, and your projected taxes, and it offers a variety of tools to help you plan. All of this information is based on data you have entered. You can adjust this data, add to it, and create reports based on it. While ultimately all tax questions

SETTING TAX ALERTS

At the top of the Tax tab in the Financial Overview Activity Center are the tax alerts.

1. Click **Set Up Alerts** and choose from the three tax sections.

2. Click **Withholding Threshold** in the left pane, click in the **Withholding Threshold** text box, and type a threshold for your projected tax liability. For example, if you type $100 as the threshold, Quicken will alert you if your withholdings are projected to be less or more than $100 of what you will owe based on the information you entered. You should consult your tax professional to ensure you've entered the appropriate information.

3. Click **Schedule A – Personal Deductions** in the left pane, and make any desired changes in the right pane to be alerted to possible personal deductions, such as employee moving expenses or personal use of an automobile for business purposes.

4. Click **Important Tax Dates** in the left pane to have Quicken remind of you filing dates, such as April 15. These dates are displayed in the Tax tab in the Tax Calendar section.

All alerts can be set to display as a dialog box or as text in the Alert List.

should be reviewed with your tax professional, Quicken provides a host of useful tools and reports to help you. To see what information is currently available in the Tax tab:

● Click the **Tax** menu and click **Go To Tax Center**. The Financial Overview Activity Center appears with the Tax tab displayed, as shown in Figure 10-6.

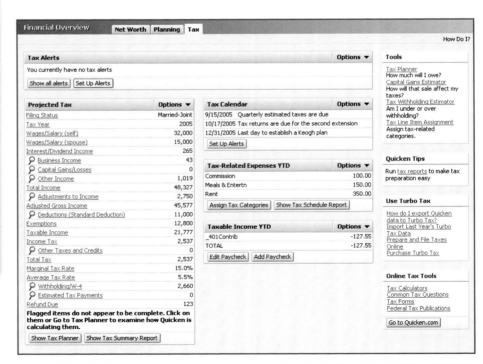

Figure 10-6: The Tax tab gives an overview of your tax information and provides you with links to several tax tools.

The Tax Calendar, which appears midway down the Tax tab, displays the important tax dates for the current year in addition to any tax alerts you have set up.

Tax Calendar   Options ▼

9/15/2005	Quarterly estimated taxes are due
10/17/2005	Tax returns are due for the second extension
12/31/2005	Last day to establish a Keogh plan

Set Up Alerts

TIP

The Projected Tax section of the Tax tab displays the information you entered into Quicken or the Tax Planner. You can click any of the links to go to the Tax Planner for that link.

Projected Tax   Options ▼

Filing Status	Married-Joint
Tax Year	2005
Wages/Salary (self)	32,000
Wages/Salary (spouse)	15,000
Interest/Dividend Income	265
Business Income	43
Capital Gains/Losses	0
Other Income	1,019
Total Income	48,327
Adjustments to Income	2,750
Adjusted Gross Income	45,577
Deductions (Standard Deduction)	11,000
Exemptions	12,800
Taxable Income	21,777
Income Tax	2,537
Other Taxes and Credits	0
Total Tax	2,537
Marginal Tax Rate	15.0%
Average Tax Rate	5.5%
Withholding/W-4	2,660
Estimated Tax Payments	0
Refund Due	123

Flagged items do not appear to be complete. Click on them or Go to Tax Planner to examine how Quicken is calculating them.

Show Tax Planner   Show Tax Summary Report

NOTE

You can assign tax lines to categories by clicking the **Tax Line Item Assignment** link under Tools on the right side of the Tax tab.

Assign Tax-Related Expenses and See Your Taxable Income

The Tax-Related Expenses YTD section of the Tax tab helps you track any tax-related expenses. To assign a tax line to an expense category:

Tax-Related Expenses YTD   Options ▼

Commission	100.00
Meals & Entertn	150.00
Rent	350.00

Assign Tax Categories   Show Tax Schedule Report

1. Click **Assign Tax Categories** at the bottom of the Tax-Related Expenses YTD section to open the Category List.

2. Select the category to which you want to assign a tax line, scroll to the right, and click the **Tax** check box for that category.

3. Click **Standard List** under the Tax Line Item Assignments section on the right of the window.

4. Click the **Tax Item** down arrow, and click the tax line that is relevant for the category. If the tax item you want to assign does not appear on the Standard List, click **Extended List** to include more tax items.

5. Click **Close** to return to the Tax tab.

Tax Line Item Assignments

⊙ Standard list   ○ Extended list

Tax item:

Form 1040:Alimony received ▼

Form 1040:Alimony received
Form 1040:Social Security income, self
Form 1040:Fed tax w/h, Soc. Sec.,self
Form 1040:Social Security inc., spouse
Form 1040:Fed tax w/h,Soc. Sec.,spouse
Form 1040:RR retirement income, self
Form 1040:Fed tax w/h, RR retire,self
Form 1040:RR retirement inc., spouse
Form 1040:Fed tax w/h,RR retire,spouse
Form 1040:Other income, misc.
Form 1040:IRA contribution, self
Form 1040:IRA contribution, spouse
Form 1040:Keogh deduction, self
Form 1040:Keogh deduction, spouse
Form 1040:SEP deduction, self
Form 1040:SEP deduction, spouse
Form 1040:SIMPLE contribution, self
Form 1040:SIMPLE contribution, spouse

The Taxable Income YTD section gives you a link to set up your paycheck if you have not already done so. For information on using the Paycheck Setup Wizard, see Chapter 5.

Use the Tools in the Tax Tab

On the right side of the Tax tab are tools you can use to help with your tax planning.

- The **Tax Planner**, which is covered earlier in this chapter, helps you determine how much you will owe in taxes.

- The **Capital Gains Estimator** helps you determine the tax implications of selling assets and investments. This wizard gives you general information about potential sales but does not substitute for a financial

Tools

Tax Planner
How much will I owe?
Capital Gains Estimator
How will that sale affect my taxes?
Tax Withholding Estimator
Am I under or over withholding?
Tax Line Item Assignment
Assign tax-related categories.

CREATING TAX REPORTS

On the right side of the Tax tab are links to other helpful tools.

Click **Tax Reports** under Quicken Tips, or, if you don't see it there, click the **Reports** menu and click **Tax**. Six reports are displayed designed specifically for taxes. These reports are only available in Quicken Premier and Quicken Premier Home & Business editions:

▼ Tax
☐ Capital Gains
☐ Schedule A-Itemized Deduction
☐ Schedule B-Interest and Dividends
☐ Schedule D-Capital Gains and Losses
☐ Tax Schedule (for export to Turbo Tax)
☐ Tax Summary

- **Capital Gains** creates a report that shows any gains you have realized from the sale of assets or securities.

- **Schedule A-Itemized Deduction** prepares a transaction report that is subtotaled by each item on Schedule A of Form 1040.

- **Schedule B-Interest And Dividends** creates a transaction report that is subtotaled by each item on Schedule B items of Form 1040.

- **Schedule D-Capital Gains And Losses** prepares a report of all gains and losses reportable on Schedule D.

- **Tax Schedule (For Export To TurboTax)** prepares a report of all of your tax-related transactions and is specifically meant to be exported to TurboTax for preparing your tax return.

- **Tax Summary** creates a report of all your tax-related transactions subtotaled by category.

or tax advisor. You can create up to three scenarios that combine with the information you entered into the Tax Planner. This wizard is discussed in Chapter 9.

- The **Tax Withholding Estimator**, which is covered at the end of this chapter, helps you determine whether you are having the appropriate amount withheld from your earnings.

- The **Tax Line Item Assignment** allows you to assign specific lines on a federal tax form to your income and expense categories, and is covered in the preceding section.

Use TurboTax and Online Tax Tools

For additional tax tools and help, Quicken gives you links to the TurboTax web site, several tax calculators, answers to common tax questions, tax forms, and federal tax publications.

USE TURBOTAX LINKS

The four links in the Use TurboTax section on the right of the Tax tab give you specific instructions on integrating your Quicken data with TurboTax:

- **How Do I Export Quicken Data To TurboTax** opens a step-by-step Help window detailing the procedure.

- **Import Last Year's TurboTax Data** opens the Import TurboTax File window from which you can choose last year's file and follow the on-screen instructions.

Use Turbo Tax

How do I export Quicken data to Turbo Tax?
Import Last Year's Turbo Tax Data
Prepare and File Taxes Online
Purchase Turbo Tax

- **Prepare And File Taxes Online** opens the TurboTax Online window from which you can create your tax return using a Web-based product.

- **Purchase TurboTax** facilitates ordering the product on a CD.

USE THE ONLINE TAX TOOLS

The several links displayed in the Online Tax Tools section of the Tax tab are direct connections to the TurboTax web site. From that web site, you can use not only the tools shown, but also find other tax-planning tools, such as the FAQ On Estimated Taxes.

Explore the Tax Menu

The Tax menu offers additional links to tax tools and planners. While many of the tools are available from the Tax tab, others are more quickly accessible from this menu.

Use Tax Menu Items

From the Tax menu you can access the Tax tab or the Tax Planner. You can open the Category List and assign tax-line times to specific categories. You can also access a utility that allows you to find potential errors in your category assignments.

1. Click the **Tax** menu and click **Tax Category Audit**. If Quicken does not detect a problem, you will see a message to that effect. If Quicken does find a problem, the Tax Category Audit window will open, as shown in Figure 10-7. This utility checks two categories:

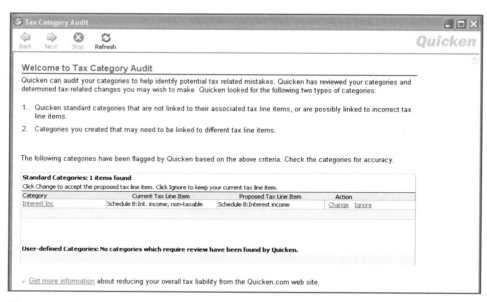

Figure 10-7: The Tax Category Audit window warns you of potentially incorrect tax-line assignments.

- Standard categories that are not linked to the correct tax line.
- Categories you created that may need to be linked to a tax-line item or categories that are linked to an incorrect tax-line item.

2. Click **Change** to open the Edit Selected Tax Audit Category dialog box, which displays a list of possible problem categories in each area:

   a. Click the **Tax Line Item** down arrow, and click the correct line item.

   b. Click **OK** to close the dialog box.

3. Click **Ignore** if you feel the tax-line assignment is correct, and the category is removed from the problem list.

4. Click **Close** to close the window.

Use the Deduction Finder

If you are not sure you have assigned tax-line items for all of your categories, or if you would just like to identify other potential deductions, you can use the Deduction Finder.

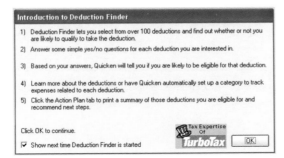

1. Click the **Tax** menu and click **Deduction Finder**. The Introduction To Deduction Finder dialog box appears explaining how it works.

2. Click **OK** to continue, and if it isn't already open, click the **Deductions** tab to begin the process.

3. Click the **Choose A Deduction Type** down arrow, and click one of the six types of deductions. A list of deductions appears on the left side of the window.

4. Click any item on the list to display questions about that possible deduction on the right side of the window. Click either **Yes** or **No** to answer each question, as shown in Figure 10-8.

5. After you have answered all the questions, a green check mark appears to the left of any deduction for which you may be eligible and a red X appears if you are not eligible. The result also is displayed at the bottom of the section.

6. Click **More Information** at the bottom of the window if you want to learn more about this deduction. Click **Create A Category** to display an explanation about a potential new category for this deduction, and then click **OK** to create it.

7. Click **Next Deduction** to go to the next deduction on the list, or select one that may pertain to your situation, and follow the same steps.

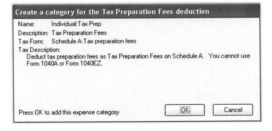

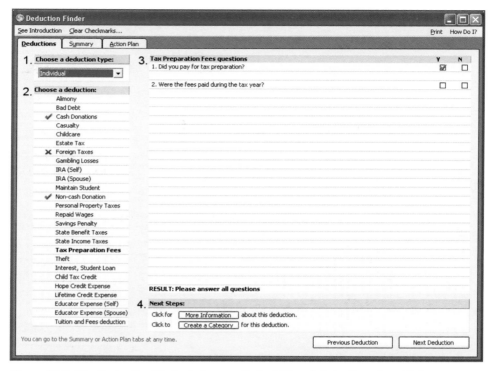

Figure 10-8: The Deduction Finder helps you find additional deductions for which you may be eligible.

TIP

If you are a teacher, you may have an additional deduction. Check the IRS regulations for the Educator Expense Deduction. Certain tuition, fees, and student loan interest may also be deductible. Check with your tax professional.

8. Click the **Summary** tab to see how many deductions are available for each deduction type, how many you have viewed and answered, and how many for which you are eligible.

9. Click the **Action Plan** tab to see the steps to take to use the deductions you have found.

10. Click **Clear Checkmarks** in the menu bar to clear all of your answers and start over.

11. Click **Close** to close the Deduction Finder.

CAUTION

Some people are not eligible to take the standard deduction and therefore must itemize. For example, if you are married and filing a separate return and your spouse itemizes, you must itemize as well. Refer to IRS publications for more specific rules on who must itemize.

Use the Itemized Deduction Estimator

You can take a wide variety of tax deductions, some of which are more common than others. Quicken provides the Itemized Deduction Estimator to ensure that you are deducting all to which you are entitled. It uses information from the Tax Planner and lets you create what-if scenarios. To use the Itemized Deduction Estimator:

1. Click the **Tax** menu and click **Itemized Deduction Estimator**. A welcome message appears, shown in Figure 10-9. The Itemized Deduction Estimator displays your projected data as you entered it in the Tax Planner.

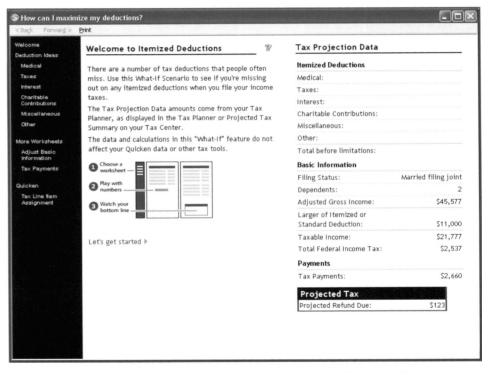

Figure 10-9: The Itemized Deduction Estimator can help you identify less well-known deductions.

2. Click **Let's Get Started** to begin the process.

3. The Medical Deductions worksheet is displayed. Each worksheet in this wizard displays the tax projection data on the right side so you can see any changes. As you make entries into the scenario, your projected tax bill changes if your scenario information decreases your liability.

4. Click in the **Miles Driven To And From Appointments** text box, and enter the number of miles you drove. Quicken will calculate the dollar value that is deductible, as shown in Figure 10-10.

5. Click in the other text boxes, select or type the requested information, and click **Next** as needed to proceed. When you have finished, click **Close** to close the Estimator.

NOTE

None of the amounts and data entered in the Itemized Deduction Estimator affects either your Quicken data or the data in the other tax tools. The Estimator only creates a what-if scenario.

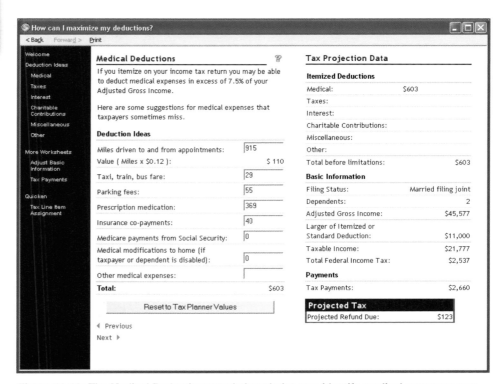

Figure 10-10: The Medical Deductions worksheet helps you identify medical expenses you may not have remembered otherwise.

TIP

Check with your tax professional to ensure that you are withholding the proper amount. This is especially true if you have income from an at-home business.

Use the Tax Withholding Estimator

The Tax Withholding Estimator Wizard allows you to determine how much you should have taken out of each paycheck. You can create a what-if scenario to ensure that you are not withholding too much or too little.

1. Click the **Tax** menu and click **Tax Withholding Estimator**. The Tax Withholding Estimator is displayed, as shown in Figure 10-11. Each worksheet has two parts. The left section allows you to enter possible changes. The right side displays the tax-projection data reflecting the current information you have entered into Quicken or into your Tax Planner. As you make changes on the left side, the right side displays the result of those changes.

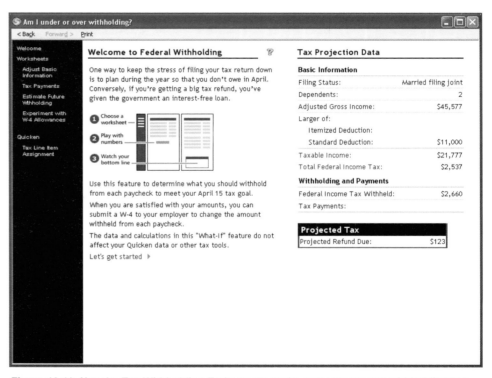

Figure 10-11: Use the Tax Withholding Estimator to make sure you are not withholding too much or too little from your paycheck.

2. Click **Let's Get Started** to display the Adjust Basic Information worksheet.

3. Click the **Filing Status** down arrow to choose another filing status, if necessary.

4. Click the **Dependents** spinner up or down to increase or decrease the number of dependents.

5. Enter any changes in the **Adjusted Gross Income** and/or **Itemized Deductions** fields.

6. Click **Next** to display the Tax Payments worksheet.

7. Click in the **Tax Payments** text box, and enter any additional payments you will be making by the end of the year.

8. Click **Next** to display the Estimate Future Withholding worksheet.

9. Enter any amounts that you want to change for yourself or your spouse. If you don't want to make any changes, or after you have made changes, click **Next** to display the Experiment With W-4 Allowances worksheet.

10. Click in the **Taxable Wages Per Pay Period** text boxes, and enter the amounts of gross wages for yourself and your spouse. This information can usually be found on your pay stub.

11. Click in the **W-4 Allowances** text boxes, and enter how many allowances you and your spouse have claimed on your latest W-4s.

12. Click in the **Additional Withholding Per Pay Period** text boxes, and enter any additional amounts you have asked your employers to withhold. The Total Withholding Per Pay Period is calculated and displayed.

13. Click **W-4 Information** to create a printed worksheet you can take to work and use to complete a new W-4.

14. Click **Form W-4 On Quicken.com** to open and print an actual W-4 from the IRS web site.

NOTE

You should provide your employer with a new W-4 each January.

Note: Italicized page numbers denote definitions of terms.

for restoring tool bar settings, 25
for Scheduled Transaction List, 92, 95
for Security List, 156
for View Loans dialog box, 111, 113, 114, 115
for Windows and Quicken, 30

L

labels under tool bar icons, changing, 25
liability accounts
    adding, 60–61
    description of, 56
    for houses and mortgages, 57
    linking assets to, 108–109
    linking to one asset account, 110
    updating for property and debts, 143
links, displaying, 29
Links bar, using with Activity Center, 28
living expenses, figuring, 185–187
loan balances, changing, 112–113
Loan Calculator, availability of, 192
Loan Setup dialog box, opening, 62
Loan Setup Wizard, starting, 114
loan summaries, printing, 115–116
Loan Wizard, using, 61–62
loans
    adjusting interest rates of, 111–112
    printing amortization schedules for, 62
    types of, 108
Loans And Debt Planner, using, 185
loans on assets, including in plans, 183
locking memorized payees, 88

M

M key, action associated with, 20
magnifying glass icon, appearance in Tax Planner, 199
Make Extra Payment dialog box, opening, 114
Manage Saved Reports window, displaying, 122
market indexes
    comparing portfolios to, 168–169
    displaying, 157
    including in graphs, 167
market value, definition of, 48
Maximize or Restore button
    description of, 14
    location of, 13
Medical Deductions worksheet, using, 215. See also deductions;
        Itemized Deduction Estimator
medical expenses, deducting from taxes, 204
Medicare taxes, payment of, 176
Memo field, displaying first, 64
Memorized Payee List, adding renaming rules from, 86
memorized payees
    changing, 85
    creating, 84–85
    locking, 88

memorizing
    from new transactions, 85
    payees, 84–85
    split transactions using percentages, 87
menu bar
    description of, 14
    location of, 13
menus, definition of, 19
mileage, deducting, 215
Minimize button
    description of, 14
    location of, 13
mini-reports, creating, 103–104
Money Market investments, account type associated with, 49
monthly transactions, scheduling, 90
Morningstar assessments, time periods in, 160
mortgage lender, entering name of, 58
mortgages
    description of, 108
    reducing interest payments on, 62
    setting up accounts for, 56–59
Mutual Fund accounts
    creating, 56
    description of, 49
    reconciling, 139–142
mutual funds
    account type associated with, 49
    definition of, 48
    ratings of, 160

N

net pay, definition of, 100
net worth, reflecting in Quicken Asset Accounts, 128
net worth reports, creating, 122–123
Next Field or Column action, keyboard shortcut for, 20
notes, adding to transactions, 78–79
Notify feature, setting preferences for, 67
Num field
    relationship to ENTER key, 70
    sorting transactions by, 78

O

One Step Update utility, managing, 154
One-Click Scorecard, using, 172
Online Account Access service, description of, 35
online banking services
    considering, 36
    implementing, 37–39
    setting up, 35, 37
Online Bill Payment service, description of, 35
online payments, scheduling, 98
Online Quotes feature, using, 150
online reconciliation, performing, 134–135
online services, using, 34–35
online tax tools, using, 210

opening balances, entering in bank statements, 130
Option buttons, using in dialog boxes, 21
other income, entering, 178–179
Other Income or Losses worksheet in Tax Planner, using,
    202–203

P

paper gain or loss, explanation of, 121
passwords
    protecting inventory data with, 126–127
    using with data files, 147
    using with Emergency Records Organizer, 147
Paste action, keyboard shortcut for, 20
Paycheck Set Up dialog box, opening, 11
paychecks, scheduling, 98–100
payee names, displaying, 120
Payee/Category/Memo field, sorting transactions by, 78
payees
    definition of, 64
    entering in Reports & Graphs Customize Transaction
        Categories tab, 120
    memorizing, 84–85
    rating in check registers, 79–80
Payment field, sorting transactions by, 78
payments
    definition of, 64
    scheduling online payments, 98
performance of investments, definition of, 48
performance research tools
    Fund Finder, 170–171
    One-Click Scorecard, 172
    Stock Screener, 171–172
Performance tab, options on, 168–172
personal loans, description of, 108
pie slices in graphs, hiding, 105
PIN Vault, accessing, 36
placeholders
    using in Gain/Loss columns, 52
    using with investment accounts, 142
Plan Results, understanding, 187–188
planned assets, including in plans, 184
Planned Loan tab in Quicken Planner, options on, 183
Planners. See also Quicken Planner
    Debt Reduction Planner, 188–192
    Loans And Debt Planner, 185
Planning Center, opening, 180
plans
    associating income with assets in, 184
    beginning, 174–175
    for college education, 186–187
    entering expected rate of return in, 182
    entering expenses associated with assets in, 184
    estimating inflation for, 180
    including assets in, 182
    including checking and savings accounts in, 180–181
    including investment accounts in, 181